John-Paul Bernbach is leadership for the 21st Century (DL21C), where he serves for Environmental Affairs and co-chair for Foreign Affairs. He is also a member of the Belgium chapter of Democrats Abroad.

During the 2008 presidential campaign cycle, Bernbach served as an official spokesman for both Democrats Abroad and the Democratic Party in Belgium. His responsibilities involved informing the press and the public, briefing European officials and organizations about (then) Senator Obama in particular, as well as Democratic Party policies and the US electoral process. He is also a debate and forum expert as a top representative of the Democratic Party, writing and speaking extensively about US policy and politics for several media outlets.

Bernbach is the co-founder and managing partner of two US based companies with operations in Brussels. Concept to Content LLC (C2C) is a communications consultancy that provides a wide range of English language solutions primarily to non-Anglophone clients. Ching Ventures LLC is a creative partnership that develops both commercial ventures and creative projects on the web.

He is a native of New York City, and has lived between Europe and the US since childhood. Today, he divides his time between New York and Brussels, whilst carrying on Party business.

BEYOND REASON

J.P. BERNBACH

ASTOR
+BLUE
EDITIONS

Published in 2016 by Astor and Blue LLC,
Suite 23A, 1330 Avenue Of The Americas, New York, NY 10019, U.S.A.
www.houseofstratus.com

Typeset by Astor + Blue

A catalogue record for this book is available from the Library of Congress and the British Library.

ISBN (Paperback):   978-1-681200-73-6
ISBN (EPUB):   978-1-681200-74-3
ISBN (EPDF):   978-1-681200-75-0
ISBN (Mobi):   978-1-681200-76-7

Contents

(continued ...)

Contents (continued)

Contents (continued)

INTRODUCTION

Everyone is entitled to his own opinion, but not his own facts.
— Senator Daniel Patrick Moynihan

Reality has a well-known liberal bias.
— Stephen Colbert

The Right's Reality Problem

The re-election of Barack Obama in November 2012 came as a surprise to many conservatives who expected not just a Republican victory, but a decisive one. Many of the most confident predictions came not from the fire-breathers and jesters of talk-radio and the Fox News Channel, but from some of the smartest and most experienced pundits in the land: the respected elders and gray eminences of American conservatism.

George Will predicted that Romney would win by 321 to 226 electoral votes and be the first Republican in forty years to win Minnesota. Michael Barone predicted a 315-223 win for Romney, including victories in Florida, Ohio, Pennsylvania, Virginia, Wisconsin, Iowa, and Colorado — all of which he ultimately lost. Peggy Noonan opined in the Wall Street Journal, "While everyone is looking at the polls and the storm, [Hurricane Sandy] Romney's slipping into the presidency. He's quietly rising, and he's been rising for a while." In the end Obama won by nearly five million votes, with a 332 to 206 advantage in the Electoral College. It was the first time a president had won a second outright popular vote majority since Ronald Reagan did it in 1984.

"I don't think there was one person who saw this coming,"[1] a senior Romney adviser told CBS News the day after the election. In fact, plenty of people saw it coming, namely anybody who had been paying attention to the polls, which conservatives disregarded in favor of their own gut instincts. Reality came as a shock to the Right because they inhabited an alternative reality of their own making. This was nothing new — it's been the Right's modus operandi for years.

The Conservative Misinformation Complex

In the fall of 2004, about a year and a half after the invasion of Iraq, the journalist Ron Suskind interviewed a "senior aide" (later identified as Karl Rove) to then-president George W. Bush. According to Suskind's subsequent article in the *New York Times Magazine*, "The aide said that guys like me were 'in what we call the reality-based community,' which he defined as people who 'believe that solutions emerge from your judicious study of discernible reality.' ... 'That's not the way the world really works anymore,' he continued. 'We're an empire now, and when we act, we create our own reality.'"[2]

The insolence of these remarks is breathtaking, but let's leave that aside for the moment and just focus on what they reveal about the conservative attitude towards facts and actuality. Someone very close to the president of the United States actually said, "We create our own reality," and he meant it.

This is not spin. This is delusion, and it's dangerous.

Whether the alternative "reality" that conservatives create is a genuine delusion or a cynical construct deliberately crafted to mislead the public is really beside the point — the ultimate impact is the same. Did the promoters of the Iraq War really believe that Saddam Hussein had weapons of mass destruction? Were they were unsure, but nevertheless content to use the claim to drum up popular support for a war they wanted to fight? Either way, the results were

2

the same: 4,486 dead American service-members; more than 30,000 wounded. More than 100,000 dead Iraqi civilians. More than a trillion dollars spent. (These are all "conservative" figures.)

As catastrophic as the Iraq War has been, the consequences of conservative heedlessness could prove to be far more destructive when it comes to the environment. At least 97 percent of experts agree that climate change is a reality and that it's caused by human activity. The level of consensus is highest among those who have the most knowledge and experience in the field of climate science. But the Right dismisses the dangers of global warming on the basis of... what, exactly? Nothing more than the fact that it doesn't fit in with their world view. They don't want it to be true; they'd prefer to create their own reality. And so they refuse to heed the consensus or even to take it seriously. They don't even pause to consider the possibility that all those scientists and experts *might* have a point. Given the stakes for everyone — including their own children and children's children — this represents more than a policy failing; it is a major moral failing.

This refusal to consider even the possibility that you may be missing something, that there may be more to the story, that the other point of view may have some merit; this close-mindedness and reflexive rejection of anything that differs from the "reality" that you have created has become the defining characteristic of conservatism in our time. Numerous surveys have demonstrated that Fox News viewers are the most poorly informed group of news consumers in the country. But it's not that they're *un*-informed — they're *mis*-informed. We might even coin a phrase and say that they are the most well-misinformed viewers in America: committed consumers of information, who are routinely misled by the conservative authorities in whom they place their trust and from whom they get their sense of reality.

If conservative claims were true — Saddam Hussein had weapons of mass destruction and was determined to use them against the U.S.; "Obamacare" has death panels; Barack Obama is a crypto-Muslim communist who wants to destroy the American way of life and replace the Constitution with Sharia law; cutting taxes always, inevitably, stimulates job-creation and economic growth; climate change is a hoax; abortion is tantamount to the murder of infants — then we'd all be crazy *not* to vote for them. The problem is not just that these conservative claims are lies, but that these lies are taken on trust by millions of Americans. And so, the conservative alternative reality abides.

The Future of a Delusion

But this approach can't work forever. Facts emerge, the truth comes out, actual results contradict the prognostications of pundits. The planet *is* getting warmer; the seas *are* actually rising. Twenty million formerly uninsured Americans now really do have health insurance thanks to "Obamacare"; none of them has encountered anything resembling a "death panel." You can only ignore reality for so long before you start looking like a fool or a fanatic or both. The G.O.P. and the conservative establishment in America are on the verge of a reckoning.

This book hopes to contribute to that reckoning. It is a collection of some of the major right-wing lies and delusions that have plagued our country over the past thirty years or so. The idea is not simply to debunk each one on its own terms (although there is plenty of that in the pages that follow), but to line them all up back to back and demonstrate a consistent, undeniable pattern of delusion and falsehood. Conservatism in our time is not just a philosophy that happens to be wrong about some important things; it is a set of beliefs and attitudes that are profoundly disconnected from, and hostile to, reality itself. It is an ideology beyond fact, beyond logic, beyond reason.

PART 1

VALUES AND PRIORITIES

THE US IS A 'CENTER-RIGHT' NATION

We are a center-right nation.

— Bill O'Reilly[3]

CONSERVATIVES CLAIM...

The views and values of conservatism reflect those of a majority of Americans or as conservatives frequently put it, "real Americans."

The myth that the United States is "a center-right" nation has become conventional wisdom in recent years - even Democrats tend not to challenge the idea when it comes up. Republican politicians and right-wing commentators have been repeating this falsehood for decades with great success, proving the theory that if you get enough people to repeat something over and over again for years and years it will eventually be perceived as true, even if it happens to be a lie — which, in this case, it most certainly is.

THE REALITY

69,498,516 citizens voted for Barack Obama on November 4th, 2008, thereby electing him president of the United States with the greatest number of votes ever cast for any candidate for any office in the entire history of the world's greatest modern democracy. The margin of victory was nine and a half million votes.[4]

Four years later, 65,915,796 Americans voted to reelect Obama — the second greatest number of votes ever cast in a U.S. election.

The margin of victory was slimmer but still substantial: five million votes.[5]

Given the tendency of conservatives to describe President Obama as "socialist," "Marxist," "un-American" and "foreign," these election results can hardly be construed to reflect the views and values of a right-leaning — or "center-right" — people.

In the past six presidential elections, Republicans have outpolled Democrats only once: in 2004, when George W. Bush defeated John Kerry by a relatively slim popular vote margin of 2.46 percent and three million votes. (In case you've forgotten, he lost the popular vote to Al Gore in 2000 by more than half-a-million votes.) 2004 was, of course, a year in which the power of incumbency was particularly strong — it was the first post 9/11 presidential election and the U.S. was in the middle of two wars which had not yet gone wrong, at least in the public mind. Four years later, Obama's 7.2 percent margin of victory over John McCain would be the widest since another Democrat, Bill Clinton, defeated Republican Bob Dole, by 8.5 points (and more than eight million votes) in 1996.

The reality is that the American people as a whole, lean to the left, if they lean at all.

Party Identification

The Gallup Organization conducts a regular survey which asks Americans whether they consider themselves to be Republican, Democrat, or independent; in the case of self-identified independents, the poll also asks which party they are more inclined to support. During the period from 2004 to 2016, the proportion of Americans who identified themselves as Republicans or Republican-leaning independents ranged between 34 and 52 percent, while Democrats and Democratic-leaning independents ranged between 40 and 56 percent.

Moreover, G.O.P. identification achieved or exceeded 50 percent on only four occasions, most recently in February 2005. During the same period, Democratic identification broke 50 percent on ninety-three occasions, most recently in December of 2012. All in all, Democratic identification has exceeded Republican identification 87 percent of the time.[6]

But that's just the last twelve years — exceptionally eventful years that have seen two major wars and a financial catastrophe followed by the worst economic crisis since the Great Depression. To be fair, we should take a longer, multi-generational view to get a better sense of where Americans have stood over time. When we do, it turns out that over time, the American people have stood more or less where they're still standing today: to the left of center.

The Gallup "generic ballot" simply asks people whether they intend to vote for a Republican or a Democrat in the next election. For the fifty years, from 1950 to 2006 (before the recent financial crisis), the Democratic Party enjoyed a constant advantage except for three brief periods: February of 1994, July to September of 1994, and October 2001 to May 2002. In other words, the Republican Party outpolled the Democratic Party for a combined not-so-grand total of 12 months in 56 years. That's less than 2 percent of the time.

A similar survey, Pew Research Center's review of party identification data from 1939 to 2012, shows that G.O.P. identification exceeded that of Democrats in only one year — 1995. The most recent survey, conducted in 2014, found that Democratic identification surpassed Republican by 9 percent.[7]

You get the point. More people consistently identify as Democrats than as Republicans. Every once in a while, there is a brief surge in Republican identification, which invariably subsides after a month or two. Then the country reverts to the left-leaning status quo.

Issues

When it comes to the issues, it's even harder to make a credible case for the argument that the United States is a center-right nation.

Clear majorities of Americans support major Democratic policies and initiatives, which Republicans oppose or have opposed in the past: Social Security, Medicare,[8] higher taxes on the wealthy, safe and legal abortion, equal rights for same-sex couples,[9] a path to citizenship for undocumented workers,[10] and numerous other liberal programs. Most of these policies and programs enjoy support in the 60 to 70 percent range.[11]

Most Americans are concerned about the federal deficit and the national debt and would like to see the Federal Government control costs. That sounds like a conservative position, but when asked to identify both the least acceptable and most acceptable budget cuts, they expressed unmistakably liberal priorities. Least acceptable were cuts to Social Security, K-12 education, Medicare and Medicaid (i.e., federal healthcare assistance to elderly, disabled, and poor Americans), heating assistance to low-income families, college student-loans, Head-Start (i.e., pre-kindergarten education), and unemployment insurance. In other words: the Liberal Agenda.

The most acceptable measures for reducing the deficit were (in order of acceptability): a surtax on millionaires, eliminating earmarks, eliminating funding for weapons systems the Pentagon considers unnecessary (i.e., defense cuts), eliminating tax credits for oil and gas companies, phasing out the Bush tax cuts for families earning more than $250,000/year. In other words: the Liberal Agenda. Indeed, with the exception of eliminating earmarks, which is a major conservative talking point (and, incidentally, completely useless as a deficit cutting measure), all of these cuts are anathema to conservatives.[12]

These priorities are confirmed in poll after poll.[13] On most of the major issues of the day, the conservative position is drastically out of sync with the views and values of a majority of Americans.

Social Security & Medicare/Medicaid

Most Americans, including a majority of self-described conservatives, approve of Social Security, Medicare, and Medicaid — the cornerstones of the liberal welfare state and the closest thing to genuinely socialist programs that the U.S. government has implemented. As the Wall Street Journal pointed out in March 2011, "Even tea party supporters, by a nearly 2-to-1 margin, declared significant cuts to Social Security 'unacceptable.'"[14]

On the other hand, all but ten Republicans in congress voted in 2012 to pass a budget plan (the so-called "Ryan Budget"), which would partially dismantle Medicare and demand severe cuts to social services in the coming decades.[15] In 2014, all but twelve G.O.P. representatives voted to pass a similar budget proposal.

Taxes on the Wealthy

64 percent of Americans support higher taxes on wealthy.[16] Conservatives not only oppose this — they actually favor tax cuts for the wealthy, which the Ryan budgets have consistently called for.

Abortion

Half of all Americans consider themselves to be "pro-choice" whereas only 44 percent of Americans consider themselves to be "pro-life."

51 percent of Americans today support abortion under some circumstances (compared to 55 percent in 1975). 29 percent believe it should be legal in all circumstances (compared to 21 percent in 1975). 19 percent believe it should be illegal in all circumstances (compared to 21 percent in 1975). These numbers have been remarkably consistent since the 1970s. At no point has support for abortion in at least some circumstances dipped below 75 percent of the population.[17] Numerous surveys reveal almost identical results.[18]

Conservatives, on the other hand, support criminalizing abortion in most cases, including those of rape and incest, and are divided over whether to allow abortion in cases when the mother's life is endangered. Many conservatives, including the G.O.P.'s last presidential candidate Mitt Romney and the current Speaker of the House Paul Ryan, have supported laws to define a human embryo as a person, which would make any abortion legally indistinguishable from murder.

Immigration

A two-thirds majority of Americans supports a so-called "path to citizenship" for illegal immigrants currently residing in the U.S., whereas less than one-fifth supports deportation.[19]

Conservatives, on the other hand, oppose this approach, calling it "amnesty."

55 percent of Americans support President Obama's policy of granting work permits to undocumented residents under the age of thirty who were brought to the U.S. as children.[20] [21]

Gay Rights

50 percent of Americans support same-sex marriage,[22] whereas every candidate for the Republican nomination for president in 2012 supported a constitutional amendment to ban it.

REASONS FOR THE DISCONNECT?

Labels — What's in a Name?

About fifty-percent more Americans describe themselves as "Conservative" than as "Liberal," which sounds pretty convincing until you start to realize that many of these self-described conservatives support Social Security, same-sex marriage, and higher taxes on the wealthy. The word "conservative" is a more respectable word than "liberal" in today's America, largely thanks to thirty years of conservative bashing of the liberal brand. The word "conservative" sounds mature, reasonable, and fair, whereas the word "liberal" has been made to sound irresponsible, counter-cultural, and maybe even subversive. Many actual liberals don't even call themselves "liberal" anymore.

But this is about labels that people apply to themselves, rather than their actual beliefs and values. If you rely entirely on self-description, you'll also find that a majority of Americans are good-looking, intelligent, and have great senses of humor.

Effective Conservative Rhetoric

Republicans and their supporters keep repeating the "center-right nation" myth over (and over and over and over), with little or no pushback from Democrats. Republicans are disciplined about staying "on message" and sticking to a coordinated and consistent set of talking points at every level, from the White House down to the local school board. After a while, these talking points start to sink in to the general consciousness and become accepted as simple reality, even though they are anything but.

Conservatives also tend to proclaim their beliefs loudly, taking up more space and getting more attention in the media and the national conversation. This creates the impression that they're more numerous than they actually are. Ten people yelling can be a lot louder than a thousand people not yelling.

Conservatives Have Claimed Universal Values as Their Own

Republicans consistently and insistently identify themselves with universal moral and patriotic values, which Democrats also happen to support but don't make such a big show of proclaiming. Republicans at every level constantly trumpet their support for the Constitution, the troops, "family values," "freedom," "faith," "morality," and "real America." Because more or less everyone supports these things, Republicans claim to represent the true feelings of the American people.

The Electoral Process Over-Represents Conservatives

Registered voters tend to be older and whiter, and therefore more conservative, than the general population. Likely voters are even more so, which means that government is almost always more conservative than the overall population, about half of whom don't regularly participate in the electoral process. Even so, a majority of registered voters consistently identify themselves as Democrats. If a majority of active participants in the electoral process aren't center-right, the country as a whole certainly isn't.

The House of Representatives is Not Representative

Of the population as a whole, that is. In the 2014 mid-term elections, Republicans won 57 percent of House seats, but only 52 percent of the total number of votes cast nationwide. That was actually an improvement over 2012, when Republicans won 54 percent of House seats while actually *losing* the popular vote.[23]

This systemic bias towards Republicans is often blamed on gerrymandering, but that is only part of the problem. (Gerrymandering is the process of designing congressional districts in such a way that their populations disproportionately represent supporters of one or the other party.) Although gerrymandering *does* ensure that a district will remain in the hands of a particular party, the process tends to produce safe districts for the other party as well. If you lump a whole lot of Republicans into one district, you're going to have to put the Democrats somewhere — more often than not, that means another equally safe Democratic district.

The problem is that safe Democratic districts tend to be located in more densely populated areas and thus tend to contain more people, while safe G.O.P. districts tend to be more rural and more sparsely populated. On average, each Republican in the House is actually representing fewer citizens than his or her Democratic counterparts.

FairVote (which defines itself as a "non-partisan Electoral Reform organization, working to make American government more representative") has estimated that the G.O.P. needs to win only 45 percent of the aggregate popular vote to maintain its majority in the House. To put it another way, Democrats could win ten million more votes than Republicans and still remain in the "minority."[24]

Equal Representation of Large (Mostly Blue) and Small (Mostly Red) States in the Senate

Every state has the same number of Senators — two — which grants disproportionate power to conservative senators who represent states with relatively small populations.

To put this into perspective: California's thirty-eight million people are currently represented by two Democratic Senators. The combined thirty-six million citizens of Wyoming, Alaska, Idaho, Nebraska, Utah, Kansas, Mississippi, Oklahoma, South Carolina, Alabama, and Georgia are represented by twenty-two Republican senators.

The Democrats are Pretty Lousy at Communicating

The evidence in this chapter is overwhelming, unambiguous, and conclusive: more Americans identify as Democrats than as Republicans, and most favor progressive policies. Yet, there's a good chance that much of this information comes as a surprise to you. Whose fault is that?

But whether people realize it or not, this the truth: the United States is not a center-right nation by any legitimate reckoning. In fact, the opposite is clear: The Republican Party represents the views and values of a distinct minority of Americans.

THE G.O.P. IS THE "PRO-LIFE" PARTY

I have always felt that it was only after a child was born and had a life separate from its mother that it became an individual person, and it has always, therefore, seemed to me that what is best for the mother and for the future should be allowed.
— W. A. Criswell, former president of the Southern Baptist Convention, responding to the Supreme Court's ruling in the case of Roe v. Wade, which established a constitutional right to abortion in 1973

Every gun that is made, every warship launched, every rocket fired, signifies in the final sense a theft from those who hunger and are not fed, those who are cold and are not clothed.
— Republican president Dwight D. Eisenhower, April 16, 1953[25]

CONSERVATIVES CLAIM...

Conservatives are the defenders of life in the midst of a liberal "culture of death." Liberal support of women's right to abortion is immoral and indicative of the fact that they value "innocent life" less than conservatives do. When it comes to the sanctity and value of human life, conservatives are more serious, more committed, and more moral than liberals.

THE REALITY

On issue after issue, conservatives favor policies that fail to protect human life and often lead directly and inevitably to the deaths of many human beings who would otherwise have lived. A majority of conservatives support foreign military intervention (i.e., war), the death penalty, and unregulated access to firearms, while opposing gun safety regulations, environmental protection, affordable healthcare for all citizens, and social programs, such as food stamps, designed to alleviate poverty, which is in itself a cause of poor-health and premature death.

Conservatives do, however, oppose abortion. Insofar as "pro-life" is a slogan that means no more and no less than "anti-abortion", there's certainly no question that the Republican Party is the "pro-life" party. But beyond that very particular meaning, the "pro-life" moniker does not represent a set of principles that affirm the value of human life or promote the quality of life for the maximum number of human beings in general.

The Death Penalty

Conservatives' pro-death position on the question of capital punishment distinguishes them not only from liberals, but from the citizens of most other advanced nations on Earth. The United States is one of only two developed nations that executes its own citizens, the other being Japan. It is the only country in the Americas with an active death penalty. It consistently ranks among the top five nations in terms of the total number of prisoners it executes, along with China, Saudi Arabia, Iran, and Iraq.[26] The only European country with an active death penalty is Belarus. Russia has not executed a citizen in more than ten years.[27]

Capital punishment has been consistently supported by a majority of Americans, but has always been most strongly supported by conservatives. Most Democrats actually oppose the death penalty (this has been true since 2010), whereas more than three quarters of

Republicans continue to support it.[28]

This conservative enthusiasm for putting guilty human beings to death is not only born out in national opinion polls, but put into lethal effect in actual policy at the state level. Of the twenty-seven states with an active death penalty, twenty are "red states" — i.e., they voted for the Republican candidate in the most recent presidential election (2012).

As of August 2015, 1,413 executions had been carried out in the United States since 1976, when the death penalty was reinstated by the Supreme Court. 1,148 of these — 81 percent of the total — have occurred in the nation's most conservative region, the South. 528 executions — 46 percent of the total - have occurred in a single state: deep-red Texas. During the same period, the total number of executions that have taken place in the nation's most liberal region, the Northeast, is four — less than one half of one percent of the total. [29]

Conservatives are not merely supportive of capital punishment, they are positively *eager* to execute people. Consider the great lengths that conservatives around the country are going to in order to preserve the death penalty at a time when overall support is declining and drugs required to carry out executions by lethal-injection are increasingly hard to obtain.

Florida (a purple state where Republicans control both legislative houses and the governorship), argued before the Supreme Court in 2014 that the state should be allowed to execute intellectually disabled prisoners. The Court rejected Florida's argument in a five to four decision. The four dissenting justices were all conservatives.[30]

The Republican governor of Nebraska has vowed to execute all inmates currently on death-row, in defiance of the legislature's bipartisan repeal of the death penalty in April of 2015. He has also sought to import banned lethal-injection drugs from a dealer in India, in contravention of U.S. federal law.[31]

In response to the decreasing availability of lethal-injection drugs, Utah has reinstated the use of firing squads,[32] Oklahoma has passed legislation authorizing the use of poison gas, and Tennessee has brought back the electric chair.[33]

There is no evidence that the death penalty deters violent crime and plenty of evidence to the contrary. 90 percent of law enforcement professionals consider it to be an ineffective deterrent. Crime rates in death penalty states are much higher on average than in those without the death penalty. Where the death penalty has been eliminated, violent crime rates have not risen; where it has been adopted, crime rates have not fallen. (These issues are covered extensively in Part 6, Chapter 5 "The Death Penalty Deters violent Crime.")

What's more, it is actually less expensive to imprison a person for life than to put him to death.[34] This may sound counterintuitive at first, but once you consider the special facilities and procedures required to house condemned prisoners, as well as the legal fees and judicial expenses associated with numerous appeals in the courts protracted over ten or more years, it is easy to see how the total cost of executing a person can be up to ten times as expensive as simply housing him within the maximum security prison system for the rest of his life. A study conducted by a senior judge and a law professor in California concluded that eliminating the death penalty would immediately save the state $170 million a year, and $5 billion over the next 20 years.[35]

If capital punishment doesn't deter crime or save money, why are conservatives so committed to condemning prisoners to death and executing them? Whatever their reasons, their position involves going to great lengths and expense to kill human beings who have ceased to pose any further threat to society. This is not in any sense a "pro-life" position.

Gun Rights vs. Public Safety

Conservatives consistently oppose any limitations on the right of citizens to acquire, carry, and use firearms. At the national level they have successfully prevented all efforts to enhance gun safety regulations, such as mandatory background checks for purchasers, which a large majority of Americans support. As a result, the United

States has by far the highest rate of gun ownership in the world and the highest rate of murder by firearms among developed nations. The chance of being killed by gunfire in the U.S. is more than four times greater than in any other developed country on Earth.[36]

Study after study has demonstrated the correlation between higher levels of gun ownership and higher levels of death by gunshot.[37] More guns mean more homicide.[38] More guns mean more suicide.[39] In a nutshell, more guns mean more death, and conservatives are all for more guns.

In the U.S. about 30,000 people die from firearms every year. In the European Union, which has far stricter gun laws and much lower levels of gun ownership, the annual number of gun-related deaths is about 6,700.[40] Europe, of course, has a much larger population — 742 million, roughly two-and-one-third times that of the U.S. If Europe had America's gun laws and gun culture, about 69,000 people would be dying annually from gunshots wounds. If the U.S. had Europe's gun laws and gun culture, the annual number of deaths would drop by a factor of ten, from 30,000 to about 3,000.

Within the U.S. the risk of death from gun violence is not evenly distributed. Firearms-related deaths occur most frequently in conservative states, which tend to have loose gun regulations and high levels of gun ownership. Firearms-related deaths occur most rarely in relatively liberal states, which tend to have the tightest regulation and lowest levels of gun ownership.

The five states with the greatest per capita rates of death by gunshot — Louisiana, Mississippi, Alaska, Wyoming, and Montana — are all red states in which more than 45 percent of households own guns. The five states with the lowest per capita rates of death by gunshot — Rhode Island, Hawaii, Massachusetts, New York, and New Jersey — are all blue states with levels of household gun ownership below 6 percent.[41]

Every time a horrific mass shooting occurs in America, liberals renew their efforts to reform gun laws and conservatives rationalize and resist and ensure that nothing gets done. Indeed, they tend to push so hard against reforms that their fervor carries them in the opposite direction. Throughout the country, conservative states have demonstrated contempt for the idea of gun safety by making it easier to obtain, carry, and use firearms.

Indiana, for instance, passed a "stand your ground" law in 2012, which makes it legal for a person to use deadly force, with no duty to retreat, if he feels his life to be threatened. To be clear: the law merely requires that a person *feel* threatened; the person doesn't actually have to be threatened in any objective sense.

At least twenty-one states have enacted similar laws (also known as "castle doctrine" laws) since 2000. Eighteen of them were red states, including every state in the Deep South; the other three — Florida, Ohio, and Michigan — were purple states under G.O.P. control when the laws were passed. There is no evidence that these laws enhance public safety — indeed there is strong evidence that they have just the opposite effect. A major study by researchers at Texas A & M University concluded that "stand your ground" laws have had no deterrent effect on the rate of violent crime but have actually increased the rate of gun-related death by 8 percent, accounting for additional 600 deaths per year.[42]

In a single year (2012), Utah, Kentucky, West Virginia, Oklahoma, Mississippi, and Virginia (a purple state fully controlled by the G.O.P. at the time) all passed laws that made it easier to obtain permits to carry concealed weapons. West Virginia repealed a law that required applicants for concealed weapons permits to undergo background checks. Utah even made it possible for convicted felons to obtain permits to carry concealed weapons. In 2013 Arkansas and Kansas each passed laws allowing employees to carry concealed weapons in schools.[43]

Every one of the states mentioned in the previous paragraph had a gun-death rate above the national average at the time the legislation was passed. Needless to say, they still do.[44]

When it comes to the rights of citizens to own, carry, and use firearms, conservatives support policies that result in exceptionally high rates of lethal violence for a developed nation. Whatever the merits of their arguments regarding second amendment rights (which are exhaustively debunked in Part 6, Chapter 3 "Gun Control Laws Are Unconstitutional"), conservatives can't credibly deny that their values prioritize a particular idea of "freedom" over life. To put it another way, conservatives are willing to tolerate thousands of avoidable deaths as the price of their desire to exercise their supposed liberties to the fullest possible extent. This is not in any sense a "pro-life" position.

War

War is an uncertain, unpredictable business which always entails unintended consequences. But there is actually one consequence of war that can be reliably predicted: death on a large scale. No matter how sound your reasons and motives may be, it is not possible to go to war without killing many, many people. We all know this. Any decision to go to war, however tactically limited and competently executed, will result in the deaths of many human beings. Soldiers, even enemy soldiers — even "enemy combatants" — are human beings, whatever else they may be to you. What's more, war always — *always* and inevitably — causes the deaths of non-combatants, which is to say human beings who have not taken up arms but just happen to be in the wrong place at the wrong time. Among the many horrors of modern warfare is that it kills and injures many times more civilians than combatants.

Even the most conservative assessments conclude that well over 100,000 innocent human beings have died as a direct result of the Iraq War, which was launched by a Republican administration, not reluctantly, but eagerly, and which still enjoys majority support among conservatives.[45]

Plenty of Democrats supported the war in 2003, but about half of the Democratic members of the House and Senate voted against it (126 out of 209 in the House; 21 out of 50 in the Senate). Republican support was all but unanimous (215 out of 223 in the House; 48 out of 49 in the Senate).

In 2013, on the tenth anniversary of the U.S. invasion of Iraq, a

Gallup poll found that a majority of self-identified Republicans still supported the Iraq War, whereas a majority of all Americans, and an even greater majority of Democrats, considered it to have been a mistake.[46]

Enthusiastic support for a war — any war, regardless of your reasons — inevitably involves supporting the deaths of many innocent human beings. This is not in any sense a "pro-life" position.

Healthcare

Conservative opposition to "Obamacare" (officially known as the Patient Protection and Affordable Care Act) was militant, often hysterical (talk of "death panels"), and monolithic (not a single Republican in the House or Senate voted in favor of the bill). From the beginning, conservatives did everything in their power to prevent the law from passing. Since its passage, they have done everything in their power to hinder its implementation, including voting more than fifty times in the House of Representatives to repeal it.

Before the implementation of "Obamacare," about forty-five million Americans lacked health insurance of any kind. The law was designed precisely to address this problem and has already managed to reduce the number of uninsured citizens by almost seventeen million (as of August 2015, a year-and-a-half after implementation).[47]

Lack of access to health insurance means lack of access to healthcare, which leads, unsurprisingly, to increased risk of illness and avoidable death. The exact number of deaths from lack of insurance is unknown, largely because nobody has conducted a thorough study of the matter in more than twenty years. The most widely cited study (from 1993) found that lack of insurance increases the likelihood of premature death by about 25 percent. A Harvard study in 2009 used the same methodologies and came up with an even higher rate of 40 percent.[48] In terms of actual numbers, the best pre-"Obamacare" estimates of annual deaths from lack of insurance range from about 20,000 to 45,000 per year — comparable to the rates of death from motor vehicle accidents (about 35,000) and suicide (41,000), and considerably greater than the murder rate (16,000).[49]

Regardless of the precise numbers, what cannot be denied is that many thousands of Americans have been dying every year because they lack access to affordable healthcare. "Obamacare" has so far extended health coverage to nearly seventeen million Americans who lacked it. This has, of course, happened over the strident objections and strenuous opposition of Republicans — that is, where it has actually been implemented. There are twenty-two states that have refused to expand Medicaid under "Obamacare," which would have made health insurance available to their poorest citizens — all of these states have Republican majorities in their state legislatures; twenty have Republican governors.[50]

As of August 2015, 57 percent of self-identified Republicans still favor repealing the Affordable Care Act in its entirety.[51]

It would be one thing if poor Americans happened to be thriving; but the opposite is true. Healthcare outcomes in the U.S. lag behind those of other developed nations, almost all of which provide their citizens with genuinely universal health coverage. The U.S. has fewer physicians and fewer hospital beds per capita than the average among the thirty-four advanced nations of the OECD (Organization for Economic Cooperation and Development). Infant mortality is higher in the U.S. than the OECD average; indeed, it's higher than that of every OECD country except for Turkey and Mexico. Meanwhile, average life expectancy in the U.S. is 78.8 years, a year-and-a-half lower than the OECD average of 80.4 years. Eighteen countries, all of which provide universal health coverage to their citizens, have an average life expectancy of more than eighty years.[52]

Conservative opposition to programs that make affordable healthcare more available to citizens is a major reason for these inferior public health outcomes. It is not in any sense a "pro-life" position.

Climate Change

The G.O.P. is the only major political party among developed nations that routinely denies climate change and opposes any measures to address it. In the rest of the world, the reality of global warming is a matter of consensus; even where there is little commitment to addressing the problem, there is at least general agreement that it *is* in fact a problem and that something ought to be done about it. Not so with America's conservatives, who are unified in denial and committed to maintaining the policies and practices that are warming the planet. As of January 2015, only 15 percent of Republicans felt that addressing global warming was a top priority, which was down from an already low 23 percent in 2003.[53]

Climate change is already a deadly problem (this issue is covered extensively in Part 4, Chapter 5 "The Evidence for Climate Change is Inconclusive"). Thousands are dying every year from conditions that are caused or aggravated by global warming. The World Health Organization has declared that climate change will cause millions of additional deaths in the coming decades from malnutrition, malaria, diarrhea, and heat stress.[54] A recent report from the DARA International Foundation concludes that the damage is already far more severe once hunger and environmental factors such as pollution are taken into account. DARA estimates that climate change is already responsible for an additional five million deaths per year, and that by the year 2030, annual deaths attributable to climate change will have risen to six million.[55]

Conservative refusal to acknowledge the consensus of more than 97 percent of the world's scientists who specialize in climate-related subjects is not just willfully ignorant, it is immoral. It represents, at best, severe negligence and, at worst, depraved indifference to human life, present and future. And it most certainly is not in any sense a "pro-life" position.

Anti-Environmentalism

Conservatives generally oppose laws designed to protect the environment. Indeed, in 2011, Senate Republicans actually introduced legislation to abolish the Environmental Protection Agency. This anti-environmentalism isn't motivated by any explicit hostility to the natural world or to the plants and creatures, including but not limited to human beings, who inhabit it. If environmental protection didn't involve regulating business practices it's unlikely conservatives would care very much about opposing it. Unfortunately for us, along with more or less all non-bacterial life forms on planet Earth, environmentalism *does* involve regulating business practices — and there's the rub.

Two-thirds of Americans support stricter limits on power-plant emissions, including more than three-quarters of Democrats. About half of Republicans oppose them. Among Tea Party republicans — i.e., the most conservative ones — opposition stands at 71 percent.[56]

Conservatives justify their anti-environmentalism on economic grounds — they argue that the need to comply with tougher regulations increases expenses, which decreases profits, which leads to less hiring and therefore fewer jobs (except, presumably, for compliance officers). The evidence doesn't actually bear this out, especially when one considers that the clean energy sector is one of the fastest growing parts of the U.S. economy. Between 2004 and 2014, total wind generating capacity in the U.S. increased by 1,000 percent,[57] while total installed solar capacity increased by 8,500 percent.[58]

Nevertheless, the conservative position isn't entirely illogical. Compliance with regulations is a hassle, and it certainly is very inconvenient and expensive to reduce harmful emissions or to dispose of toxic waste in a manner that doesn't endanger public health. Regardless of the debatable merits of this thinking, people who think this way can't credibly deny that they are willing to tolerate higher levels of pollution than would occur with more regulations in place. And the thing about pollution is: it kills people.

A team of researchers at MIT has determined that air pollution causes 200,000 premature deaths in the U.S. every year, including 52,000 from power plant emissions, and 53,000 from road vehicle exhaust.[59] A 2010 report by the Clean Air Task Force demonstrated that between 2004 and 2010, premature deaths from power plant emissions had been reduced from roughly 24,000 to 13,000 per year *owing specifically to increased regulation*. Their report concluded: "Strong regulations that require stringent emission controls can have a dramatic impact in reducing air pollution across the country, saving lives, and avoiding a host of other adverse health impacts."[60]

Conservatives can't credibly deny that they favor the interests of corporations over public health. Even if they are genuinely blind to the economic benefits of clean energy and believe sincerely that their policies are better for the economy, they are prioritizing economic prosperity over the well-being and even the lives of many thousands of human beings, not to mention animals. This is not in any sense a "pro-life" position.

The Battle to Defund Planned Parenthood

Planned Parenthood is a non-profit organization that provides reproductive health services to 2.7 million Americans every year. It is the largest provider of abortions in the United States, but abortion accounts for only 3 percent of its activities. 97 percent of its activities are not related to abortion. Every year, Planned Parenthood provides hundreds of thousands of Pap tests, HIV/AIDS tests, and breast cancer screenings, as well as a range of family planning services.

The organization receives roughly half of its funding from federal and state governments, mostly in the form of reimbursements for medical services covered by Medicaid and Medicare. None of these funds are used for abortion, since federal law forbids any tax dollars to be allocated for that purpose. Numerous investigations and audits have confirmed that Planned Parenthood abides by the law and has not used any tax-payer dollars to fund abortions. Nevertheless, Republicans at the state and federal levels have been seeking to cut off all government funding to Planned Parenthood, in hopes that the lack of funds will put the organization out of business altogether.

In August of 2015, Republicans in the U.S. Senate introduced "A bill to prohibit Federal funding of Planned Parenthood Federation of America." The measure was supported by 51 of 54 Senate Republicans and opposed by 44 of 46 Senate Democrats, including the two independents who caucus with the Democrats. It did not obtain enough votes to overcome a filibuster.[61] One month later, the U.S. House of Representatives passed the "Defund Planned Parenthood Act of 2015". As with the Senate measure, the House bill received almost unanimous support from Republicans (239 of 246 in favor) and almost unanimous opposition from Democrats (184 of 188 opposed).[62]

At the state level, Republican-dominated legislatures in Indiana, Texas, Arizona, North Carolina, Tennessee, and Kansas have passed legislation to block funding for Planned Parenthood. These measures have all been stopped in the courts, since federal law protects the right of Medicaid recipients to seek care from any qualified provider.[63]

If government support for Planned Parenthood were withdrawn, it would have no effect on the number of abortions the organization provides, since government funds aren't used for abortion. It would, however, have a severe negative effect on the ability of the organization to provide women's health services, including cancer screenings and preventive care, which would cause direct harm to the health of women in America; particularly that of poor women, many of whom rely on Planned Parenthood as their sole source of medical care.[64] Without access to affordable testing and early intervention, women will find themselves at greater risk of dying from breast cancer and AIDS.

What's more, by driving Planned Parenthood out of business and thus eliminating a primary source of family planning services for millions of American women, conservatives would cause hundreds of thousands of unintended pregnancies, about half of which would result in abortions. This is worth emphasizing: family planning services, which include access to affordable contraception, prevent unintended pregnancies and thus prevent abortions.

Approximately half of all abortions are obtained by women who did not want to become pregnant, but failed to use contraception. In 2010, for example, the number of abortions reported to the Center for Disease Control was 765,651,[65] which means that more than 350,000 abortions could have been prevented in that year alone if family planning services, including contraception, had been universally available and accessed.[66] In a 2009 report, the Guttmacher Institute estimated that publicly-funded family planning services prevent more than 1.9 million unintended pregnancies and more than 800,000 abortions annually in the U.S. If these services were eliminated, the rates of unintended pregnancy and abortion would increase by hundreds of thousands every year.[67]

Planned Parenthood may be the largest abortion provider in America, but it is also the largest abortion preventer. If "pro-life" conservatives manage to put it out of business, they will not only eliminate vital health services for millions of women throughout the U.S., but they will actually bring about tens of thousands — perhaps even hundreds of thousands — of abortions which would otherwise not have occurred. An agenda that deliberately places hundreds of thousands of women at greater risk of dying while actually increasing the number of abortions due to unintended pregnancy can hardly claim to be either reasonable or moral. And it is not, except in the narrowest possible sense, a "pro-life" position.

REASONS FOR THIS DISCONNECT?

Propaganda

There is no question that the G.O.P. is the party that affixes the "pro-life" label to itself. But what does this label actually mean? "Pro-life" is not a coherent system of values. It's a slogan that stands for a single principle: opposition to abortion. If we take "pro-life" to be a precise synonym for "anti-abortion" then of course the G.O.P. is the "pro-life" party.

About 75 percent of Americans, and even a majority of Republicans, support women's right to abortion in at least some circumstances (e.g., in cases of rape, incest, and/or when the life of the mother is endangered). Yet almost half of Americans consider themselves "pro-life."[68] Who, after all, wants to declare, even if only by implication, that they're not on the side of "life?"

"Pro-life" is a perfect slogan. It instantly polarizes the issue into a "pro" and an "anti." By characterizing their opposition to abortion in terms of life itself, conservatives place themselves on the "pro" side, automatically placing those who disagree with them on the "anti" side, without any possibility of complexity or middle ground. Simple logic dictates, after all, that anyone who's not "pro-life" must be "anti-life" or even "pro-death." It's an effective rhetorical trick.

Piousness

Conservatives' focus on eradicating abortion allows them to present themselves as defenders of human life, while somehow overlooking the impact of other policies which are anything but pro-life and even in some cases literally pro-death (death penalty, war, gun "rights").

There's something more here, though. As was pointed out above, G.O.P. attempts to put Planned Parenthood out of business would inevitably lead to *more*, not fewer, abortions. You'd think that if "innocent human lives" were genuinely important to conservatives, they would at least pause to consider the actual impact of the legislation and policies they support. But their commitment to ideology blinds them to the real-world consequences of the policies they support. To put it another way, their ideology is more important to them than actual human beings, whether born or unborn.

Conservatives want to think of themselves as virtuous and life-affirming even though they promote a variety of policies that are aggressive, vengeful, stingy, and neglectful of actual suffering. The "pro-life" moniker is a fig leaf — it allows them to pretend to themselves and to others that their agenda is benevolent, virtuous, and respectful of life when it is, in many respects, the opposite.

CONSERVATIVES ARE STRONGER ON "FAMILY VALUES" THAN LIBERALS

We insist that public policy, from taxation to education, from healthcare to welfare, be formulated with attention to the needs and strengths of the family.
— 2012 Republican Party platform

It is time for those who talk about family values to start valuing families.
— Presidential nominee John Kerry, at the 2004 Democratic National Convention

CONSERVATIVES CLAIM...

Conservatives are more moral in general than liberals, especially when it comes to families. Conservative social policies promote moral behavior; they support families and help to keep them together. Liberal policies encourage immorality and lead to broken homes. Families benefit more from conservative policies than liberal ones.

THE REALITY

While conservatives frequently talk about their support for "family values," they consistently fail to support policies that actually allow families to thrive. The result is one of America's weirder paradoxes, which is saying something. Conservative social policies have led to the destruction of millions of families through higher rates of teen pregnancy, higher rates of divorce, higher levels of poverty, and higher levels of injury and death from gun violence.

"Family values" is a flexible phrase that is open to different interpretations but conservatives are quite clear about what they mean by it. They value the "traditional family" — i.e., two parents of different sexes and their biological or adopted offspring — as the essential unit of society and the only domestic arrangement that is entitled to be recognized as a family. The Family Research Council (one of America's two or three most prominent and powerful conservative pro-family organizations) describes the family as "the foundation of civilization, the seedbed of virtue, and the wellspring of society."[69] Accordingly, they are committed to supporting and strengthening this institution and promoting "a culture in which human life is valued, families flourish and religious liberty thrives."[70]

These are fine and laudable sentiments. Indeed, even most liberals (certainly your liberal author and the liberals he knows) support the very same principles. So have we found some common ground at last? A way of emphasizing the "unum" rather than the "pluribus" for once in these parlous times?

You'd think so. And if we take conservatives at their word, then the answer should certainly be "yes." After all, if you are truly dedicated to strong marriages, flourishing families and religious liberty, then there's no more admirable and successful a place than the very blue state of Massachusetts, where teen pregnancy is rare (second lowest in the nation), divorce is rarer still (lowest in the nation), and religious freedom is so absolute as to be a non-issue.

But, of course, "family values" is not a matter of consensus; it's a matter of contentious disagreement and heated conflict. It turns out that whereas liberals, such as the people of Massachusetts, support policies that actually help real families to thrive in the literal sense — i.e., to be less poor, less hungry, less sick, less prematurely pregnant — conservatives prefer to praise families in the abstract, while withholding support of a more practical nature.

How to explain this? How is it possible that families tend to do poorly whenever the party of "family values" has the power to enact its ostensibly pro-family agenda? The answer to this question is rich and complicated, rather like life itself, but it starts with a single little three-letter word (also like life itself, come to think of it), namely...

Sex

When conservatives talk about "family values," what they're usually talking about is sex. For whatever reason, they don't seem to like it and they don't want anyone else to like it either. When it comes to valuing families, the conservative position consists mostly of verbally promoting chastity before marriage and monogamy within marriage until death. It doesn't seem to matter so much whether the policies they promote actually make people more chaste or committed to monogamous marriage; the important thing is the rhetoric.

Conservative rhetoric and policies are highly effective at expressing disapproval of sexual activity outside of marriage, whether pre-marital or extra-marital. The problem is that the policies that conservatives support are ineffective at actually promoting behavior that conforms to their standards, which is either a sign of fecklessness, or perhaps an ingenious plot to ensure that there will always be enough licentious behavior around to provide opportunities for them to express disapproval and take stands.

Teen Pregnancy

The teen pre-marital birth rate is highest in the most politically conservative region of the country — the South. The ten states with the highest teen birthrates in the U.S. are Southern states with conservative-majority legislatures.

The lowest rates of teen pregnancy occur in the some of the most liberal parts of the country: the North East, the upper Mid-West, and Washington State. The thirteen states with the lowest teen birthrates are all blue states (this includes New Hampshire).[71]

34

High rates of teen pregnancy are actually a direct consequence of conservative social attitudes and policies, since the disapproval of sexual activity before or outside of marriage prohibits making contraception available to unmarried teens. Red states tend to promote abstinence-only sex education, which has been shown to be ineffective in reducing sexual activity among teens. If teens in red states have the same amount of sex as teens in blue states but less access to contraception, it stands to reason they'd get pregnant more often.

This issue presents a painful dilemma to conservatives, since the only way to effectively lower the rate of teen pregnancy is to make contraception available, which would at least tacitly condone pre-marital sexual activity. Since expressing disapproval of sex is the actual priority, high levels of teen pregnancy are a regrettable but unavoidable consequence of the conservative "family values" agenda.

Maternity Leave

If the cornerstone of the traditional family is the mother, conservatives have an especially paradoxical approach to valuing families when it comes to supporting motherhood. Republicans have consistently opposed regular attempts by Democrats to provide paid leave for new mothers. As a result of this conservative resistance to what most nations — developed and undeveloped alike — consider to be a basic human right, the United States is one of only four countries in the world that does not mandate any paid leave for new mothers. The others are Papua New Guinea, Swaziland, and Liberia.[72] By comparison, the UK provides thirty-nine weeks of paid maternity leave;[73] France, a minimum of sixteen weeks;[74] Germany, a minimum of fourteen weeks;[75] Russia, a minimum of 140 days (i.e., twenty weeks);[76] China, a minimum of ninety days (i.e., thirteen weeks);[77] India, a minimum of twelve weeks;[78] Iran, a minimum of twenty-four weeks;[79] Israel, a minimum of fourteen weeks.[80]

The United States does have the Family and Medical Leave Act of 1993, which was passed by Democratic majorities in the House and

Senate and signed into law by Democratic president Bill Clinton. The law provides up to twelve weeks of *unpaid* leave and covers only employees of businesses that employ 50 or more people. It's pretty feeble by international standards, but better than what conservatives supported, which was nothing at all.

Democrats have regularly attempted to pass bills mandating paid leave, which would allow the U.S. finally to meet a standard of civilization which every developed nation and the great majority of undeveloped nations have long-since achieved. Every attempt has been opposed by a majority of Republicans.[81] [82] [83]

Divorce

Given the stresses and burdens that conservative "family values" impose on actual individuals and families, it should come as no surprise that the highest divorce rates in America occur among some of the most politically conservative Christian denominations, including Evangelical protestants.[84] Christians in general have a divorce rate that is higher than the national average. Indeed, Christian marriages fail more often than those of atheists and agnostics. For the record, the lowest rate of divorce in the U.S. occurs among Hindus.[85]

Divorce occurs most frequently in the most conservative states in the Union. Twelve of the fifteen states with the highest rates of divorce are red states.[86]

The lowest divorce rate in the nation is in the very blue state Massachusetts, which was also the first state in the U.S. to legalize same-sex marriage, in 2004.

Same-Sex Marriage

Conservatives characterize their position on same-sex marriage as "support for traditional marriage." But nobody is trying to limit, let alone ban, so-called traditional unions between a man and a woman. It is more accurate to describe the conservative position in terms of its opposition to expanding the rights and benefits of marriage to all adults above the age of consent. The conservative position is entirely negative: it involves denying rights to a class of citizens — denying the right to marry the person they love, denying the right to hold property jointly, denying the right to have a family that is legally recognized as such by the state.

The conservative position actually seeks to limit rather than expand the number of families in America. If it were to prevail, there would be fewer married couples in the U.S. and more children living in homes with unmarried parents.

As noted above, the first state to legalize same-sex marriage, Massachusetts, has the lowest divorce rate in the nation today. The state has actually seen a decline in the divorce rate since same-sex marriage was legalized in 2004.[87]

Poverty

In March of 2012, the House of Representatives voted to adopt the so-called "Ryan Budget" — a ten-year federal budget proposal covering fiscal years 2013-2022, designed by Congressman Paul Ryan, then the chairman of the House Budget Committee, who has long been regarded as the conservative movement's vision leader in fiscal matters. The measure passed by a vote of 244-191. All but ten Republican members voted for it. Every Democratic member voted against it.[88]

The Ryan budget takes an especially severe (one might say "severely conservative") approach to reducing support for poor families. It cuts income security programs — i.e., programs designed specifically to alleviate poverty, such as food stamps — by 16 percent, and "education, training, employment, and social services" by 33 percent.

The Ryan budget would also repeal the comprehensive health reform bill ("Obamacare"), which provides affordable health insurance coverage to most Americans, including 95 percent of children. It also cuts Medicaid — i.e., medical assistance for the poor and disabled — as well as grants for college students. This sort of thing is what the language gods had in mind when they invented the word "draconian."

At the same time, the Ryan budget would cut taxes for the wealthy and corporations by 10 percent. All in all, the plan would reduce tax revenues by $4.6 trillion over ten years, which is why draconian spending cuts would be required in order to avoid massive increases in the deficit. The fiscal philosophy couldn't be plainer — it divides the world into "makers" vs. "takers" and seeks to reward the former while penalizing the latter.

This conservative dream budget would be a nightmare for families who struggle to make ends meet and hope to provide a better life for their children. It effectively robs families not only of material support, but of the opportunity to improve their circumstances. Robert Greenstein of the Center for Budget and Policy Priorities described it as "Robin Hood in reverse — on steroids."[89]

The good news is that the Ryan budget will never be implemented as long as there is a Democratic president. The Republicans who devised and declared their public support for this bill knew that, which makes their "yes" votes essentially symbolic — a sort of declaration of principles rather than a serious attempt at legislation. (Again — the conservative penchant for "making statements.") So what principles were they declaring? Basically, that poor families do not deserve government support, especially if it comes at the expense of the wealthy. In their view, wealth is worth, not just in the material sense, but also in a moral sense. Poverty is therefore quite literally unworthy of assistance. God helps those who help themselves, and the Ryan budget helps society's worthy "makers" help themselves to an increasing share of the nation's wealth, while the worthless poor become ever poorer and thus ever more unworthy of respect and support. This is the message that conservatives went out of their way to declare, by passing a symbolic budget that has no chance of being implemented.

Although the Ryan budget won't be enacted at the federal level, conservatives have been able to apply their fiscal principles at the state level. The results have been predictably grim for families.

Seventeen of the twenty poorest states in the union (in terms of median household income) are red states, with consistently conservative government.

Sixteen of the twenty states with the highest levels of child poverty are red states.[90]

Sixteen of the twenty states with the highest levels of economic distress (in terms of a combination of housing foreclosures, unemployment and participation in the food stamp program) are red states.[91]

Nationally, child poverty has tended to decrease under Democratic presidencies and increase under Republicans — a pattern that goes back at least 50 years.[92]

Violent Crime and Public Safety

Gun violence is a major public health problem in the United States. Every year, firearms kill more than 30,000 Americans,[93] including 2,500 children and teens. Conservatives have consistently failed — or, more accurately, refused — to even acknowledge this problem, let alone propose any serious measures to deal with it. Instead, they insist that any attempt to pass gun safety laws would constitute an intolerable threat to their Second Amendment rights.

In 2010, homicide by firearm was the fourth leading cause of death for children between the ages of 5 and 14.[94] Every year more children and teens die from gunshot wounds than troops have died in the War in Afghanistan, which is the longest war in American history. On average, guns kill more than fifty children and teens in America every week.[95]

Republicans in congress have consistently resisted Democratic efforts to enact gun safety legislation, claiming that it would violate the Second Amendment, and that, in any case, it wouldn't be effective. Yet, they have offered no proposals of their own to address one of the most devastating threats to families in America, which is tantamount to denying that gun violence is even a problem worth attempting to solve.

There is in fact a proven correlation between the availability of guns and violent death or injury from guns.[96] In those parts of the country where gun ownership is more prevalent, death and injury due to firearms, whether intentional or accidental, is higher.[97]

Among the twenty states with the highest levels of gun violence (i.e., gun deaths per capita), eighteen are conservative Red states (the exceptions are D.C. and New Mexico). Seventeen of the bottom twenty are relatively liberal blue states (the exceptions are Nebraska, North Dakota and South Dakota).[98]

The most politically and socially conservative region in the country — the South — is also the most violent region by far, with 40 percent more violent deaths per capita as the next most violent region, the West, and 75 percent more than the least violent — and most liberal — region, the Northeast.[99]

In fairness, we must recognize that there are some Republicans who acknowledge the problem of gun violence in America and believe the government should act to address it. But we should also recognize that the measures currently under discussion — requiring background checks for all gun purchasers; making it illegal to buy weapons in order to resell them to third parties; limiting the maximum capacity of magazines for semi-automatic weapons; an outright ban on assault weapons (which is not considered likely to pass) — are all long-standing Democratic proposals which have been resisted by a large majority of Republicans for years.

Destruction of the Environment

Conservatives in the United States are the only major political faction among all the nations of the developed world that consistently denies climate change and opposes any and all measures to address it. This comes from both right-wing Christians and anti-regulation corporatists.[100] It's understandable that oil and coal companies oppose climate change legislation that would limit the use of their products — it's a simple matter of the bottom line. But it is perverse for conservatives to place their devotion to the interests of corporations above those of their own descendants.

The conservative denial of climate change places the material interests of people today above the well-being of people in the future. If their attitude prevails, the weather will continue to become more severe. Food will become scarcer. The conditions of life will become harsher. The refusal to acknowledge global warming reflects a lack of concern for the conditions in which future generations will live. This disregard for the well-being of one's children and children's children is perfectly antithetical to real family values.

REASONS FOR THE DISCONNECT?

Sex

Conservatives get credit for being concerned with family values because they speak about "family values" all the time. Talking about something a lot suggests that you really care about it. And, of course, conservatives do in fact care a great deal about "family values" insofar as the term describes a certain standard of moral conduct or to be precise, sexual conduct. That is the real issue here.

Conservatives disapprove of sexual conduct that occurs outside of traditional marriage, as they define it. They believe that premarital sex is immoral; extramarital sex is immoral; homosexual sex is immoral. When it comes to expressing disapproval of the wrong kinds of sex, they are indeed steadfast in their commitment to upholding "family values."

Semantics

For conservatives, "family values" is not about promoting policies that help all families to thrive. It's about promoting a particular view of what a "traditional family" is: one man and one woman bound in holy matrimony, along with their children. Moreover, it's also about condemning conduct or family arrangements that don't conform to

41

their particular standards. In their view, any arrangement that does not conform to the conservative standard cannot be considered a legitimate family and is thus unworthy of support.

If on the other hand, we take the words literally, "family values" must refer to a set of principles that support families, both morally and materially. As we've seen, America's most liberal state — Massachusetts — does very well by this standard. It has the lowest rate of divorce and the second lowest rate of teen pregnancy, which ought to attract the admiration of all proponents of family values. Instead, Massachusetts is a regular object of contempt among conservatives — one need only to mention the word "Massachusetts" to evoke eye rolls and disapproving head shakes in conservative circles.

The truth is that "family values," like much of what we hear from Conservatives, is little more than a slogan — a virtuous sounding phrase that conceals an agenda that is anything but supportive of the great majority of real families who are struggling to survive with a modicum of security and dignity in the United States. The point of the conservative "family values" agenda is to exclude Americans who don't conform to or comply with their particular standards or views. It is precisely this concept of "family values" that prevents conservatives from supporting policies that actually value families.

THE U.S. IS A CHRISTIAN NATION

The Government of the United States of America is not, in any sense, founded on the Christian religion.
— The *Treaty of Tripoli*, ratified by the United States and signed by President John Adams in 1797[101]

We establish no religion in this country, we command no worship, we mandate no belief, nor will we ever. Church and state are, and must remain, separate. All are free to believe or not believe, all are free to practice a faith or not, and those who believe are free, and should be free, to speak of and act on their belief.
— Ronald Reagan, October 26, 1984[102]

CONSERVATIVES CLAIM...

The United States of America is founded on Christian principles. The Founders were inspired by the Bible, which is as important a guide as the Constitution. American civilization has a distinctively Christian character and, what's more, the United States has been singled out by the Christian God to fulfill a unique and pre-eminent role among all the nations of the Earth.

THE REALITY

Christians of all denominations made up about 70 percent of the U.S.

population in 2014, so it is certainly true that the United States is a nation in which the majority of citizens identify themselves as Christians.[103] By the same standard, the U.S. is also a right-handed nation, a brown-eyed nation, and a nation of people with Type O-positive blood.[104] Even by a purely demographic standard, the U.S. is becoming less Christian. The percentage of Americans who identify themselves as Christian declined by 8 percent between 2007 and 2014, while the percentage of religiously unaffiliated Americans increased by 7 percent.[105]

However, when conservatives insist that the U.S. is a Christian nation, they're not talking about demographics alone — they mean that the nation has a distinctively Christian character and identity. And while it is certainly true that American civilization has been influenced by the beliefs of many Christian citizens and politicians, it is equally true that the nation was founded by men who deliberately sought to exclude religion — including Christianity — from the public sphere.

The U.S. Constitution does not promote Christianity over other creeds. There is no reference to Jesus Christ or Christianity in the Constitution, nor does the word "God" appear anywhere in the document. Religion in general is only mentioned twice. Both mentions are negative — Article VI prohibits any religious test for holding public office, and the First Amendment explicitly forbids establishing an official state religion or prohibiting citizens from practicing whatever religion they like.

Faith

The Founders' personal religious convictions continue to be matters of debate, but their words leave little doubt that they had no intention of establishing a nation that was Christian in any sense of the term.

We actually have a careful record of the discussions surrounding the writing of the Constitution. On August 15th, 1789, during the debate about the wording of the First Amendment, James Madison made his intentions very clear: "Congress should not establish a religion, and enforce the legal observation of it by law, nor compel men to worship God in any Manner contrary to their conscience."[106]

Several years before, Madison had declared, in a speech before the Virginia General Assembly, "During almost fifteen centuries has the legal establishment of Christianity been on trial. What have been its fruits? More or less in all places, pride and indolence in the Clergy, ignorance and servility in the laity, in both, superstition, bigotry and persecution."[107]

Thomas Jefferson produced his own version of the New Testament, entitled *The Life and Morals of Jesus of Nazareth*, in which he eliminated every mention of Jesus's divinity, along with all the miracles and supernatural events, including the resurrection. Jefferson's Jesus was a virtuous and enlightened human being, but pointedly not a supernatural figure, let alone the son of God.

Thomas Paine, whose pamphlet *Common Sense* was the spark that ignited popular support for independence from Britain in 1776, later published *The Age of Reason*, which was brutally critical of organized religion in general, and Christianity in particular. "All national institutions of churches, whether Jewish, Christian, or Turkish [i.e., Muslim], appear to me no other than human inventions set up to terrify and enslave mankind, and monopolize power and profit."

John Quincy Adams, not a Founder himself, but the son of a Founder, took the presidential oath of office in 1825 by affirmation, not by swearing to God. Nor did he place his hand on a Bible — instead he used a law book, which contained the text of the Constitution.

Works

Let's also consider how the United States conducts itself, and how this conduct compares with the actual life and teachings of Jesus Christ.

Poverty & Wealth

Jesus gave comfort to the poor and admonished the rich, saying that "it is easier for a camel to go through a needle's eye, than for a rich man to enter into the kingdom of God." (Luke 18:25).

Contrary to the teaching and example of Christ, Americans don't have any problem with wealth. As a society, we don't even have mixed feelings about it. Americans work hard at accumulating as much wealth as possible, and they're very, very good at it. With over $63 trillion held in private hands, Americans possess more than 40 percent of the world's total wealth while accounting for less than 5 percent of the world's population.[108] The next wealthiest nation, China, has a little over 10 percent of the world's wealth, distributed (not very evenly) among a population four times as large.

Despite being the world's wealthiest nation by far, the United States has one of the highest rates of poverty among developed nations. More than 17 percent of U.S. citizens live in poverty. That amounts to more than fifty million people. According to the Organization for Economic Cooperation and Development (OECD), only four developed nations (Mexico, Turkey, Israel, and Chile) have a higher percentage of citizens living in poverty.[109]

Clearly, the U.S. has the means to alleviate poverty if it wanted to do so. The high levels of poverty and economic inequality in America are a matter of choice — a distinctly unchristian choice.

Death Penalty

Christianity is a religion of forgiveness. Jesus said, "Blessed are the merciful: for they shall obtain mercy" (Matthew 5:7). And Saint Paul preached, "Avenge not yourselves, but rather give place unto wrath: for it is written, Vengeance is mine; I will repay, saith the Lord" (Romans 12:19), which means that it is not up to human beings to exact revenge in this life — that's God's prerogative. Americans, however, have demonstrated that they aren't satisfied with the Christian attitude to revenge. As we've already seen (in chapter 2 "The G.O.P. is the Pro-Life Party"), the United States consistently ranks among the top five nations in the world in terms of the total number of prisoners it executes, along with China, Saudi

Arabia, Iran, and Iraq.[110] The only other developed nation that executes its own citizens is Japan. One thing all these nations have in common is that they put convicted prisoners to death. Another thing they have in common is that none of them can legitimately be described as a Christian nation.

War

War is just about the most un-Christ-like activity imaginable. Jesus was clear and firm on this subject: "A new commandment I give unto you, That ye love one another; as I have loved you, that ye also love one another." (John 13:34-35) "But I say unto you, love your enemies, bless them that curse you, do good to them that hate you, and pray for them which despitefully use you, and persecute you." (Matthew 5:44)

The United States is the most formidable military power in the history of the world. We fought four major wars in the 20th century (five if you include the first Gulf War). We have been constantly at war in the 21st. Our military budget accounts for between forty and 50 percent of all military spending on planet Earth in any given year. Military spending accounted for 17 percent of the federal budget in 2014, more than all other discretionary spending combined. The United States is by far the largest manufacturer and exporter of arms in the world, accounting for almost a third of all weapons sales.[111] The U.S. is the only country in history to have used nuclear weapons in war, which it did twice, knowingly causing the deaths of two-hundred thousand innocent civilians.

The Iraq War was a war of choice, waged against a country that had not attacked us, or been complicit in any attack against us. Well over a hundred thousand innocent human beings (mostly civilians) have been killed as a direct result of this war, which was entered into with the support of a majority of Americans, and which a majority of conservative Americans continue to support.

Even if Iraq had somehow been involved in the 9/11 attacks, which it was not, and even if all the victims of the Iraq War had been enemy combatants, which they were not, the toll of this retribution would represent a ratio of one-hundred dead Iraqis for each victim of 9/11. You'd think that Christians would be familiar with the biblical law of proportional retribution — an eye for an eye. That's one eye for one eye; one life for one life. Of course, that law is found in the Old Testament. The New Testament — the specifically Christian one — goes further and forbids revenge altogether. "Ye have heard that it hath been said, An eye for an eye, and a tooth for a tooth: But I say unto you, That ye resist not evil: but whosoever shall smite thee on thy right cheek, turn to him the other also." (Matthew 5:38-39) Almost every page of the New Testament features a rebuke to some aspect of the American way of life. The many ways in which the United States fails to walk the Christian walk despite all its Christian talk could be the subject of a book twice as long as this one. But we need to move on.

We'll let Jesus have the last word. "Why do you not understand what I say? It is because you cannot accept my word." (John 8:43)

REASONS FOR THE DISCONNECT?

Pilgrims vs. Founders

The first settlements in the North America were founded by the pilgrims, who were puritan Christians seeking to establish a Christian society. But these puritans were British subjects; the colonies they founded were chartered by the British crown. They were not attempting to create a politically independent nation.

The United States of America did not come into existence until more than 150 years after the arrival of the Mayflower and the foundation of the Massachusetts Bay Colony. As we've seen, the leaders of the American Revolution and writers of the Constitution had no intention of establishing a Christian nation — indeed they deliberately sought to exclude religion from the nation's official

identity.
Revisionism vs. Communism

Phrases such as "under God" in the pledge of allegiance and "In God We Trust" on our currency give the impression that religion has always been a prominent part of our official political culture. In fact, these words were not introduced until the 1950s, just as the Cold War was intensifying against the Soviet Union, with its official creed of "godless" Communism.

The original text of the Pledge of Allegiance, composed in 1892 (by a self-proclaimed socialist, no less), was: "I pledge allegiance to my Flag and the Republic for which it stands, one nation, indivisible, with liberty and justice for all." The text was amended on several occasions in subsequent years, but not until 1954 was the phrase "under God" added.[112]

The motto "In God we trust" began to appear on U.S. coins around the time of the Civil War and was used intermittently on various coins in subsequent decades, but it was not adopted as the official motto of the United States until 1956. It first appeared on paper bills in 1957.[113]

Conservatives vs. Reality

Many conservative Americans are Christians. So are many liberal Americans. In fact, the number of Christians who identify as Democrats (40 percent) is only slightly lower than the number who identify as Republicans (43 percent).[114]

Whereas liberals and Democrats in general are comfortable with the separation church and state, many conservatives are not. They want to believe that they live in an America that fully reflects their particular values and priorities, including their religious convictions. This accounts for the distinction they often make between "real Americans" and everybody else. By claiming that America is a Christian nation, they define America in terms that exclude and delegitimize other Americans with different views and lifestyles.

America's diversity is a threat to conservatives who don't want to believe that they are no longer the majority, if they ever were. The problem for this type of conservative is that there's more of everybody else that there is of them, but they can't face the prospect of being in the minority.

LIBERALS ARE WAGING A "WAR" ON CHRISTIANITY

I'm not ashamed to admit that I'm a Christian, but you don't need to be in the pew every Sunday to know there's something wrong in this country when gays can serve openly in the military but our kids can't openly celebrate Christmas or pray in school. As president, I'll end Obama's war on religion, and I'll fight against liberal attacks on our religious heritage.
— G.O.P. presidential candidate and Texas governor Rick Perry, in a campaign ad, December, 2011[115]

CONSERVATIVES CLAIM...

Liberals are generally hostile to the Christian religion. They are "secular humanists" who want to suppress or even eradicate any open expression of Christianity from American culture. There is a liberal "war on Christmas."

THE REALITY

Until very recently, more Christians in the United States identified themselves as Democrats than as Republicans. Of all Christian denominations in America, only two — Evangelicals and Mormons — identify more as Republicans than as Democrats.[116]

In December of 2007, the U.S. House of Representatives (then held by the Democrats), passed House Resolution 847, "Recognizing the importance of Christmas and the Christian faith." Here is the complete text of the resolution:

Resolved, That the House of Representatives

1. recognizes the Christian faith as one of the great religions of the world;
2. expresses continued support for Christians in the United States and worldwide;
3. acknowledges the international religious and historical importance of Christmas and the Christian faith;
4. acknowledges and supports the role played by Christians and Christianity in the founding of the United States and in the formation of the western civilization;
5. rejects bigotry and persecution directed against Christians, both in the United States and worldwide; and
6. expresses its deepest respect to American Christians and Christians throughout the world.

The final vote tally was 372 in favor, nine opposed (forty did not vote and 10 voted "present").[117] 195 of the "yea" votes were Democratic and 177 were Republican. The Democrats were in the majority at the time and thus had control of the voting agenda — they could easily have prevented the bill from ever coming to a vote. But they didn't.

Among recent Democratic presidents, Jimmy Carter and Bill Clinton are Baptists, and Barack Obama is currently unaffiliated, having publicly broken in 2008 with his congregation of twenty years, the Trinity United Church of Christ in Chicago. That break occurred because of remarks made by the Reverend Jeremiah Wright, a controversial Christian minister.

Since entering the White House, the president and his family have attended services at numerous Christian churches in the Washington D.C. area, including, according to Politico.com, "19th Street Baptist Church, the Washington National Cathedral, Allen Chapel A.M.E. Church, Vermont Avenue Baptist Church, Metropolitan A.M.E. Church, Shiloh Baptist Church and multiple services at St. John's Episcopal Church and Evergreen Chapel at Camp David."[118]

All three recent Democratic presidents have led the nation in prayer on numerous occasions. All have attended the annual National Prayer Breakfast in Washington and engaged in public prayer at these occasions. Former presidents Bill Clinton and Jimmy Carter have both been leaders in the movement to establish a "New Baptist Covenant" as an alternative to the increasingly conservative-dominated Southern Baptist Convention. This movement represents an attempt to reclaim the Christian religion for liberals and other non-conservatives — it's the very opposite of a "war on Christianity."

The benediction at Barack Obama's first inauguration was delivered by Reverend Joseph Lowery, a minister in the United Methodist Church and a former president of the Southern Christian Leadership Conference, a position once held by Dr. Martin Luther King Jr., who was himself both a Christian minister and a liberal icon. The benediction at Obama's second inauguration was delivered by another Christian minister, the Reverend Luis Leon, pastor of an Episcopal church in Washington D.C.

Even the 2012 Democratic Party platform firmly embraced religion: "There is no conflict between supporting faith-based institutions and respecting our Constitution, and a full commitment to both principles is essential for the continued flourishing of both faith and country."[119]

If you are a Christian who thinks that you are being discriminated against, try this thought experiment: you go to the DMV to renew your driver's license and there is a menorah in the lobby and a Star of David on the wall, prominently displayed next to the American flag.

Or imagine this: your kids come home from school and you ask how their day was. They tell you it was interesting: from now on, at certain appointed hours, all students and teachers will stop whatever they're doing and turn towards Mecca to offer a prayer to Allah.

How would you react to this? If you find it disturbing, but believe that it would be different if Christianity were the religion being promoted because America is a Christian nation, then you have a bone to pick with the founding fathers.

The issue is not whether you are allowed to practice or to profess your own religion, but whether you are compelling others to profess and practice a religion not their own. This position is not only grounded in the liberal values of religious toleration and openness, it is dictated by the First Amendment to the U.S. Constitution itself: "Congress shall make no law respecting an establishment of religion, nor prohibiting the free exercise thereof..." In other words, the government and its instruments (such as schools and court rooms) is forbidden from embracing a particular religion, or granting a privileged position to any particular religion's doctrine, messages, or symbols.

The Real War on Christmas

Having said all of the above, it would be incorrect to suggest that Christmas has never been threatened in America. Although there is nothing to justify current fears about a war on Christmas, there is a precedent in America's past. The celebration of Christmas was actually banned at one time — and in the bluest of all blue states, Massachusetts. We do have to go back a bit, though — to the seventeenth century. Christmas was banned by the puritans in Massachusetts from 1659-1681. Anyone caught celebrating the holiday was subject to a fine of five shillings, which was nothing to sneeze at back then.[120] So it seems that the only actual war on Christmas was waged by Christians, and pretty conservative Christians at that.

According to the standards of today's Christmas vigilantes, the founders of the nation weren't much better. There is no mention of Christmas — or, indeed, Christianity — in the Constitution or the Bill of Rights. Indeed, Christmas was not even made a federal holiday until 1870.[121] But it has remained so ever since, under Democratic and Republican presidents alike.

For each of the past eighty-nine years, since the presidency of Calvin Coolidge, there has been a national Christmas tree displayed in Washington. Since 1978 — during the presidency of Democratic president Jimmy Carter — the tree has stood on the Ellipse, immediately South of the White House grounds. Every year, the president personally lights the tree in a nationally televised ceremony broadcast by public television stations nationwide — your tax dollars at work![122] At the most recent ceremony, President Obama's remarks included the following Christian sentiments: "More than 2,000 years ago, a child was born to two faithful travelers who could find rest only in a stable, among the cattle and the sheep. But this was not just any child. Christ's birth made the angels rejoice and attracted shepherds and kings from afar. He was a manifestation of God's love for us. And He grew up to become a leader with a servant's heart who taught us a message as simple as it is powerful: that we should love God, and love our neighbor as ourselves. That teaching has come to encircle the globe. It has endured for generations. And today, it lies at the heart of my Christian faith and that of millions of Americans. No matter who we are, or where we come from, or how we worship, it's a message that can unite all of us on this holiday season."[123]

From President Obama's remarks at the National Prayer Breakfast, February 2, 2012: "I have fallen on my knees with great regularity... asking God for guidance not just in my personal life and my Christian walk, but in the life of this nation and in the values that hold us together and keep us strong. I know that He will guide us. He always has, and He always will. And I pray his richest blessings on each of you in the days ahead."[124]

The world's most prominent Christmas tree is displayed every year at Rockefeller Center in New York City, which is not only the most liberal big city in America but the literal epicenter of the allegedly liberal media — 30 Rockefeller Plaza, the building that houses the headquarters and studios of NBC and MSNBC.[125]

There is no liberal war on Christmas or Christianity.

REASONS FOR THE DISCONNECT?

1st Amendment Confusion

The 1st Amendment to the Constitution prohibits the establishment of a state religion, which means that the government is forbidden from promoting a particular religion or religion in general. Successive legal decisions over the decades have made it clear that the prohibition extends to the states as well. But this does not mean that American citizens are not free to practice whatever reason they choose more or less whenever, wherever, and however they like. The Constitution bans directed prayer in public schools, because a public institution can't promote religion; but the Constitution also *protects* the right to pray in schools. Students and teachers have a right to pray on school property in their own time or even to form religious clubs or prayer groups — public schools just can't take the lead in making them do so.

The Fox Factor

In December 2011, the O'Reilly Factor devoted three times as much coverage to the non-existent "War on Christmas" as to the ongoing war in Afghanistan,[126] where 560 American service members died during the course of the year, twenty-seven during that month alone.[127] Evidently, ratings are better for coverage of fictional wars than for actual ones.

God Knows

A small number of conservative Christians seem to feel permanently threatened by any sign of official respect for religions other than their own. You can pray anywhere and everywhere, even in school, except under a few very limited circumstances. You can profess your religion anywhere and everywhere, except under a few very limited circumstances. Conservative Christians believe that limitations on their ability to use every occasion freely to promote their creed constitutes some kind of oppression. Christianity is by far the dominant religion in the United States. Christmas is a national holiday and there is a national Christmas tree. Nearly 80 percent of Americans identify themselves as Christian.[128] How could anyone honestly believe that Christianity in America is under serious attack? And yet they do.

AMERICA IS THE FREEST NATION ON EARTH

If a nation expects to be ignorant & free, in a state of civilization, it expects what never was & never will be.
— Thomas Jefferson

We must be free not because we claim freedom, but because we practice it.
— William Faulkner

CONSERVATIVES CLAIM...

The United States is a uniquely free country and is a beacon of liberty to the rest of the world. Other countries may be free and democratic, but none is as free and democratic as America. Our freedoms are the envy of the Earth — which is why other countries look up to us and terrorists want to destroy us.

THE REALITY

To begin at the beginning: for the first eighty-nine years of its existence, the U.S. economy depended on the institution of chattel slavery. Millions of human beings were held in bondage, utterly deprived of any and all rights, privileges, or liberties. Millions of other human beings profited directly and indirectly from this system of oppression; the entire society was implicated, both practically and morally. The people of the North did not hold slaves, but they certainly benefitted from cheap cotton and other products of slavery. Abolitionists became active in the North in the decades leading up to the Civil War, but they did not represent a majority of Northerners, let alone of Americans as a whole — in 1860, Abraham Lincoln, the only candidate running on an abolitionist platform, won the presidential election with a majority of electoral votes, but only 40 percent of the popular vote. (It was a four person race.)

The Emancipation Proclamation technically freed all slaves in 1863; the 13th Amendment effectively ended the institution of slavery in 1865. But crimes against freedom did not just magically cease. Oppression and exclusion of African Americans persisted to such a degree that a full century later the Civil Rights Act (1964) and the Voting Rights Act (1965) had to be passed in order to guarantee them the most basic privileges of citizenship. And, of course, the civil rights laws of the 1960s were no more magical than the presidential proclamation and the constitutional amendment of the 1860s.

Laws are only as strong as the will to enforce them. In America, that will has been inconsistent at best. Today, millions of Americans who are the descendants of slaves still do not enjoy the whole set of privileges and opportunities available to their fellow citizens.

That a country with such a history can have always, from its foundation, considered itself a beacon of liberty — indeed, the very "land of the free" — says a lot about its character. We don't see the present clearly; we don't fully reckon with the past. America is not quite the beacon of liberty that it imagines itself to be.

A Free Country in an Increasingly Free World

Freedom House rates 44 percent of the world's countries — from Chile to Mongolia — as fully free; together, these countries provide 40 percent of the world's citizens with freedom of expression, assembly, and worship, and freedom of movement within and across borders. The United States is among the freest countries in the word, but Freedom House rates forty countries as freer. Moreover, the U.S. was one of sixteen countries that have become less free in recent years "because of the cumulative impact of flaws in the electoral system, a disturbing increase in the role of private money in election campaigns and the legislative process, legislative gridlock, the failure of the Obama administration to fulfill promises of enhanced government openness, and fresh evidence of racial discrimination and other dysfunctions in the criminal justice system."[129]

According to *The Economist's* "Democracy Index," the U.S. is the twentieth most democratic country on Earth. Fifteen Western European nations are considered more democratic, as are Canada, Australia, New Zealand, and the tiny island nation of Mauritius.[130] *The Economist* bases these rankings on a combination of five factors: electoral process and pluralism; functioning of government; political participation; political culture; and civil liberties.

The libertarian Cato Institute offers a similar assessment in their 2015 *Human Freedom Index*, which considers seventy-six different factors, including the rule of law, civil society, security and safety, size of government, property rights, regulation of credit, labor and business conditions, and freedom of movement, religion, association, assembly, expression, and relationships. Their working definition: "Freedom in our usage is a social concept that recognizes the dignity of individuals and is defined by the absence of coercive constraint." Their conclusions: "The top 10 jurisdictions in order were Hong Kong, Switzerland, Finland, Denmark, New Zealand, Canada, Australia, Ireland, the United Kingdom, and Sweden. The United States is ranked in twentieth place."[131]

The Power of Elites

A major study released in 2014 determined that the United States is not a functioning democracy. The authors of the study, Professors Martin Gilens of Princeton University and Benjamin I. Page of Northwestern analyzed more than 1,800 policy initiatives during the period from 1981 to 2002 and concluded that the American political system is one of "Economic Elite Domination." They found that the level of popular support for a particular policy has no statistical bearing on whether it will be taken up and passed by Congress. On the other hand, support from elites and special interest groups is highly correlated with the likelihood that a policy will be implemented. In other words, the preferences of economic elites and special interests drive policymaking; public support, on the other hand, has little if any effect.[132]

In an interview about the study's findings, Gilens said that "ordinary citizens have virtually no influence over what their government does in the United States. And economic elites and interest groups, especially those representing business, have a substantial degree of influence."[133]

Consider, for example, the question of mandatory background checks for all gun purchasers. Polls consistently show very high levels of support — in the range of 90 percent of all Americans — and yet Congress has yet to pass any laws that reflect this overwhelming public consensus.[134] Instead, lawmakers do the bidding of the National Rifle Association, a lobbying organization that represents the interests of the firearms industry.

The Power of the Two Parties

Compared to other advanced democracies, U.S. citizens have fewer choices at the ballot box. Most advanced democracies have a wide variety of political parties to choose between — the U.K. has twelve; France has eighteen; Germany, seven; Japan, eight; India, seventeen; Israel, fourteen; Spain, more than twenty; and Brazil, more than thirty.[135] Many of these parties are relatively small and inconsequential most of the time, but they do have enough of a public profile to offer citizens a broad spectrum of alternative views and policy proposals.

The U.S. has, for all intents and purposes, two parties. There are technically dozens of others, some of them serious — the Green Party, for instance — but these alternative parties are precluded from any serious consideration, since the two major parties literally control the electoral process in the U.S. Moreover, the campaign finance system, which provides no public funding for national races, requires that any candidate who wants to vie seriously for federal office be able to raise many millions of dollars in private money — a virtual impossibility for anyone who is not a member of one of the two major parties.

The Republican and Democratic Parties may be political rivals, but they are also partners who together dominate American government much as a cartel dominates an industry. The parties differ on many issues, but they also see eye-to-eye on many issues of enormous consequence to the American people — free trade; prosecuting a "war on drugs" that emphasizes criminalization over rehabilitation; spending a half-trillion dollars annually on the military; perpetuating the system of privately-funded campaign finance. When it comes to these policies, the American people don't even have the pretense of a choice in the matter.

Since the two major parties actually run the electoral process itself, including state primaries and caucuses, as well as the presidential debates, Americans' choices at the ballot box are severely limited by a system that effectively excludes any alternative voices from even being heard.

Vote Suppression

Voting practices vary by state, but it is certainly fair to observe that voting in United States is generally more complicated than it needs to be. Americans who wish to vote in an election face a series of annoying obstacles that may not rise to the level of outright suppression, but do cause a variety of inconveniences that discourage participation in the electoral process. Only two states, Oregon and California, automatically register citizens to vote; eleven states allow citizens to register on election day; the rest require citizens to register in advance. Election day is not a holiday, as it is in many countries — in many states, the voting system is so inefficient that it is impossible to participate without having to take several hours off from work, which is not an option for many people, especially the poor.

In recent years, G.O.P. controlled states have passed a variety of laws that restrict access to the polls, or at least to make voting more difficult. The most notorious of these are "voter ID" laws that require voters to present approved forms of identification, which places another time-consuming burden on poorer citizens who may not already have a legally required form of I.D.. According to the National Conference of State Legislatures, eleven states have "strict" voter ID laws.[136] Throughout the country, G.O.P. controlled states such as Arizona, and North Carolina have also shortened early-voting periods and limited the number of polling stations on election day.

In twelve states, convicted felons are prohibited from voting — not only while they are in prison or on parole, but for the rest of their lives. By contrast, the European Union has declared voting to be a human right. Most E.U. member nations don't automatically deny voting rights to convicted felons even while they are in prison. Almost six million U.S. citizens who have already "paid their debt to society" are permanently deprived of the right to vote — that amounts to about 2.5 percent of the voting age population.[137] Because a higher proportion of African Americans are convicted of felonies, a higher proportion — more than 7.5 percent — are permanently disenfranchised.[138]

Prisons

In one category, the United States is literally the *least* free nation on Earth. The U.S. has the world's largest prison population, both in terms of absolute numbers — about 2.2 million — and as a percentage of the overall population — about 0.67 percent. (According to the most recent available statistics (as of March 2016) the U.S. actually has the second highest per-capita rate of incarceration, after the Seychelles, which has a tiny population of about 90,000. The total prison population of the Seychelles is 735 — that's seven hundred and thirty-five individuals.

The U.S. incarcerates more people than China, despite the fact that it has a population less than one-fourth the size. We have a billion fewer people, and yet keep about half-a-million more behind bars. [139]

In 2011, the Justice Policy Institute compared the sentencing practices of five advanced nations with similar crime rates — the U.S., the U.K, Germany, Finland, and Australia. The study found that the U.S. resorts far more often to incarceration than to other methods of punishment, such as parole, fines, and community service, whereas the other countries in the study favored fines and parole. In total, 70 percent of convictions in the U.S. result in prison sentences. None of the other countries are anywhere close to this — Canada, the next most punitive country in this category, imprisons 34 percent of its convicted criminals; the U.K., less than 10 percent.[140]

Not only do American courts send more convicted criminals to prison; they also impose harsher sentences. The average prison sentence in the U.S. is sixty-three months, almost twice as long as that of the next most punitive country, Australia, which has an average of thirty-six months. In the U.K. the average sentence is thirteen months. In Germany, it's less than a year.

It's worth restating that these are all countries with similar crime rates. A historically more draconian approach to crime in the U.S. has not lead to lower crime rates.

Militarization of the Police

Law enforcement in the United States is also exceptionally brutal and repressive for an advanced democracy. *The Economist's* Democracy Index report observed that the country has become less free in recent years owing to "the use of excessive violence by the state, as perpetrated by law-enforcement officers." The editors go on: "The US law-enforcement system is violent and punitive, to the extent that not only blacks, but a large percentage of whites, do not have confidence in the police or the criminal justice system more broadly (37% of blacks have confidence in the police, compared with 59% of whites). The para-militarized police force, now equipped with grenade launchers and armored cars, is lethal. In 2015, more than 1,100 Americans died at the hands of US law-enforcement officers, according to a database compiled by a UK newspaper, The Guardian (the US government does not keep a comprehensive record of people killed by law-enforcement officers). The US jails 1 percent of the adult population, more than five times the developed-country average, and sentences are harsh (the US is the only developed country to impose life without parole for persistent, non-violent offenders)."[141]

This sort of state-perpetrated violence is virtually unheard of in other advanced democracies.

REASONS FOR THE DISCONNECT?

History vs. today

Throughout its history the United States has been pre-eminent in establishing the freedoms and democratic values that were once rare, but which most of the world now enjoys. Today, however, in the second decade of the 21st century, America is no longer *exceptionally* free. Many countries have caught up to the U.S.; quite a few have surpassed it.

Eagles, Flags, Guns

America may not actually be the freest country in the world, but it is certainly the world leader in brandishing symbols of liberty. Our liberties may be eroding, but our rich iconography of freedom — eagles, flags, public recitals of the Pledge of Allegiance — is still going strong.

Conservatives may support the very policies that are actually making America less free, like voter ID laws, "tough on crime" law-enforcement policies, but they are always ready to wave the flag, invoke the Constitution, and fight for ever looser gun laws, as though these symbols are what liberty is really all about.

"We're Number One" Mentality

From the Conservative point of view, America's primacy among nations does not depend on our actions or attitudes — it is simply an incontrovertible existential fact. Anyone who denies this fact is ipso-facto unpatriotic. America simply is — and must be — the best at everything that is deemed good. Freedom is good; therefore America must be the best in the world at being free. QED.

PART 2

THE ECONOMY

THE ECONOMY DOES BETTER UNDER REPUBLICANS

It just seems that the economy does better under the Democrats than the Republicans.
— Donald Trump[142]

CONSERVATIVES CLAIM...

Republicans are the business-friendly party. Democrats are hostile to private enterprise and clueless about how to grow the economy — when it comes to economic policy, their mantra is "tax and spend." Democrats place onerous regulations on businesses which make it difficult for them to succeed in a competitive economy. Republicans are far more competent at helping the marketplace to thrive, mostly by getting out of the way and letting the "job creators" in the private sector do what they do best.

THE REALITY

If by "economy" you mean jobs, productivity, the stock market, and corporate performance, and by "does better" you mean that all these things go up as opposed to down, then the economy does much better under Democrats.

Jobs

From 1937 to 2009, each party held the White House for an equivalent period of time: 36 years. During this period, 102.4 million jobs were created in the U.S. economy. 34.6 million were created under Republicans, 67.8 million — nearly twice as many — under Democrats. The average increase in employment per presidential term was 1.2 percent for Republicans and 3.02 percent for Democrats.[143]

If we rank presidential terms according to job growth rate during this period, eight of the top ten are Democratic, while nine of the bottom ten are Republican.

On the day Ronald Reagan took office, there were about ninety-one million Americans in the workforce. When he left office eight years later, there were about 107 million, representing a gain of about sixteen million jobs. When George H.W. Bush left office four years after that, the U.S. economy had added about three million more jobs.

On the day Bill Clinton took office, there were just under 110 million Americans in the workforce. When he left office eight years later, there were about 133 million. An increase of roughly twenty-three million jobs — the strongest eight-year period of job creation since the end of World War II.

On the day George W. Bush took office, there were a little under 133 million Americans in the workforce. When he left office eight years later, there were about 133.5 million. Over the course of his presidency, net job creation in the private sector was actually negative. The modest gain in jobs was entirely owing to the public sector.

On the day Barack Obama took office, there were about 133.5 million Americans in the workforce. As of February 2016, there are about 143.5 million, representing a net gain of ten million jobs, with eleven months to go in his second term.

Between 1981 and 2016, Republicans held the White House for twenty years, during which time about 19.5 million jobs were created. During the fifteen years that Democrats held the White

House, about 33 million jobs were created. That works out to an average of less than one million jobs per year for Republicans and more than two million per year for Democrats.

No matter how you look at it, the U.S. economy creates about twice as many jobs when a Democrat is in the White House.

The Stock Market and Corporate Profits

The stock market has also done much better under Democrats, even if we leave aside the fact that the two catastrophic stock market crashes of the past hundred years — namely those that preceded the Great Depression and the Great Recession — both occurred under Republicans.

On second thought, before we leave them aside, let's note in passing that these catastrophes each came in the aftermath of a period of sustained G.O.P. control of the White House and both houses of congress. Before the crash of 1929, the Republicans held the White House, the House, and the Senate for twelve years. Before the crisis of 2007, the Republicans held the White House and the House for six years and the Senate for four of those six. These two periods were the only times during the last hundred years when Republicans held both houses of congress and the White House at the same time for a period of more than two years. Both of these periods ended in economic catastrophe for millions of people not just in America but around the world.

Under Democrats, the stock market has thrived. Since 1900, the Standard & Poor's 500 stock index (S&P 500) has risen at an average rate of 5.1 percent per year under Republicans. Under Democrats it has risen at an annual rate of 12.1 percent.[144]

In the post World War II era, corporate profits have risen less than 9 percent per year under Republicans while growing 10.5 percent per year under Democrats.[145]

Even in the wake of the worst financial crisis since the Great Depression, under Democratic president Barack Obama the stock

71

market has more than doubled. The day of Barack Obama's first inauguration, the Dow Jones Industrial Average closed at $7,949.09. Six years into his presidency, in May of 2015, it hit an all-time high of $18,252. Under Obama, corporate profits have also achieved a series of all-time highs.

If Democrats really are seething socialists hostile to private enterprise, as Conservatives claim, then they have been spectacularly inept at implementing their anti-capitalist agenda.

Economic Growth

Given the enormous economic production associated with World War II, it would be unfair to include this period in a comparison of GDP growth. So let's start after the war, and look at annual GDP growth between 1948 and 2012. Under Republican presidents, the economy grew at an average of 2.6 percent per year, while under Democrats it grew by 4.33 percent. That translates to average growth of 18.5 percent per presidential term under Democrats, compared to 10.6 percent under Republicans.[146]

The most thoroughgoing comparison of economic performance under the two parties in the post-World War 2 period was published in 2014 by the economists Alan Blinder and Mark Watson, of Princeton University. They determined that not only did the economy grow much more rapidly under Democrats — it slowed down much more often under Republicans. Over the course of the period surveyed, the economy was in recession for a cumulative total forty-nine fiscal quarters — i.e., the equivalent of twelve years and one month. Republicans were in the White House for 41 of those quarters; Democrats for eight. Since the end of World War II, the U.S. has spent the equivalent of ten years in recession under Republicans and only two years in recession under Democrats.[147]

Blinder and Watson observe: "The superiority of economic performance under Democrats rather than Republicans is nearly ubiquitous; it holds almost regardless of how you define success...By many measures, the performance gap is startlingly large."

There is much uncertainty and no consensus as to why the economy performs so much better under Democrats, but there is no denying that it does.

REASONS FOR THE DISCONNECT?

Propaganda

Republicans have spent generations establishing their reputation as the party of business. They talk all the time about the importance of the private sector. They trumpet their support for the "free market," while deriding Democrats as "tax and spend" liberals who think that government is the solution to every problem. Democrats, on the other hand, don't talk much about this stuff, and when they do, they tend to speak in terms of wonky specifics rather than catchy generalities. Republicans are less successful stewards of the economy, but they are very accomplished at proclaiming their support for "job creators" and the "free market."

Amnesia

The superior performance of the economy under Democratic leadership is so clear and impressive that it's hard to explain why everyone isn't aware of it. Democrats are generally poor at trumpeting their achievements, not necessarily because they're modest, but because they're disorganized when it comes to messaging.

But there's something more to this, which would require a separate book to explain, namely: Democrats don't seem to remember their own successes. From 1933 to 1981, Democrats controlled both houses of congress the entire time except for two brief periods of two years each; they also controlled the White House for two thirds of the time. During that period, they created Social Security and the FDIC, waged and won World War II, integrated the U.S. Army, created the G.I. Bill, enacted the Marshall Plan, passed Civil Rights and Voting

Rights legislation, created Medicare and Medicaid, Pell Grants and student loans for college, passed the Clean Air Act and put a man on the moon. And yet we rarely if ever hear Democrats claim ownership of this legacy of successes. For whatever combination of reasons, Democrats don't take credit for many of their greatest accomplishments. Sound management of the economy is one of those accomplishments.

WHAT'S BEST FOR CORPORATIONS IS WHAT'S BEST FOR THE REST OF SOCIETY

Corporations are people too, my friend.
— G.O.P. presidential candidate Mitt Romney, campaigning at the Iowa State Fair, August 11, 2011

There is one and only one social responsibility of business — to use its resources and engage in activities designed to increase its profits so long as it stays within the rules of the game, which is to say, engages in open and free competition without deception or fraud.
— Milton Friedman, *Capitalism and Freedom*

CONSERVATIVES CLAIM...

Private enterprise and the free market invariably ensure the greatest levels of prosperity for all levels of society. The self-interest of entrepreneurs and CEOs is entirely consistent with the best interests of society as a whole, since the success of their enterprises creates jobs and has a trickle-down effect that enriches everyone. The best thing that government can do is to get out of the way of business and stop interfering with the magic of the marketplace.

75

THE REALITY

Publicly traded companies have no mandate or duty to be patriotic, or public spirited, or to create jobs. What they do have is a fiduciary duty — a *legally enforceable* obligation — to operate in best interests of shareholders. If that means reducing the cost of labor by closing down a factory in Michigan or Ohio and opening one in China or India, then so be it. If that means exploiting every possible loophole in order to avoid complying with anti-pollution laws or workplace safety regulations, then so be it. If that means replacing workers with cheaper, more efficient robots that don't need coffee breaks, and don't take sick days, and never get pregnant, then so be it.

Unlike the U.S. government, corporations are under no obligation to promote the general welfare, and it is usually not in their practical interest do so. The essential mission of a corporation is to maximize shareholder value by maximizing profits. When this mission happens to coincide with the public interest, then society will benefit. But the operative word there is "coincide" — as in "coincidence." A corporation cannot act effectively in the public interest unless its own interests coincide with those of the public, or unless it is regulated in such a way as to compel it to do so. This is the case even if the individuals in the company are good and honorable people who have the very best of intentions.

Consider, for example, a hypothetical unregulated market for petrochemical products, in which there are no laws against polluting. If companies may legally dump their toxic waste into the nearest river, any company that chooses to dispose of its waste in a more conscientious — and more costly — manner will put itself at a competitive disadvantage. This more socially conscious company will incur higher operating costs than the other companies, which means that, all other things being equal, it will have to accept lower profits, or off-set the higher cost of its socially beneficial waste disposal practices by raising prices. Either way, it will find itself handicapped in a competitive marketplace.

Acting in the public interest is rarely profitable. It usually entails extra costs, or lower revenues, or both. At the very least it requires a less than optimally efficient allocation of resources. Unless all companies in the same sector are functioning under the same set of regulations, it will usually be to a company's disadvantage to engage unilaterally in practices that benefit society while, to whatever extent, reducing its own profitability.

Of course, a hugely profitable company such as Google can afford to not "be evil" because it has money to burn. So long as a company has very high profit margins, it can choose to provide free food for employees and donate to charitable causes and establish foundations to make the world a better place. But most companies must function in a highly competitive marketplace that allows for relatively slim profit margins. They can't be expected unilaterally to sacrifice profits, and thus endanger their own prospects of survival.

Once again, it's not because capitalists are evil or don't love their country. It's because they don't have much of an alternative if they're going to thrive in a competitive marketplace.

Jobs, Jobs, Jobs

Companies employ people not because they want to but because they have to. Employee compensation is an enormous bottom line expense. As with all expenditures, companies want to minimize payroll as much as possible — not because they're mean and uncaring, but because they are legally obligated to do so according to their fiduciary duty to shareholders. There are two ways to minimize payroll: (1) keep wages as low as possible, and (2) employ as few people as possible. One of the richer ironies of conservative rhetoric is that the last thing in the world the so-called "job creators" want to do is to actually create more jobs.

Productivity is one arena where the interests of companies can come into conflict with those of workers. It's reasonable for employers to want to get as much work as possible out of each individual worker — the more productive workers are, the fewer of them are required to produce the same amount of goods. It's also reasonable for workers to expect their wages to rise in proportion to their productivity — if the company is getting more out of each of them; it seems only fair that they should be compensated accordingly. But higher compensation for workers means lower profits, so companies have a natural interest in maximizing productivity while keeping wages as low as possible.

Since about 1980, worker productivity in the U.S. has been steadily increasing while wages have stagnated. That means that companies are getting more out of each worker in exchange for not much more compensation. Another way of describing this is that today's workers are getting paid less per unit of productivity than their counterparts in the past.

During the first three decades of the post World War II era, wages more or less kept pace with increases in productivity. From 1947 to 1973, productivity increased by an average of 2.8 percent per year, while wages increased by 2.6 percent. From 1973 to 1979, productivity increased by 1.1 percent per year, while wages increased by 0.9 percent per year.

In the three decades since, the gap has steadily widened. In the 1980s, productivity increased by an annual average of 1.4 percent, while wages increased by 0.5 percent. In the 1990s, productivity increased annually by 2.1 percent and wages by 1.5 percent. And in the 2000s, productivity increased annually by 2.5 percent and wages by 1.1 percent.[148] All in all, between 1979 and 2009, productivity of American workers increased by 80 percent while compensation increased by only 10.1 percent.[149]

To put this in perspective, imagine that thirty years ago, a worker was producing ten widgets per hour for a salary of ten dollars an hour. The company would have been paying one dollar in wages per widget. Today, the same worker would be producing eighteen widgets per hour and being paid eleven dollars an hour, so the company would be paying eleven dollars for eighteen widgets, or about sixty cents per widget. This is more or less what's been happening throughout the U.S. economy.

The last thirty years have been increasingly good for corporations and increasingly bad for workers — i.e., the rest of society. Employee compensation as a share of the economy has been steadily plummeting for the past forty years. In 1970, wages accounted for 53.5 percent of GDP; in 2011, they hit an all-time low of 43.5 percent.[150] Meanwhile, corporate profits have been increasing. In the third Quarter of 2012, after-tax corporate profits accounted for 11 percent of GDP, a post World War II high.[151] There is no clearer or starker demonstration of the premise of this chapter than the contrast between those two facts.

Corporate Profits and Excess Cash

It only makes sense that in an era of maximal profitability, excess cash reserves held by corporations in the U.S. are the highest they have ever been. As of March 2012, they were estimated to be about $1.7 trillion. That sounds like a lot of money, and of course it *is* a lot of money. But that already staggering figure does not include offshore holdings, which swell the total to more than $5 trillion. This money is not being used for any constructive purpose, let alone employing U.S. workers. As David Cay Johnston observes, "For workers, idle cash means idle hands and minds. With one in five Americans unemployed or underemployed, and real median wages in 2010 back down to the level of 1999, this is no time for capital to go on an extended holiday."[152]

During a period of persistently high unemployment and underemployment, when wages are as low as they have ever been (as a percent of GDP) and corporate profits are at an all-time high, U.S. corporations are investing their unprecedented reserves of capital in — nothing.

No doubt each individual company has its own reasons for sitting on excess cash and it is not our purpose here to question the soundness of their business strategies. The point worth noting is this: at a time of unprecedented profits, when companies have plenty of money to spend, they're not hiring. In pursuing their own best interests and those of their shareholders, companies are deciding to hold on to their capital rather than spend it in ways that could make an enormous positive difference to a society still struggling to recover from a major economic crisis. In other words, what corporations have determined to be in their own best interest is not what's best for the rest of society.

Let's look at a few examples of actual industries that affect the lives of almost every American, to get a sense of how the interests of corporations and those of society can diverge and even, in some cases, conflict.

Health Insurance and Healthcare

The U.S. is the only country in the developed world that lacks a universal public health insurance program. In most developed nations, it is actually illegal for basic health insurance to be sold on a for-profit basis. Private insurers can provide basic health coverage, but just not at a profit. The reason for this is simple to grasp: when it comes to health insurance, what is best for corporations is unavoidably contrary to the public interest, insofar as the public interest consists of ensuring that the maximum number of citizens have access to good and affordable healthcare.

Private insurers maximize profits by raising premiums as high as possible while keeping payouts as low as possible, which means, among other things, denying coverage to people with pre-existing conditions (which has recently become illegal, thanks to "Obamacare"), or finding reasons to refuse to pay for expensive medicines and procedures. This isn't because they're evil — it's because for-profit enterprises have an obligation to maximize profits, regardless of whether the individuals who work for those corporations would prefer to do the right thing. In other words, what's in the best interests of health insurance companies is not in the best interest of society.

The United States has the highest per-capita healthcare costs among the thirty-four developed nations of the OECD (Organization for Economic Cooperation and Development), including countries that provide "free" universal health coverage to all citizens. ("Free" is in quotation marks because it's not actually free — it's paid for by tax dollars, which come out of the pockets of citizens.) In 2010, total health expenditure for each American — $8,233 — was two and a half times the OECD average ($3,268), more than 50 percent higher than the next most expensive country, Norway ($5,388), almost twice as high as Germany ($4,338), and more than twice as high as France ($3,974), the U.K. ($3,433), and Japan ($3,035).[153]

Not only do other developed countries manage to provide universal health insurance for much less — they do it while assuring a generally better quality of care. The U.S. has fewer physicians and fewer hospital beds per capita than the OECD average. Infant mortality is higher than the OECD average; indeed, it's higher than that of every OECD country except for Turkey and Mexico. Meanwhile, average life expectancy in the U.S is 78.7 years, more than a year lower than the OECD average of 79.8 years. Eighteen countries have an average life expectancy over 80 years.[154]

If our more expensive market-based health insurance system were providing superior results, it might be possible to argue that it's worth the cost because it provides for a healthier society. Sadly, this is very far from being the case.

Postal Service vs. Private Carriers

The U.S. Postal Service is entirely funded by its own operations and has not cost the taxpayers any money since 1982 (except for some services to the disabled and election-related services, such as handling absentee ballots, which the federal government pays for with tax dollars). In fact, the Postal Service is required by law to be revenue neutral; more often than not over the past thirty years, it has actually turned an annual profit. All the while, it has managed to provide the same range of services as private enterprises such as FedEx and UPS, at much lower cost to consumers.[155] And, unlike FedEx and UPS, the Postal Service has always delivered on Saturdays at no extra charge (although this may change soon — see below).

The Postal Service's recent budget problems began in 2007, when an act of Congress required them to set aside over five-and-a-half billion dollars a year for ten years in order to fully fund their pension program for the next seventy-five years. In other words, the USPS is required by law to accumulate a surplus of more than $55 billion — a unique and unprecedented burden that no other federal agency, and certainly no private company, in the U.S. must bear. Without this pension requirement, the USPS would be running a $1.5 billion surplus.

This unique burden is the result of an especially sinister piece of legislation, the 109th congress's H.R. 6407, the "Postal Accountability and Enhancement Act," which was passed in December 2006 by Republican majorities in the House and Senate, and signed into law by President George W. Bush.[156] It could very well put the postal service out of business; at the very least, it creates enormous pressure to increase rates, cut payroll, and reduce services, including Saturday delivery — i.e., the very things that the USPS has traditionally done better and/or more cheaply than its private competitors.

In passing this so-called "accountability" law, conservative legislators abused their lawmaking power to interfere with the marketplace in order to destroy a successful and efficient quasi-governmental enterprise that effectively contradicts their pro-market, anti-government economic ideology. What's more, they passed this law in order to actively promote the interests of private corporations over those of the public. On a level playing field, the USPS would be in surplus and more than holding its own against more expensive alternatives like FedEx and UPS. So the Republicans tilted the playing field steeply in favor of the private enterprises. And then they point to the Postal Service's struggles as a vindication of their free-market principles.

Conservatives in government have come up with a way to eliminate competition so that private corporations can command higher prices for more limited services. It's obvious how this benefits FedEx and UPS, but how does it benefit society? The answer is equally obvious: it doesn't.

Energy

Oil company profits have never been higher than they were in 2012, mostly because oil prices have also never been higher. Conservatives try to blame the current Democratic administration for high prices for fossil fuels, but it is market forces that have set these prices high, not the government. Indeed, if the government could intervene directly in order to affect prices, that would be socialism.

Oil is becoming scarcer and more difficult to extract from the ground. At the same time, the world's population is increasing, and high-population countries such as India and China (which together account for a third of the world's population) are becoming wealthier and demanding more and more energy. This is what's causing prices to rise, and it's not going to stop.

At the same time, solar and wind power are becoming cheaper — the sources themselves are free and infinite, while the technology to turn them into usable energy is becoming more efficient and less expensive every year. However, renewable energy is still a risky sector for investors — there is still much uncertainty about which particular new technologies will succeed, and the cost of generating energy from renewable sources is still high in relation to fossil fuels in all but a few markets. In other words, movement toward the renewable energy economy will be slower and less direct if left to market forces alone — i.e., what's best for corporations — whereas government investment and incentives can hasten and stabilize progress, which will be in the best economic interests of society.

(This subject is covered extensively in chapters 4 and 5 of this volume, "Renewable Energy is not a viable Alternative to Fossil Fuels" and "Increasing Domestic Oil Production Promotes Energy independence".)

"It's Just Business"

We've all heard the expression, "It's just business." This is something people say when they feel bad about doing something unpleasant, but which they feel powerless to prevent because the exigencies of business leave them no alternative. The interests of the enterprise — i.e., maximizing profit — are always paramount.

The point of this chapter is not to denigrate or demonize free enterprise or business in general, which have been the engine of America's extraordinary growth and prosperity across many generations. The point is to demonstrate that corporations do not come into existence in order to create national prosperity or to promote the general welfare or even to create jobs. They come into existence in order to make money for the people who own them. In and of itself, there's nothing wrong with that, so long as we have other means of ensuring that all of society's interests are promoted, or, at the very least, protected.

Conservative ideology seeks to diminish the responsibilities of government, which is ultimately accountable to the people, on the pretext that corporations, which are not accountable to the people, are better suited to promoting the public interest. Society suffers when we leave it to corporations to provide social benefits that they are neither designed to provide nor interested in providing.

REASONS FOR THE DISCONNECT?

Negative propaganda

In his first inaugural address, Ronald Reagan stated: "In this present crisis, government is not the solution to our problem; government *is* the problem." In the years since Reagan spoke these words, they have become a conservative credo, with one significant omission: the first clause of the sentence. Whereas Reagan condemned government in the context of "this present crisis," conservatives since Reagan have developed a habit of relentlessly demonizing government at every opportunity.

The attitude has devolved over time into the simple, automatic assertion that government — any government; all government — is bad just because it's government. Never mind that government provided Social Security and Medicare, won World War II, put a man on moon, developed the internet, provides roads, bridges, cops, firefighters, teachers, weather reports and disaster relief...It must always be denigrated, anathematized, and minimized. Rhetorically, that is. Republicans don't actually limit government when the have the opportunity and the power to do so (as we'll see in a later chapter "The G.O.P. is the Party of Small Government").

Thirty years of conservative anti-government propaganda and nattering about "socialism" has turned much of the public against the government, while converting them to the view that the private sector will better provide for all of society's needs.

Positive propaganda

In 1971, a lawyer named Lewis Powell (who went on to become a Supreme Court justice) prepared a memorandum for an executive at the U.S. Chamber of Commerce, which contained this remarkable observation:

> "As every business executive knows, few elements of American society today have as little influence in government as the American businessman, the corporation, or even the millions of corporate stockholders...One does not exaggerate to say that, in terms of political influence with respect to the course of legislation and government action, the American business executive is truly the 'forgotten man.'" [157]

Things certainly have changed since 1971. They've changed in no small part because of that very document, known as "The Powell Memo" or, rather more dramatically, "The Powell Manifesto," which outlined a comprehensive strategy for promoting the interests and reputation of business in America.

Powell recommended that business adopt "a more aggressive attitude" and recognize "that political power is necessary; that such power must be assidously [sic] cultivated; and that when necessary, it must be used aggressively and with determination -- without embarrassment and without the reluctance which has been so characteristic of American business."

The memo presented a multi-pronged strategy to promote a pro-business outlook throughout society, including initiatives in education, public relations, news media, and politics. Some examples:

Education: "evaluation of textbooks," "balancing of faculties," "action programs, tailored to the high schools [i.e., to promote a pro-business outlook]." Public relations; businesses should dedicate up to 10 percent of their operating budgets to communicating a positive message to the public. News media: "the national television networks should be monitored in the same way that textbooks should be kept under constant surveillance." Think tanks: the Chamber of Commerce should consider establishing its own "faculty of scholars;" Powell also observed that "incentives might be devised to induce more 'publishing' by independent scholars who do believe in the system." [NB: the quotation marks around the word "publishing" are Powell's; the present author is at a loss to explain what precisely is meant by these.] Politics: business should "consider assuming a broader and more vigorous role in the political arena."

Of course this is just one document, prepared by a lawyer functioning as a consultant to an executive of a voluntary association of business leaders. But some documents have a way of making change happen (see "Independence, Declaration of"). The Powell memo became the template of one of the most successful propaganda campaigns of modern times. It gave rise to the Heritage Foundation (founded in 1973) and the Cato Institute (founded in 1974); it inspired and established a major, multi-pronged movement dedicated to shifting public opinion in favor of free-market solutions.

To get an idea of how successful this movement has been, consider how utterly strange that first quoted paragraph from the Powell memo sounds today. The notion that the "American business executive is truly a 'forgotten man'" is as remote from today's reality as top-hats and hoop-skirts.

The CEO Effect

CEOs have become culture heroes, regularly featured on magazine covers and as guests on talk shows. In the 1980s, Lee Iacocca was the rare corporate leader who became a household name. Today, dozens of CEOs are famous personalities, who wield enormous influence beyond their business sectors. Warren Buffett is considered a national treasure. Steve Jobs was the subject of a best-selling biography and an Oscar-nominated movie. Richard Branson and Jeff Bezos are household names. Billionaire Michael Bloomberg became a three-term mayor of New York, America's largest city. Donald Trump had a series of TV show that aired on a major network during prime time and has lately secured the G.O.P. nomination for president. As a culture, we have come to admire CEOs and look to them as paragons of competence.

Money

The U.S. Chamber of Commerce alone spent $135 million on lobbying in 2012.[158] Other business associations as well as individual companies spend untold millions more on lobbying and campaign contributions. Corporate lobbying and influence over campaigns ensure that legislators hear the concerns of corporations on a daily basis, and also understand that their electoral prospects depend on how responsive they are to those concerns.

Confusing Ends and Means

Conservatives frame the economic debate between left and right as one about means rather than ends — in other words, they suggest that Democrats and Republicans both care about assisting the poor and promoting the general welfare, but just disagree about how best to accomplish these ends. But this is not the actual debate. The debate is about whether helping the poor and promoting the general welfare are worthwhile goals if accomplishing them would require limiting the free enterprise system in some way, or promoting government solutions rather than business ones. Conservative policies plainly reveal that the answer, as far as they're concerned, is no.

Conservatives claim that the free enterprise system will ensure the greatest prosperity for all, including the poor. But this is clearly not the case, which is why Democrats, who also support the free enterprise system, insist on social programs to provide a degree of economic security that free-enterprise can't. Conservatives, on the other hand, are willing to accept high levels of poverty, misery, and social distress as perhaps regrettable but nevertheless unavoidable consequences of free enterprise — a social cost worth paying so long as businesses can be free to thrive without any constraints.

ECONOMIC STIMULUS DOESN'T WORK

So this is surely the time for economic stimulus.
— Mitt Romney, December 8, 2008[159]

I was pleased that the primary objectives of their project will allow residents and businesses in the partner cities to reduce their energy costs, reduce greenhouse gas emissions, and stimulate the local economy by creating new jobs.
— Paul Ryan, October 28, 2010, in a letter to the Department of Energy requesting stimulus funds for the Wisconsin Energy Conservation Corporation[160]

CONSERVATIVES CLAIM...

The $787 billion American Recovery and Reinvestment Act of 2009 — a.k.a. the stimulus package — was a colossal waste of taxpayer dollars which had no positive impact on the economy and failed to create jobs. In general, government can't do anything constructive to stimulate economic growth; the best thing it can do is stay out of the way, do nothing, and allow the private sector manage the economy.

THE REALITY

The American Recovery and Reinvestment Act prevented the United States from slipping into a depression in 2009.

In January 2009, the month Barack Obama became president, the

U.S. economy lost over 800,000 jobs. As staggering as that number is, it was typical of the monthly job losses around that time. December of 2008 saw more than 600,000 jobs were lost. February, March and April of 2009 each saw job losses of more than 700,000.[161] The word that many have applied to the economy at that time is: "freefall."

During the same period, the U.S. economy was shrinking. GDP had contracted by $314 billion in the last quarter of 2008, which made for an astounding annualized <u>negative</u> growth rate of 8.8 percent. This trend continued through the first half of 2009, with GDP declining by $158 billion in the first quarter and $38 billion in the second quarter.[162]

The stimulus halted a downward slide towards depression and stopped the hemorrhaging of jobs, reversing both trends soon after it kicked in. By the end of President Obama's first year in office, both employment levels and economic output were rising, as they have continued to do since. Surveys indicate 80 percent of economists believe that this economic turnaround was at least partially owing to economic stimulus.

The American Recovery and Reinvestment Act — the so-called "stimulus package" — was passed by the House and Senate on February 13th, 2009 and signed into law by the president on February 17th. The law authorized $787 billion worth of economic stimulus measures, only about a third of which was allocated to direct investment, such as infrastructure spending. Another third went to temporary tax relief, such as payroll tax cuts and increased deductions for depreciation of business equipment. And the final third went to extending benefits, such as unemployment insurance and food stamps, for people hit hardest by the economic crisis.[163]

As provisions of the new law began to kick in during the summer of 2009, the economic freefall was arrested. GDP stopped declining and began to grow again in the third quarter. In the fourth quarter, the economy grew fast enough to make 2009 a year of net positive growth. The unemployment rate peaked at 10 percent in October of 2009 and has been on a path of gradual decline since. The non-partisan Congressional Budget Office estimates that the stimulus package increased the number of full-time jobs by a minimum of 400,000 and by as many as 2.6 million.[164]

The most authoritative survey to date of how distinguished economists assessed the impact of the stimulus package determined that 80 percent agreed with this statement: "Because of the American Recovery and Reinvestment Act of 2009, the U.S. unemployment rate was lower at the end of 2010 than it would have been without the stimulus bill." When weighted for each expert's level of confidence in their view, the positive result increased to 93 percent. A plurality of 46 percent agreed that benefits of the stimulus would outweigh its costs, while only 9 percent disagreed and 29 percent were unsure or provided no opinion.[165]

The survey was conducted early in 2012, among a panel that included, "Distinguished experts with a keen interest in public policy from the major areas of economics, to be geographically diverse, and to include Democrats, Republicans and Independents as well as older and younger scholars. The panel members are all senior faculty at the most elite research universities in the United States. The panel includes Nobel Laureates, John Bates Clark Medalists, fellows of the Econometric society, past presidents of both the American Economics Association and American Finance Association, past Democratic and Republican members of the President's Council of Economics, and past and current editors of the leading journals in the profession."[166] If you feel qualified to disagree with these folks, then why on Earth would you still be reading this?

REASONS FOR THE DISCONNECT?

Bad Economic Thinking

It may be counter-intuitive, but the economics of running a country are not the same as the economics of running a household or a company. It seems to make sense that a government should not be spending more money during a time of economic calamity — after all, if you suddenly found yourself unemployed, up to your ears in debt, and unable to pay your bills it would be the height of recklessness to increase your borrowing and spending. The same goes for running a business. Tightening your belt, getting your house in order, balancing the books...all of this sounds like the sober, responsible way to react to an economic crisis.

But if the government stops spending, then everything comes to a halt. Consumers aren't buying, so businesses aren't selling. If businesses aren't selling, then they have to lay off workers and unemployment rises. If unemployment rises, then fewer people are earning and spending money, which means even fewer consumers are buying, which causes businesses to cut back even more.

The government can prevent this stagnation of the overall economy during a crisis by spending when nobody else is. This is why it's called "stimulus" — government spending, or tax cuts, or extension of benefits, puts more money into the pockets of consumers and businesses so that they can continue to spend and the economy can begin to grow again.

Anti-Government Ideology

Conservatives are passionately dedicated to the proposition that government solutions are always inferior to those of the private sector, no matter what the problem or predicament. For those who adhere to the view that government is always the problem and never the solution, it would be paradoxical to acknowledge that stimulus — i.e., a government program — could ever work. Ideological conservatives refuse to admit that the government could ever benefit the economy in ways that the private sector can't. To do so would be to discredit their entire world view (which is my job, not theirs).

Politics

Republicans in the Senate and the House of Representatives were committed to thwarting Barack Obama from day one of his presidency. Accordingly, the G.O.P. developed a policy of deliberate obstruction of the president's efforts to promote recovery. The American Recovery and Reinvestment Act, which was designed along economic principles that both parties had supported routinely for decades, received precisely zero G.O.P. votes in the House and only three in the Senate. However, that did not stop dozens of G.O.P. legislators from requesting, and obtaining, stimulus money for their own states and districts, once the law had been passed without their support.

RENEWABLE ENERGY IS NOT A VIABLE ALTERNATIVE TO FOSSIL FUELS

We are like tenant farmers chopping down the fence around our house for fuel when we should be using nature's inexhaustible sources of energy — sun, wind and tide...I'd put my money on the sun and solar energy. What a source of power! I hope we don't have to wait until oil and coal run out before we tackle that.

— Thomas Edison, in conversation with Henry Ford and Harvey Firestone, March 1931[167]

There is no free market for oil.
— T. Boone Pickens

CONSERVATIVES CLAIM...

Renewable energy is pie in the sky. Wind, wave, and solar power sound great in theory, but they're just not practical — they're inefficient and expensive. Meanwhile, there's plenty of oil left in the ground, and that, combined with abundant supplies of coal and natural gas, can provide all our energy needs for the next hundred years or more.

THE REALITY

A hundred years from now, within the lifetimes of your great-grandchildren, there will be no longer be any major use of oil or coal. Power will be generated from wind, water, and sunlight — some of it will come from large power plants, but much of it will be generated on people's own properties, perhaps even on their own persons, from fabrics that absorb the sun's rays and convert it into usable power. The air in cities will be as fresh as air in the mountains, and the word "smog" will be the quaint relic of a more backward age.

This is not a dream. It will happen, because it has to happen — fossil fuels are becoming scarce while demand for energy is increasing. The only question is: when will it start to happen?

It turns out that the question has already been answered, and the answer is: yesterday. Humanity's long process of conversion to an all-renewable energy economy is well underway, and not a moment too soon.

Renewable Energy is Already Viable

The technology already exists to turn wind and sunlight into useable electricity on a large enough scale to power entire towns. Not only does the technology exist, it is in use today and powering millions of homes around the world.

In 2011, renewable sources accounted for about 11 percent of the energy generated for human consumption on planet Earth. In the U.S., which is by far the world's largest consumer of energy, renewables supplied 9.5 percent of the power consumed.[168]

The largest renewable source of energy is hydroelectric power, which has been in use since the 19th century, but wind and solar are now growing much more rapidly. The total amount of power generated from wind doubled in the three years from 2007 to 2010 (from 170.5 to 341.5 billion kilowatt hours). During the same period, all non-hydroelectric renewable sources combined increased by 55 percent, (from 483 to 752 billion kilowatt hours).[169] The pace is accelerating. In the single year from 2010 to 2011, global capacity of solar power generated by photovoltaic cells (e.g., solar panels), increased by 67 percent while installed wind capacity increased by 21 percent.[170]

Wind alone produced about 3 percent of the world's electricity in 2015. That may not seem like much, but think again. The age of large-scale wind power is still in its infancy and already almost one thirtieth of all power consumed by human beings is being generated by wind turbines. In the U.S., wind generated more than 4 percent of all power consumed in 2013. The state of Iowa, the U.S. leader, already generates 25 percent of its power from wind.[171]

Spain has been a world leader in developing and deploying both wind and solar technology on a large scale. Already in 2006, five provinces in Spain were generating more than half of their power from renewable energy sources. Two provinces — Galicia and Castile y Léon — were generating 70 percent or more.

The Gemasolar plant in Andalucia is capable of gathering and concentrating enough solar energy to generate 20 megawatts of power twenty-four hours a day — sufficient to supply about 20,000 homes. It has fifteen hours of energy storage, using a molten salt system, which allows it to produce power even when the sun is not shining.[172]

Germany supplies about 25 percent of its energy from renewable sources. On May 25 and 26, 2012 German solar plants produced power at a rate of over 22 gigawatts per hour — equal to twenty nuclear power stations running at full capacity — which was enough to supply one half of the total electricity requirements of a fully-industrialized country with a population of more than eighty million.[173]

In the U.S., The Military is Leading the Way

Given that renewable energy is usually associated in the media with environmentalist movements, it may come as a surprise to many that the military has already committed itself to a sustainable energy future.[174] The U.S. Army and Air Force have set an overall goal of developing 1 gigawatt, equivalent to 1 billion watts, of renewable power on their installations by 2025.[175]

The Army has established a series of "Net Zero Energy" initiatives aimed at making bases self-sufficient, so that they consume no more energy than they are able to produce on site. What's more, the U.S. Army has already converted 70 percent of non-tactical vehicles to renewable sources of fuel, and is "well on the way to 100 percent," according to the assistant secretary of the Army for Installations, Energy and Environment.[176]

While it would be nice to believe that the military is committed to a clean environment, the real incentive is economic. Fossil fuel is increasingly expensive, while renewable energy is increasingly cheap. This is all the more true for operations abroad. A 2001 Defense Department report assessed the true cost of fuel to be at least $17.50 per gallon for "tanker-delivered fuel" and up to "hundreds of dollars per gallon for Army forces deep into the battlespace."[177] And keep in mind that those are pre-9/11 estimates, when the cost of gasoline was around $1.30 per gallon.

The military has been using portable solar-powered generators in Afghanistan, not only to save on the cost of fuel itself, but to minimize the additional costs and safety risks associated with having to transport thousands of gallons of fuel through dangerous territory.[178]

Renewables are Superabundant

The sun provides hundreds of times more harvestable energy than is necessary to meet all of humanity's demands, and it will continue to do so for several billion years. That's just harvestable energy — i.e., the proportion of solar energy that is accessible to our current technologies for conversion into usable power. The total amount of solar energy reaching planet Earth is many hundreds of times greater still. Wind also provides far more harvestable energy than the human race requires — at least four times as much, although most estimates place it closer to ten times as much.

The National Renewable Energy Laboratory (NREL) estimates that the total amount of wind and solar energy available for conversion into useable power in the U.S. amounts to almost 450,000 terawatt-hours per year. That certainly sounds like a lot, especially after you've converted the units to 1.54×10^{18} British Thermal Units ("btu"). That's 1.54 *quintillion.*

But how much exactly is that in relation to total domestic demand at current levels? About fifteen times as much. In other words, if we built and installed the maximum number of wind turbines and solar panels and solar power plants to capture all the energy that can be harvested with currently existing technologies, we'd be generating fifteen times as much power as the American people consumed in 2011.[179] Needless to say, that's quite a bit more than we need.

Keep in mind that this assessment is not an inventory of the total amount of wind and sunlight that actually falls upon and blows across U.S. lands and territorial waters — it's only the portion of the those winds and rays that are capable of being captured and converted into useable power by *currently existing* technologies.

To put this in another perspective: total U.S. energy consumption in 2011 (28,633 terawatt hours, or 97.7 quadrillion British thermal units, for those of you who are keeping score at home) represented just 6.4 percent of the country's total supplies of harvestable sunlight, and about 72 percent of what could potentially be generated in the state of Texas alone.[180]

The Future is Even Brighter…and Windier

The International Energy Agency's "World Energy Outlook 2012" predicted that renewable sources of energy would become the world's second largest source of electric power, after coal, by 2015, and will surpass coal by 2035. "A steady increase in hydropower and the rapid expansion of wind and solar power has cemented the position of renewables as an indispensable part of the global energy mix; by 2035, renewables account for almost one-third of total electricity output. Solar grows more rapidly than any other renewable technology. Renewables become the world's second-largest source of power generation by 2015 (roughly half that of coal) and, by 2035, they approach coal as the primary source of global electricity."[181]

These projections are based on current trends — they don't count on new government initiatives, such as major investment programs, or additional rebates and tax incentives. Nor do they assume the development of as-yet-unanticipated breakthrough technologies, which are actually more likely to emerge than not (as we will see below, breakthroughs are happening right now). The IEA bases their projections on likely scenarios, given the state of current technologies, as well as the nature of our public institutions and the character of our present leaders. They take for granted the political factors and market forces that prevail in the world today. These projections should therefore be considered conservative.

Ambitious Comprehensive Plans

If we leave aside the political obstacles and consider not just what is probable but what is feasible, we see that the technological possibilities are far-reaching. Indeed, political and market forces are the only things preventing the world from converting to an all-renewable energy economy within a few decades.

In recent years, numerous credible plans and studies have demonstrated that it's possible to convert the world to an entirely renewable energy economy before the middle of the 21st century. All are visionary and ambitious, but the most remarkable thing about these plans is the fact that they're entirely feasible.

The Delaware Study

A study conducted by scholars at the University of Delaware found that a major regional electricity grid, covering fifteen states in the Northeast, could derive 99.9 percent of its power from a combination of renewable sources by 2030 — "at costs comparable to today's."

The study was almost ridiculously comprehensive, incorporating over 35,000 hours (i.e., four years' worth) of actual historical data on weather conditions and fluctuating demand levels for electricity. Computer models then ran over twenty-eight billion scenarios, each with a different combination of renewable sources and storage systems, in order to determine the most efficient, productive, and cost-effective possible system. The model ultimately produced a plan for a system that would provide close to 100 percent of the region's energy needs, twenty-four hours a day, by 2030.[182]

Indeed, the system would exceed demand much of the time. The authors of the study reported that "the least cost solutions yield seemingly-excessive generation capacity — at times, almost three times the electricity needed to meet electrical load. This is because diverse renewable generation and the excess capacity together meet electric load with less storage, lowering total system cost."[183]

The Dutch Plan

A team of scholars in the Netherlands have proposed a plan to convert the global energy economy to 95 percent renewable by 2050 *using only currently available technologies*. This plan addresses both supply (by fully exploiting the wide variety of available sources of renewable energy) and demand (by maximizing efficiency to lower the level of aggregate demand). The proposal recognizes that its goals can't be achieved with "small, incremental changes" but will require a "paradigm shift towards long-term, integrated strategies" — in other words, it faces serious political challenges. But in terms of technology and economics, the plan, while certainly ambitious, is realistic.[184]

The California Solution

In 2009, professors Mark Z. Jacobson of Stanford and Mark Delucchi of the University of California at Davis proposed a comprehensive plan to supply 100 percent of the world's energy needs from renewable sources by 2030.[185] The plan exploits the full range of renewables, including wind, wave, geothermal, hydroelectric, and both types of solar energy (photovoltaic — i.e., solar panels — and solar concentrating thermal power plants, like the Gemasolar plant discussed above).

The proposal is, of course, highly ambitious, requiring, for instance, the manufacture and installation of 3.8 million wind turbines and 90,000 solar power plants worldwide. This sounds enormous, until you consider that human beings currently produce about eighty million motor vehicles every year.[186] Industrial production on a massive scale is something that human beings do pretty well.

We are perfectly capable of ramping up production to extraordinary levels when necessity, or opportunity, demands. During World War II, the U.S. increased the manufacture of military aircraft by 4,400 percent over a period of five years. Output tripled in 1940, tripled again in 1941, more than doubled in 1942, almost doubled again in 1943, and increased by 12 percent in 1944, when we produced 45 times as many aircraft as we had in 1939.[187]

In other words, when we need to do something, or want to do something, no matter how immense the challenge, we have a history of doing it. That should encourage us.

Fossil Fuels Will Become More Expensive

Since we're not assessing the viability of renewable energy in a vacuum, but rather in relation to that of fossil fuels, let's take a look at the current and future state of "traditional energy sources" (as proponents of fossil fuels like to call them, apparently disregarding the fact that people have been using energy from wind and water for thousands of years).

The one thing we all know about oil, besides the fact that it's black and sticky, is that they're not making any more of it. The more we consume, the closer we get to the day when there won't be any left. Global oil consumption is currently about ninety-one million barrels per day and rising. Oil is becoming more expensive and will only continue to do so until it runs out.

At the same time, spare capacity is becoming narrower and less constant as demand increases, which means that the global market is less able to adjust smoothly to events, such as wars in the Middle East, that may disrupt oil production — which makes us even more vulnerable to sudden spikes in the cost of oil.[188]

The law of supply and demand already dictates that increasing levels of demand for a finite resource will lead to higher prices, but an additional factor ensures that the price of oil is likely to remain volatile. The oil that has already been extracted from the Earth was the easiest to access. All those large pools of oil directly underfoot have been drilled dry. Whatever oil is left in the ground today is harder to access, either because it's more remote (e.g., under the ocean), or deeper underground, or mixed with other substances (e.g., tar sands). In other words, it's more difficult and therefore more expensive to extract and refine into useable petroleum products. So, even as demand is rising for this increasingly scarce commodity, the commodity itself is becoming more difficult and expensive to produce.

What's more, the high price of oil is precisely what provides the incentive for oil companies to drill in remote and hard-to-access places. When the price drops, so does the incentive. Supplies then have to dwindle until the price rises to high enough levels to entice the oil companies to start drilling again. So, long story short: even though the price of oil may come down from time to time, sooner or later it will go up again.

Oil dependency is hugely stressful to the economy — it is a burden that we bear collectively as a society. Fossil fuels are inextricably linked with economic growth. The economy runs on energy — which, for now, still means that it runs on fossil fuels. Every business uses energy, whether to produce its goods, or to light and heat (or air condition) its buildings and factories, or to transport its goods to market. The more expensive and/or scarcer the sources of energy, the harder it is for the economy to expand. Volatility in the price of oil means uncertainty throughout the economy.

This isn't a pessimistic picture of an apocalyptic future — it's a description of the reality we already inhabit. Every spike in oil prices in the last forty years has been associated with a global recession.[189] In the 21st century so far, the price of oil has more than tripled, only to fall again to 2000 prices in 2015.[190] Meanwhile, GDP growth has been sluggish and employment stagnant. This was the case even before the economic collapse of 2008, but it has only gotten worse. In 2011, the median American household spent more than $4,000 — almost 8 percent of its income — on gasoline alone.[191] In 2016, the price of oil is lower, and Americans will probably be paying less at the pump for a while, but who knows how long that will last?

The United States of America is the wealthiest nation on planet Earth, and yet we find ourselves beleaguered by an oppressive sense of scarcity and limited potential. We feel that our power, both figuratively and literally, is becoming more and more limited. The American character has always been characterized by optimism, determination and a sense of endless possibilities, but today Americans are obsessed with cutting costs and lowering expectations as we hunker down in preparation for a long, oppressive era of lack. Winter is coming.

But wait. It gets worse.

Externalities

The cost of fossil fuels isn't limited to the price of gasoline and heating oil and coal-generated electricity. Once we consider "externalities" — i.e., the social costs of air and water pollution, greenhouse gases and other environmental damage — these fuels are revealed to be much more expensive. Consider, for instance, that motor vehicle and power plant emissions from oil and coal account for about 20,000 premature deaths and over $100 billion in health costs in the U.S. each year.[192]

Coal — which many to believe to be the cheapest source of energy currently available — is actually more expensive than renewables, when externalities are factored in. The price of coal-generated power is currently averaging about 9 cents per kilowatt-hour, which is relatively cheap compared to other sources of energy. But the externalities add anywhere from 9 to 27 additional cents, which makes coal considerably more expensive. At the current rate of consumption, externalities from burning coal are costing society an extra $300 to $500 billion a year.[193]

By comparison, wind purchase agreements (i.e., long-term contracts for wind power) are setting rates at levels ranging from 4 to 9 cents per kWh, depending on the region. Externalities associated with wind power are somewhere between minimal and non-existent. So wind is already cheaper than coal in many parts of the country. In Michigan, for instance, a recent government study found that wind power is 12 percent cheaper than the most favorable estimate of the cost of coal, even before externalities are considered.[194]

And the price of wind energy is only going to fall over time, while the price of coal is only going to rise, as are the externalities associated with coal.

What about natural gas? Isn't that the clean and cheap answer to all our energy woes? The price of natural gas is relatively cheap (4 cents per kWh) and it has relatively low externalities compared to coal and oil. But, compared to wind and solar, natural gas is not a good deal for society. Natural gas is a potent greenhouse gas — at least 25 times as potent as carbon dioxide. A certain amount of gas escapes into the atmosphere during the extraction process, especially if that extraction process involves hydraulic fracturing, or "fracking," which is responsible for most of the newly available natural gas. Assessments of externalities associated with natural gas are likely to rise, as recent measurements of methane leakage at drilling sites have revealed that previous estimates were drastically understated (i.e.,, between 4 percent and 9 percent, as opposed to the 2 percent that the EPA and industry sources had initially claimed).[195] [196]

Renewables are Becoming Cheaper

Actually, that's not quite right. Renewable sources of energy aren't getting any cheaper for the simple reason that they can't get any cheaper — because they're already free. That's one of the many virtues of renewables. Another virtue is that supplies are so abundant as to be virtually unlimited. So, if you divide the available supply of renewable energy (infinity) by the cost (zero) you get...my calculator just exploded.

Of course, energy derived from renewable sources does have a price — but this has to do with the cost of equipment to convert wind, sunlight, water-pressure, geothermal heat, or whatever the source, into usable power, rather than with the cost of the energy sources themselves. Large-scale renewable systems require a considerable up-front investment in technology, but thereafter the cost of energy is reduced to the expense of operating and maintaining that equipment. The cost of technology has been dropping year after year — in 2011 alone, the price of solar panels dropped by 50 percent, while the price of wind turbines fell by almost 10 percent.[197] Prices will continue to fall as the technologies become more efficient and more widely implemented, and as new discoveries are made and cheaper technologies are developed.

In late December 2012, the supply of wind power drove the wholesale cost of electricity in Europe below zero on five consecutive days.[198] Yes, you read that correctly. During certain periods of low demand and high wind production, utilities received energy from producers for free. This was not an anomaly; the same thing has occurred within the past couple of years in other places, including South Australia and Texas, and will no doubt happen more often in the future as increasingly efficient wind and solar plants are constructed around the world.[199]

How can the wholesale price for electricity drop below zero when enough electricity is still being provided to meet demand? It sounds too good to be true. There must be a catch. What is actually going on here? There were periods when the supply of electricity so far exceeded demand that electrical utilities were able to pay nothing to producers for power generated during those periods. It doesn't mean that customers paid nothing, since the wholesale price is what utilities pay to producers of electricity, not what utilities charge their customers. Indeed, there's little evidence at this point that utilities are passing the savings on to their customers. What is incontrovertible, however, is that renewable energy is already driving down the cost of electricity, and that this is only the beginning.

The Future

As we've seen, even with today's technology, renewable energy is already a viable alternative to fossil fuels. But we won't have to continue relying on today's technology. Every year sees major improvements to existing technologies, as well as the introduction of new technologies, which will drive the costs of implementation ever downward. Indeed, one of the reasons that some manufacturers of solar panels (most notoriously, Solyndra) have struggled financially in recent years is that prices have plummeted, making it difficult or impossible for some of them to turn a profit.[200] While the plummeting cost of solar panels may be bad news for some manufacturers, it is paving the way for wide scale implementation of solar energy. As with wind, solar-generated electricity is already as cheap as or cheaper than fossil fuels in many places, even before externalities are considered, and this trend is increasing.

There are many promising developments underway in the area of renewable energy and potentially game-changing technologies on the horizon, which we haven't discussed because they are still theoretical or at least many years from being ready for wide scale use. The point of this chapter is to demonstrate that renewable technologies in their current state are *already* viable alternatives to fossil fuels. But it is far more likely than not that the future of renewable energy technology is even brighter than it now appears. If, after all of the facts and figures we've surveyed in this chapter, we wanted to allow ourselves a moment of sheer speculation, we might consider what the experience of recent decades has taught us about the evolution of technologies in our lives. Consider, for instance, the personal computer, the mobile phone, the DVD player and the flat-screen TV. Consider the Internet. Can anyone name a major technology that has become less efficient and more expensive over time?

It is certainly possible, for instance, that in the coming decades we will be able to generate pure hydrogen via electrolysis from inexpensive artificial leaves submerged in jars of water exposed to sunlight. Perhaps we'll store that hydrogen in fuel cells and use it to power vehicles that emit nothing more noxious than water vapor. All of the technologies involved already exist, just not yet in efficient enough forms to be widely practical or cost-effective. Major auto manufacturers — including Ford and Nissan — are developing hydrogen-powered vehicles that they hope to bring to market within as little as four years. Will they be economically viable? And, if so, at what point? Who knows? But nobody who can remember trying to download a high-resolution digital photograph over a 28,800 bps dial-up internet connection is in a position to doubt that we have unanticipated technological revolutions in our future.

You Don't Have to Be an Environmentalist to Appreciate the Benefits of Renewable Energy

Perhaps you've noticed that this chapter has not yet mentioned climate change or carbon footprints. That's not because climate change and the environment are not important issues — they're crucial. But it's important to demonstrate that renewable energy is a distinct, if related, issue, and that renewables provide benefits that can be readily appreciated by everyone, including those who aren't especially concerned about the environment.

In addition to all of the benefits discussed so far, renewable energy also happens to be good for the environment — its early and swift adoption could help us to avoid a global climate catastrophe. So there's that, too. As we look to the future, the question we should really be asking ourselves is: are fossil fuels a viable alternative to

107

renewable sources of energy? But that's really just a rhetorical question. The answer is, plainly, no.

REASONS FOR THE DISCONNECT?

Inertia

More than 90 percent of the energy we consume still comes from fossil fuels. There is a vast, global system of energy exploration, extraction, and distribution, which permeates every aspect of the global economy and our individual lives. The sheer scale and momentum of this global operation is awesome. There are over a billion internal combustion vehicles on the world's roads. It's overwhelming to contemplate that all of this could be significantly modified, let alone replaced by another system, despite the fact that it's actually happening already.

Myopia

It takes a bit of imagination to see the world as it could be rather than as it currently is. We're still surrounded by the smokestacks and exhaust pipes that have been synonymous with energy production for more than a hundred years. Car exhaust and smog and factories spewing geysers of dirty smoke into the air are normal to us — that's what energy looks like. All those clouds of smoke can blind us to the possibility of a totally different looking — and smelling — future. It just doesn't seem real or possible.

By the same token, people associate renewable energy with environmentalist concerns about pollution and global warming, which means that they also tend to associate it with conservation. There is a tacit assumption that solar, wind, geothermal and other renewable sources are attractive because they're clean, but that they're not necessarily practical or affordable. Environmentalists rarely emphasize the economic merits of renewables, which is a lost opportunity, since it allows people to assume incorrectly that renewables, though virtuous, aren't as cheap or efficient as fossil fuels.

Dementia (i.e., Free Market ideology)

If left to the free market alone, it will take a long time for renewables to scale up. Government investment is necessary to develop the infrastructure to support a large scale renewable energy economy. Free market ideologues believe that the fact that government investment is required somehow invalidates renewable alternatives to fossil fuels — according to their free-enterprise ideology; they believe that until renewable energy can be competitive in the marketplace for energy, it's a non-starter. If this attitude had prevailed forty or fifty years ago, there would never have been a man on the moon and the Internet would not exist.

Propaganda

Exxon/Mobil alone spent more money on lobbying the U.S. government than all renewable energy companies combined.[201] This stands to reason, since the more renewable energy we use, the less of their products we'll buy. What's good for America, and the rest of the world — economically, environmentally, and in terms of public health — is what's bad for the fossil fuel industries. The longer they can delay the development of renewable energy, the longer they can continue to profit from the global economy's dependence on the increasingly scarce and expensive petroleum products they supply.

A HEALTHY STOCK MARKET MEANS A HEALTHY ECONOMY

If farming were to be organized like the stock market, a farmer would sell his farm in the morning when it was raining, only to buy it back in the afternoon when the sun came out.
— John Maynard Keynes

CONSERVATIVES CLAIM...

The rising and falling of the Dow Jones Industrial Average represents the strength of the American economy as a whole. When the Dow is up, the economy is strong. When the Dow is down, the economy is weak. It's critical that government policies work to reassure Wall Street investors so that the stock markets continue to rise.

THE REALITY

On October 9th 2007, the Dow Jones Industrial Average closed at 14,164.53, an all-time high.

Exactly one year later, on October 9th 2008, the Dow closed at 8,579.19, having lost 40 percent of its value over the course of the preceding year (and over 7 percent of its value on that day alone).[202] That made 2008 the worst year since 1937. The U.S. economy was in free-fall, hundreds of thousands of jobs were being eliminated every month, and the Secretary of the Treasury, Henry Paulson, was considering partial nationalization of the banking system in order to forestall the possibility of economic collapse. In other words, the Dow had posted its all-time high on the very eve of an economic catastrophe.

Observing the Dow in the fall of 2007, one would never have suspected that the seeds of financial disaster had already been sown. But, as we know now, they had. Officially, the Great Recession began in December of 2007. Millions of jobs would be lost and trillions of dollars of wealth would be wiped out in the ensuing crisis. It took until the spring of 2014 for the economy to replace the jobs that had been lost in the Great Recession that followed the crash, which the Dow had failed to see coming.

Of course, the Dow Jones Industrial Average is not the only stock market index — there are a number of others, most notably the S&P 500 and the NASDAQ composite. But they all tend to fluctuate in parallel and trace the same pattern of ups and downs over time. On that magical day in October of 2007, when all seemed right with the world from the trading floor of the New York Stock Exchange, not only did the Dow achieve its highest level ever, but the S&P 500 index also hit an all-time high and the NASDAQ composite index hit a six-and-a-half year high.[203] They all declined more or less in parallel over the course of the following year, and all bottomed out in early 2009, at which point they all began their gradual climb to pre-recession levels.

The economy as a whole has fared very differently from the Dow and the other stock market indexes. By the spring of 2011 the stock markets had already rebounded to pre-recession levels, while unemployment remained above 9 percent and GDP growth was sluggish. Wall Street was booming again while millions of Americans continued to struggle with a brutally slow economic recovery that felt indistinguishable in real-life terms from the recession that had officially ended almost two years earlier, in the summer of 2009. The disparity between the fortunes of Wall Street and those of Main Street continued to widen throughout 2012: markets continued to rise, as did corporate profits, which hit an all-time high June and again in

December of that year. At the same time, wages hit an all-time low (calculated as a percentage of GDP).[204]

The stock market has very little to do with the economy as it is experienced directly by the great majority of citizens. This is not to say that it's irrelevant — many people depend on retirement accounts and pension funds that invest in the stock market. Millions of Americans saw their retirement savings wiped out in the financial crisis because the stock market tumbled. But the day-by-day — or hour-by-hour, or even minute-by-minute — fluctuations of the stock market do not reflect fluctuations in the state of anything other than the hunches, fears, and expectations of investors. Those hunches, fears, and expectations may or may not turn out to have been justified, but they are only remotely related to the everyday economic reality that most Americans inhabit.

REASONS FOR THE DISCONNECT?

The Dow is Not the Stock Market

The Dow Jones Industrial Average represents only a small slice of the stock market — it is a composite of the values of thirty particular stocks out of the hundreds that are traded on the New York Stock Exchange. None of these stocks are small businesses, which represent 99.7 percent of US employer firms.[205] It is not an indicator of the actual state of the economy — it is an indicator of how a certain group of investors feel about a limited number of specific components of the economy, i.e., thirty particular companies, all of which are atypical of the great majority of U.S. employers.

Force of Habit

In the first several decades of the post World War II era — until the 1980s — the stock market rose in parallel with a number of other economic factors that reflected general levels of prosperity, such as median wages and household income. That correlation allowed stock market indexes such as the Dow to stand as a convenient standard by which to judge the health of the economy as a whole. But that correlation was to some degree a coincidence — this was a period of unusual growth and improvement at all levels of society. Businesses were booming and the rich were getting richer, but so too were the middle class and the poor. Since the 1980s, however, income has been stagnating for a majority of Americans, while the rich have continued to get richer and the stock market has continued to rise. Yet we still maintain the habit of correlating stock market performance with national prosperity.

Whose Economy?

As a general rule, stock prices go up when profits go up. A business may increase profits by laying off workers and getting more productivity out of the workers that remain. During the recent financial crisis, millions of workers were laid off and unemployment remained high for years, while corporate profits reached all-time highs and the stock market rebounded to pre-recession levels and kept on rising. The resurgent Dow reflected the well-being of businesses, which is only one part of the overall economic situation.

Perception vs. Reality

Stock price is a reflection of perceptions, not necessarily reality. The perceptions of investors may reflect a realistic sense of the strength of a particular company's present condition and prospects, but they may also be wildly optimistic or irrationally pessimistic based on unsubstantiated rumors or the reported opinions of noted experts, who may ultimately turn out to have been wrong.

Moreover, many of the decisions of major investors are not based on assessments of the actual strength of companies, but rather on assessments of how those companies' stocks are likely to perform in the short-term — for instance, investors may recognize an overvalued stock and keep investing in it (thereby helping to drive the price up) in order to maximize their profits by selling at the highest possible price before it starts to fall.

The point is that investors have an interest in driving the prices of stocks as high as possible, regardless of whether those prices are based on reality or illusion. A company's stock may be sky-high because the company's fundamentals and prospects are strong (e.g., Apple) or because of misinformation and hype (remember Enron?).

This isn't to say that there is no correlation between stock prices and the state of the economy as a whole, only that the Dow, along with the other indexes, is just one of a number of indicators of overall economic well-being. And it's certainly not an accurate barometer — after all, the point of a barometer is to anticipate the weather, not tell us about a storm that's already happened.

PART 3

TAXES

CUTTING TAXES INCREASES REVENUE

You cut taxes and the tax revenues increase.
— President George W. Bush (February 8, 2006)

As a general rule, I don't believe that tax cuts pay for themselves.
— Bush Administration Treasury Secretary Henry Paulson (June 27, 2006)

CONSERVATIVES CLAIM...

Cutting tax rates always stimulates economic growth and creates jobs, and thus leads to increased tax revenues.

THE REALITY

There is no evidence to support this theory. In fact, actual historical experience decisively disproves it — which is too bad, because it would be a wonderful thing for all of us if we could pay less in taxes every year without reducing services or benefits, and without accumulating any debt. Unfortunately, like many wonderful ideas, this one is a fantasy.

The reality is less wonderful, but certainly more logical: when tax rates are cut, revenues fall; when rates are increased, revenues go up.

At the beginning of Ronald Reagan's first term in office, the top marginal income tax rate was 70 percent; when he left office eight years later it was 28 percent. In that period, the national debt tripled — from $994 billion to $2.8 trillion. In other words, those tax cuts did not increase revenues. They didn't even pay for themselves. They were paid for by unprecedented deficit spending.

After President Reagan signed the "Economic Recovery and Tax Act" in 1981 (often referred to as "Kemp-Roth"), tax revenues fell and did not recover to 1981 levels until four years later, even though the economy expanded at an historically above average rate during that time. In other words, tax cuts did not lead to increased revenues.[206]

After his initial foray into tax-cutting, Ronald Reagan actually signed tax increases into law in every year of his presidency except 1988.[207]

In 1993, President Clinton enacted a major tax increase, which conservatives deplored as one of the largest in U.S. history — and yet, revenues increased and the U.S. economy thrived. Tax revenues rose steadily throughout the 1990s as the economy expanded, without the help of any major tax cuts. By 1998, the federal budget was in surplus for the first time since the last fiscal year of Lyndon Johnson's presidency, 1969.[208]

When taxes were cut in 2001 and again in 2003 (the so called "Bush tax cuts") revenues fell immediately and did not return to 2000 levels until 2006.[209]

The same pattern applies when revenues are computed as a ratio of GDP — in other words, as a proportion of the economy as a whole. Federal tax revenues in the United States have not risen when tax rates have been cut, nor have they fallen when rates have been increased. In 2010, when tax rates were at their lowest levels since the late 1980s, tax revenues were also exceptionally low — 14.9 percent of GDP, well below the post World War II average of 18.5 percent. In 2000 — after the Clinton tax increases and before the Bush cuts — revenues stood at 20.6 percent of GDP.

If all of this seems a little academic, think of it in terms of Robin Hood: the Sheriff of Nottingham wasn't going around lowering people's taxes in order to fill King John's coffers. If the conservative theory of taxation applied, the king would have maximized his revenues by cutting taxes and Robin Hood would have been out of a job.

None of this should be hard to grasp — it simply makes sense that when tax rates rise, tax revenues increase and when they fall, revenues decrease. There is simply no legitimate case to be made that cutting taxes raises revenues.

REASONS FOR THE DISCONNECT?

Mumbo Jumbo

This stuff is not actually too complicated for most people to understand if they're willing to put in the time and do the math — but it is complicated. Following and assessing the validity of various arguments about tax policy requires patience, focus and a fair amount of mental work which most people find unpleasant and even mind-numbingly boring.

Magical Thinking

During the 1980 primary campaign for the Republican presidential nomination, George H.W. Bush famously derided Ronald Reagan's program of tax cuts as "voodoo economic policy" because it seemed so obviously disconnected from reality. Bush lost and Reagan went on to become president. G.O.P. politicians who promote this oxymoronic theory (whether sincerely or cynically) have not suffered at the ballot box — quite the contrary.

Wishful Thinking

It's tempting to believe that we can lower everybody's taxes and still raise enough revenue to pay for all the things that most Americans

— right, left and center — expect the government to provide, from national defense to Medicare. Who *wouldn't* want this to be true? Unfortunately, one of life's more difficult lessons is that if something sounds too good to be true, then it probably is — and in this case, it certainly is.

THE GOVERNMENT WASTES YOUR TAX DOLLARS

Taxes, after all, are dues that we pay for the privileges of membership in an organized society.
— Franklin D. Roosevelt

It is desirable to have some money spent by government for those things, those services that we believe we can get more usefully and more effectively through government. If people are getting their money's worth, fine.
— Milton Friedman[210]

CONSERVATIVES CLAIM...

Government doesn't work for average Americans. Hard-earned tax dollars are wasted on programs that don't benefit the public and which they don't even support. The American people would be better off if taxes were lower and they could spend more of their own money on the things that matter to them.

THE REALITY

According to a Gallup poll conducted in 2014, Americans believe that more than half of their tax dollars are wasted by the federal government. The same poll showed that people believe that state government wastes about 42 cents out of every dollar of tax revenue, and that local government wastes about 37.[211] These results were consistent with previous polls conducted by Gallup in 2011 and 2009, and with a CNN poll conducted in 2010.[212]

When the results were broken down by political affiliation, self-identified Republicans found government at all levels to be more wasteful than did self-identified Democrats. At the federal level, where the divergence was greatest, Democrats believed that government wastes 42 percent of revenues while Republicans believe it wastes 59 percent. No wonder they hate the federal government.

Of course, the question of whether the government is spending money on worthwhile programs is personal and subjective. Some people think it's a "waste" to spend half-a-billion dollars a year on public television; others think it's a "waste" to spend more than half-a-trillion dollars a year on the military. Some people even think the government itself is a waste of money.

Until his retirement in early 2015, the fiscally conservative Oklahoma Senator Tom Coburn was the Senate's leading deficit hawk. Every year, he published a catalog of what he considered to be the most egregious examples of wasteful government spending. Known as the 'Wastebook," each edition described dozens of programs that sound ridiculous, absurd, or pointless — in a word: wasteful. The Wastebook makes for fun reading, describing all sorts of silly sounding programs, including a study to determine the effects of Swedish massages on rabbits ($387,000); a grant to a company that turns alpaca droppings into fertilizer ($50,000); and a Pentagon program to destroy surplus quantities of perfectly good ammunition ($1 billion). All in all, the 2014 edition included 100 items whose total cost to taxpayers amounted to roughly $25 billion.[213] That sounds like a lot of money until you compare it to the overall size of the federal budget, which, in 2014, was just over $3 trillion.

Here's the notable point: the premier deficit hawk in the U.S. Senate, whose highest priority is to make government more fiscally responsible, and whose primary motivation is to bring attention to government waste, found that wasteful spending accounts for less than 1 percent of the federal budget — 0.83 percent to be exact.

The reality is that your taxes pay mostly for things that significant majorities of Americans not only support, but value: Social Security, Medicare and Medicaid, national defense, roads and bridges and tunnels, public schools, veterans' benefits, local police and fire departments, municipal water supply, maintaining food and drug safety standards, to name only a few.

Every time you turn on a water faucet and water actually comes out, you're receiving the benefit of the government putting your tax dollars to work on your behalf. You can even take it for granted that the water will be clean enough to bathe in, cook with, and drink. But, of course, it's not granted. It's been paid for by you — with tax dollars.

Conservatives' attitude to taxes is paradoxical: they deplore taxation while expecting to benefit from the services that government uses their tax dollars to provide. What's more, they fiercely oppose any cuts to the services and programs they support, such as Social Security, Medicare and Medicaid, and the military. Those three items alone account for about two thirds of the federal budget, leaving only 33 cents on the dollar left for everything else.[214] The government simply doesn't have enough revenue to waste the kind of money people think it does.

REASONS FOR THE DISCONNECT?

Benefits from Tax Dollars are Indirect

The benefits and services that come from taxation are not delivered directly, in tangible form, upon payment of your taxes. Because these benefits are indirect or delayed, it's easy not to connect them with the taxes you've paid in order to receive them.

Many Benefits From Tax Dollars are Intangible

People don't always notice the ways in which they benefit — directly or indirectly — from services provided by tax dollars. We notice when there's a pothole in the road, but we rarely notice the road when there's no pothole to remind us that our tax dollars pay to maintain it.

Occasional outbreaks of E. coli or tainted medicine become major news stories precisely because they are rare events, thanks to the system of regulatory agencies that monitor the quality of our food and drugs.

We rely on law enforcement and the criminal justice system to ensure public safety. We expect the police to come quickly when we call 911. We hope never to need the services of the local fire department, but we expect them to show up promptly if we do.

Americans don't have to worry about the possibility of foreign invasion because their tax dollars provide them with the most powerful military on planet Earth.

Demagoguery

Nobody likes paying taxes. For that matter, nobody likes paying for anything — in a perfect world, we'd get everything we want for free. Even those who generally support taxation naturally resent the need to pay taxes to the government.

It's all too easy — almost irresistible, in fact — for politicians to gain popularity by taking advantage of people's resentment. Politicians who rail against taxes and against the government are positioning themselves "on your side" against an enemy — "Government" — that has no voice with which to defend itself or make its own case.

Defending Taxation is Politically Risky

Few, if any, public figures are willing to mount a passionate public defense of taxation for the sensible reason that in most cases it is tantamount to political suicide.

Demonizing Government in Order to Dismantle the Social Compact

Many conservatives have long wished to modify or eliminate popular and successful social programs, such as Social Security and Medicare, but could never hope to garner public support. By demonizing government in general, they hope to discredit any and all programs administered by the government, including the ones that actually work well, benefit the public, and enjoy the support of huge majorities of voters.

Public Ignorance

Millions of Americans are poorly informed about what the government actually spends money on - e.g., foreign aid, the Environmental Protection Agency and public broadcasting. Foreign aid makes up less than 1 percent of the federal budget and the EPA about 0.67 percent.

An egregious example of this sort of misinformation is a recent flap over the federal funding of public broadcasting. A 2011 CNN poll found that 77 percent of Americans believed the Corporation for Public Broadcasting receives more than 1 percent of the budget and 37 percent believe that it receives more than 5 percent. The real number is 0.014 percent.[215] If you prefer fractions, that's 14/100,000 — fourteen one-hundred-thousandths! — of the federal budget. If citizens and politicians are really concerned about the budget, then the amount of time and energy devoted to trying to defund CPB was a scandalous waste. Demagoguery and public ignorance aggravate each other — it's a vicious circle. Politicians have more to gain by taking advantage of ignorance than by correcting it. A misinformed electorate frees them from the need to be true to the facts and allows them to formulate positions that inflame the voters' passions instead of calming them.

None of this is to say that government is perfectly efficient — far from it. Tens of billions of dollars can be saved by addressing redundancy, waste, fraud, and abuse. And even if the government were perfectly wise and efficient in spending our tax dollars, there would still be plenty of room for vigorous arguments about the overall size of government and what programs or policies are worth spending money on. But to say that the government wastes most of our money is simply wrong.

TAXES IN THE UNITED STATES ARE

TOO HIGH

$0.00
— Total amount of federal taxes paid in 2010 by GE, the world's largest corporation

The truth of the matter is that federal taxes in the United States are very low. There is no reason to believe that reducing them further will do anything to raise growth or reduce unemployment.
—Bruce Bartlett, former economic advisor to Ronald Reagan[216]

CONSERVATIVES CLAIM...

American citizens and companies suffer from an unfair burden of taxation. High top marginal tax rates on individuals punish success and dampen the entrepreneurial spirit. U.S. corporate taxes are the highest in the world, which places a huge burden on businesses and thereby suppresses job creation, innovation, and global competitiveness.

THE REALITY

Taxes in the United States are not high, either in comparison with U.S. rates in the past or with current rates in other developed countries. In fact, they are among the lowest in the developed world. This is equally true of personal and corporate taxes.

Let's start with personal income taxes.

Current federal income tax rates are lower than at any point since before World War II.[217]

Effective tax rates ("effective" refers to the actual amount paid, after deductions and refunds) in the U.S. have fallen over the past ten years, whether calculated per capita[218] or as a percentage of Gross Domestic Product — i.e., the total amount of all goods and services produced within the country in a given year. Throughout the 1970s, 1980s and 1990s, individuals consistently bore a tax burden of around 27 percent of their income. By 2000, that burden had risen to 28.7 percent. By 2010 it had been reduced to 23.6 percent - a drop of over 5 percent.

When calculated as a percentage of GDP, in 2000 tax revenues stood at 20.6 percent; by 2010 they had fallen to 14.9 percent - also a drop of over 5 percent.[219] By 2015, they had risen again to 18.1 percent. To put that into a larger perspective, federal tax receipts in the period since World War II have averaged about 18.5 percent.

For a large majority of Americans, effective tax rates are at or near their post World War II lows.[220] Indeed, the total current tax burden on U.S. citizens has been calculated to be at its lowest point since 1958.[221]

Taxes in the U.S. are also low when compared to other countries. The overall effective federal income tax rate in the U.S. is about 19 percent, which increases to about 25 percent when payroll taxes are included. This is well below the global average — in fact, more than fifty countries have higher effective tax burdens.[222]

U.S. individuals' total tax burden (including federal, state and local taxes) in 2009 ranked 15th among the developed nations of the world, as represented by the Organization for Economic Co-operation and Development (OECD).[223]

In terms of taxes as a percentage of GDP, the U.S. ranked 26th among OECD nations in 2006. U.S. taxes at all levels of government accounted for 28 percent of GDP, compared with the OECD average of 36 percent of GDP.[224]

That's a lot of numbers to follow, but they all add up to the same thing: Americans have a relatively low tax burden, whether compared to Americans in the past, or to the citizens of other developed nations.

Now, let's take a look at corporate taxes.

U.S. corporations are not highly taxed relative to other developed countries.

Although the top marginal corporate rate in the U.S. is relatively high, at 40 percent, the average effective rate — i.e., what corporations actually end up paying — is considerably lower, at about 25 percent, which is the same as China's.[225]

From 2000 to 2008, while corporate profits grew by more than 11 percent, corporate tax receipts actually declined by 8 percent.[226]

Despite the relatively high statutory rate, U.S. corporations are able to take advantage of a variety of credits, loopholes, and deductions that ensure they actually bear a comparatively low tax burden. In fact, U.S. corporations consistently enjoy one of the lowest tax burdens among all developed nations — in 2008 it was the lowest of all, when calculated as a percentage of GDP.[227]

Companies that have the resources to organize themselves so as to exploit all available loopholes and deductions can drive their effective rates much lower. In 2010, Google paid 2.4 percent in taxes,[228] while the world's largest corporation, General Electric, paid nothing at all. In fact, they actually received over a billion dollars in benefits from the government — paid for by your tax dollars. [229]

REASONS FOR THE DISCONNECT?

Demagoguery

Nobody likes paying taxes. Even those who generally acknowledge the need for adequate levels of taxation naturally resent the need to pay taxes to the government. It's all too easy — almost irresistible, in fact — for politicians to exploit people's resentment in order to gain their support. By relentlessly harping on the evil of taxation, conservative politicians have created a general impression that taxes are much more unreasonable than they actually are.

It's an effective tactic. As we've seen, taxes are actually lower today than they've been for generations, and yet more Americans believe that their taxes are too high than believe that their taxes are too low or about right. And the percentage of Americans who believe that their tax rates are fair has actually fallen in the years since the second round of Bush tax cuts, in 2003.[230]

Voodoo Economics

The prevalent conservative misconception that cutting taxes leads to increased revenues contributes to a false belief that even relatively low levels of taxation are unnecessarily high. In a (fantasy) world where tax cuts are the solution to every economic problem, any tax burden, no matter how low, will be perceived as too high.

Failure to Follow the Money

Many people don't know what their taxes are used for. Social Security, Medicare and military spending account for about 60 percent of the federal budget. Federal, state and local taxes pay for roads and bridges, schools, water supply, food inspection, police and fire departments. In other words, large majorities of Americans — liberals and conservatives alike — support most of the things their tax dollars are used to provide, but they don't always connect the dots.

Confusion of Statutory and Effective Rates

The statutory rate represents the rate of taxation before credits, deductions, and loopholes are taken into account. The effective rate represents the amount of taxes actually owed, which is usually considerably lower.[231]

The top statutory corporate tax rate in the U.S. is 40 percent, which really is among the highest in the developed world. But the average effective rate is closer to 25 percent, which is about average. The top statutory personal income tax rate is 39.6 percent, which is not especially high by global standards, but the effective rate for the top 1 percent of earners is closer to 27 percent.

HALF OF AMERICANS DON'T PAY TAXES

50 percent of Americans households no longer pay taxes.
— Sean Hannity, Fox News Channel, April 9, 2010[232]

HALF of America pays NO taxes. ZERO. So they're happy for tax rates to be raised on the other half that DOES.
— Rick Warren on Twitter, July 25, 2011

There are 47 percent of the people who will vote for the president no matter what...who are dependent upon government, who believe that they are victims...These are people who pay no income tax.
— G.O.P. presidential candidate Mitt Romney, May 17, 2012

CONSERVATIVES CLAIM...

Roughly half of Americans pay no taxes while benefiting from programs and entitlements that the rest of us pay for with our tax dollars.

THE REALITY

The claim that half of Americans pay no taxes at all is false.

While it's true that almost half — 46 percent in 2015, to be precise — of U.S. households typically do not pay federal income taxes, there are plenty of other federal, state and local taxes which everybody pays, including the poorest Americans.[233]

132

All U.S. residents who are employed pay payroll taxes, usually by having them withheld from their wages. And even the unemployed pay a variety of federal and state sales taxes and excise taxes on the goods and services they consume every day, including groceries, clothing, and gas.

When all taxes are considered, the median U.S. household, which earns about $51,000 a year, pays about 18.5 percent of its income in taxes.[234]

In 2010, the poorest 20 percent of Americans earned an average of $12,500, of which $2,025 went towards federal, state and local taxes. This amounts to an effective tax rate of 16.2 percent.[235]

Not all Americans who don't pay federal income taxes are poor. Many of the country's wealthiest citizens manage to avoid paying any federal income tax at all, thanks to a range of deductions, loopholes, deferments and write-offs designed specifically for the investor class.[236] According to the IRS, about 1,470 millionaires paid no federal income tax at all in 2009.[237] So that 46 percent who don't pay federal income taxes includes not only the poorest Americans, but some of the richest as well.

REASONS FOR THE DISCONNECT?

Confusion

Americans are subject to many kinds of taxes, some more apparent than others. It's easy to focus on the striking statistic that almost half of American households pay no federal income taxes without putting it into the larger context of the numerous other taxes that people actually do pay.

Distortion

Many conservatives in politics and the media exclude all but federal income taxes from the discussion of taxes in order to create the impression that half of all Americans are living off the rest of us. This is at best irresponsible, since the facts are readily available to anyone who has two minutes to spare, an internet connection, and a genuine interest in knowing the truth. At worst, it represents a willful misrepresentation of the facts that is explicitly designed to mislead the public and foment hostility towards the poorest members of society.

THE RICH PAY MORE THAN THEIR FAIR SHARE IN TAXES

It is not very unreasonable that the rich should contribute to the public expense, not only in proportion to their revenue, but something more than in that proportion.
— Adam Smith, *The Wealth of Nations*

CONSERVATIVES CLAIM...

The wealthy pay more than their fair share in taxes. They are the job creators. Democrats want to soak the rich and punish success, while redistributing the wealth to a growing class of poor Americans who don't pay income taxes. The society is becoming increasingly divided into the "makers" and the "takers."

THE REALITY

When all taxes — federal, state and local — are reckoned, the overall distribution of tax burdens in the U.S. is revealed as neither progressive nor regressive. Each income bracket pays a share of total taxes that is very close to its share of total income. In 2011, the lowest-earning quintile (i.e., bottom 20 percent), who had an average annual income of $13,000, received 3.4 percent of the income and paid 2.1 percent of the taxes, while the top 1 percent received 21 percent of the income and paid 21.6 percent of the taxes.[238] Thus, according to this most basic measure, the rich don't pay more than their fair share in taxes.

The argument that the rich pay more than their fair share almost invariably depends on a single statistic: that the wealthy pay a disproportionately large share of federal income taxes, and that this share has increased over the past thirty years or so.

The portion of total federal income tax liabilities borne by the wealthiest Americans has indeed increased over the past thirty years. For the top 1 percent, it almost doubled, from 15 percent in 1979 to 28 percent in 2007. The federal income tax burden of the top 10 percent rose from 41 percent to 55 percent during the same period.[239] This would seem to argue that the rich do indeed pay more than their fair share, until we look more deeply into the numbers and discover that they are paying a larger portion of the income taxes because they possess a larger share of the wealth. In effect it is a reflection of the growing gap between the very wealthy "1 percent," and the increasingly poorer "99 percent" in America.

What's more federal income taxes accounted for only about 47 percent of federal revenues in 2015. 33 percent came from payroll taxes, which, being capped at $118,500 (in 2015 - the number increases slightly each year), become less burdensome the richer you are. 9 percent of federal revenues came from excise and other taxes, which are by nature more regressive — i.e., their burden falls disproportionately on the middle class and the poor.[240] Indeed, when it comes to sales and excise taxes, the poorer you are, the greater the relative burden, since you pay the same amount as a rich person pays.

Tax Rates vs. Tax Burden

Tax rates on the wealthy today are low by historical standards. The top federal income tax rate is 39.6 percent. Aside from the periods from 1988 to 1993, when the top statutory rate was 28 percent, and the period from 2001 to 2014, when the top rate was 35 percent, the current rate is the lowest since before the Great Depression.

The top marginal income tax rate was 50 percent through the first seven years of Ronald Reagan's presidency — he lowered it to 28 percent in his final year. His successor, George H. W. Bush, raised it to 31 percent (thereby breaking his "no new taxes" pledge). In 1993 Bill Clinton raised the top rate to 39.6 percent where it remained until the early 2000s, when George W. Bush reduced it to 35 percent. The "Bush tax cuts" were set to expire after ten years, but were extended by Barack Obama for two years, and then ultimately made permanent for all but those making more than a quarter of a million dollars per year.[241]

More importantly for the wealthy, the long term capital gains tax rate for wealthy individuals is also at a historically low level of 20 percent. This rate was cut to just below 16 percent by the Bush tax cuts and allowed to rise under Obama. The wealthiest 1 percent of Americans derive more than a third of their income from capital gains, so the much lower rate of taxation on this type of income is a major boon to the wealthy, which most of society doesn't benefit from at all.

When all taxes are included, the effective tax rate of the wealthiest 1 percent of Americans fell from 37 percent in 1979 to 26.1 percent in 2009.[242] "Effective" tax rates reflect the actual amount of money paid, after deductions and credits. During this period, effective tax burdens have fallen across the board, but nowhere more than for the top 1 percent. At the same time, the rich have come to possess an unprecedented share of the country's total wealth.[243]

Well, not entirely unprecedented. According to IRS data, in 2007 the top 1 percent received 23.5 percent of the nation's income, which is the highest level since 1928.[244] This share fell to about 18 percent in the aftermath of the financial crisis, but has been rising again since 2010. According to Nobel Prize winning economist Joseph Stiglitz, twenty-five years ago the wealthiest 1 percent earned 12 percent of America's annual income and owned 33 percent of its wealth; today they earn 25 percent of income and possess 40 percent of the national wealth. During the same period, the middle class has actually seen their share of income fall.[245]

As of 2007, the bottom 50 percent owned only 2.5 percent of the wealth of the United States, while the top 10 percent owned 71.5 percent. What's more, the top 10 percent own over 90 percent of all stocks, bonds and mutual fund shares.[246] While unemployment and underemployment have remained high and GDP growth has remained sluggish in the aftermath of the financial crisis, the stock market has rebounded to well beyond pre-recession levels, having reached an all-time high in May of 2015. And, of course, gains realized from investment in the stock and bond markets are taxed at a maximum of 20 percent, not at the higher income tax rates.

Income Inequality

Nobody denies that the divide between rich and poor in America has widened over the past generation. The question is: are the poor and middle classes of the past three decades lazier and less responsible than those of previous generations?

Alternatively, is there something about the way the economy has changed, or indeed the tax structure, that has allowed the wealthy to amass an increasingly greater portion of the total wealth of the nation? In other words: has it become gradually more difficult for average, hard working people who play by the rules to simply get by?

The conservative argument depends on the first answer: it's the poor's fault; it's the middle class's fault that they can't get ahead. The conservative view is that an increasing number of Americans have become spoiled by "government handouts", which makes them lazy and less willing to seek gainful employment. This was Mitt Romney's point when he asserted that there are 47 percent of Americans "who are dependent upon government, who believe that they are victims, who believe the government has a responsibility to care for them, who believe that they are entitled to health care, to food, to housing, to you name it. That that's an entitlement. And the government should give it to them."

But the reality for working Americans is drastically different. Over the past thirty years, U.S. Gross Domestic Product — basically, the size of the entire economy — has more than doubled. During the same period, median household income has stagnated and the cost of living has increased, while workers have become more productive at an average rate of about 2 percent per year.[247] In other words, people are working harder and producing more, in exchange for less. The economy as a whole is better off, while the majority of workers are worse off.

By every significant measure, income distribution in the United States has become steadily more polarized over the past thirty years or so, while GDP has continued to grow. According to the U.S. Census bureau, household income stagnated or increased only marginally over past 30 years for the least well-off 60 percent of the population. During the same period, incomes for the next 20 percent increased by 25 percent, and for the top quintile increased by over 40 percent.[248] The minimum wage, adjusted for inflation, has declined by 20 percent since 1967.[249]

To put all these numbers into words: it's been getting consistently harder for middle-class and poor Americans to make ends meet. Working hard and playing by the rules gets you less far in today's America than it did a generation ago. The reason 47 percent of Americans are not liable for federal income taxes is that they are too poor.

Another method of quantifying income inequality is the GINI coefficient, which measures the degree of inequality in the distribution of household income in a particular country, or region. A GINI coefficient of 0 indicates perfect equality; a coefficient of 100 indicates perfect inequality. According to the C.I.A.'s World Factbook, the world average in 2007, before the financial crisis hit, was 39. That year, the United States had a GINI coefficient of 45, up from 40 in 1997. That made the U.S. the 42nd most unequal country in the world, which places it in the economic, if not the geographical, neighborhood of Jamaica, Bulgaria, Cameroon, Guyana, Uruguay, Iran, Cambodia, and Uganda.[250]

Among the developed nations of the OECD (Organization for Economic Cooperation and Development), the U.S. ranks 31st out of 34 in terms of equality, ahead of Turkey, Mexico and Chile.[251] This is true even after taxes and transfers have been taken into account.

If all these numbers and coefficients seem a little abstract, we can look at another statistic that hits us where we live, quite literally. This is the "Toil Index," devised by the economist Robert Frank, which measures the number of hours of work per month required for the median earner to make enough money to pay for the median rent. ("Median" refers to the exact mid-point of a sample — in the case the total number of households, with half of households earning more and half earning less. This is distinct from "average," which adds up all income and then divides by the number of households.)

In 1950, the toil index was 42.5 — in other words, the median rent cost 42.5 hours' worth of the median worker's monthly salary. By 1970, the toil index had fallen to 41.5, while GDP had more than doubled. Those were good times. From 1970 to 2000, GDP increased by another 163 percent,[252] but the toil index increased by over 60 percent, to 67.4, which means that the median worker had to work 22 more hours every month to cover the rent.[253]

The toil index demonstrates that average Americans have become increasingly worse off in an age of increasing income inequality.

"Handouts"

Most government benefits are not funded via the income tax. Social Security, Medicare — the largest entitlement programs buy far — are funded with payroll taxes, which are not applied to income beyond the first $118,500. Everyone who is employed pays these taxes. Unemployment insurance is not funded through the income tax, but through state and federal payroll taxes.[254]

So, the wealthy are not paying a disproportionate amount to subsidize entitlements. The largest single portion of the federal budget that is paid for by federal income taxes actually goes to the military. So, if the wealthiest 1 percent want their taxes lowered, they may want to consider lobbying the government to cut military spending.

Contributing to Recovery

The wealthy are not spending their money at the same rate as the less well-off, which means they're not contributing to economic recovery — by saving the money they earn, they are effectively withdrawing money from the economy.[255] As a rule, the poorer the household, the more of their income they spend, regardless of whether that income comes from wages or some form of government benefit or assistance. So, leaving aside the moral arguments for or against public assistance programs, there is a fair argument to be made that these programs help to sustain local economies in times of recession. The billions of dollars that the federal government spends on transfer programs, such as unemployment benefits and food stamps, pass almost immediately back into the economy because they are spent by their recipients. In other words, it circulates. Some of that money will come back to the government in the form of various taxes, such as sales taxes on the products purchased, or the payroll and income taxes of the employees who are able to remain in the workforce because the local businesses that employ them are supported by those very government "handouts" and thus don't have to lay them off.The wealthy, on the other hand, are not doing "their fair share" when it comes to helping the economy to recover. According to Robert Frank of the Wall Street Journal (a different Robert Frank from the one who devised the "toil index"), "the top 5 percent of earners account for more than a third of consumer outlays. If they're hoarding cash and worried about their companies, they're not hiring or spending—and thus, not creating jobs...Their savings rate soared to 34 percent in the second quarter of 2012, up from 12 percent in 2007. Higher savings would normally be good for the economy. But not now, when capital is needed to invest in growth and jobs. The One Percenters put 56 percent of their available cash into savings accounts and money markets in 2012 — that's up from 24 percent in 2007."[256]

141

Burdens

We have been speaking entirely in terms of numbers — percentages and dollar amounts. This makes sense, since the discussion about taxation and representation rarely transcends the realm of the quantifiable. And yet, there is another dimension to consider.

The word "burden" is a useful one. It may refer to taxes, yes, but it can refer to other things that are just as onerous, just as unpleasant to endure. The rich may argue that they bear their fair share of taxes, but they cannot seriously claim to bear a fair share of the struggle, distress, deprivation and, occasionally, humiliation that millions of hard-working Americans endure every day. The rich are asked to part with some of their money, just like everybody else. But the rich are not asked to sacrifice their dignity, or their peace of mind, or the opportunity to provide a better life for their children. The statistics make clear that we are living in an increasingly unfair and unequal economic system, in which the rich get disproportionately richer as everybody else gets poorer. The burdens of this system are born exclusively, and increasingly, by the middle class and the poor.

REASONS FOR THE DISCONNECT?

Misleading Emphasis on Income Taxes

While the wealthiest Americans certainly do pay a very high proportion of federal income taxes, those particular taxes only account less than half of federal tax revenues. About a third of those revenues come from payroll taxes, which are assessed as a percentage of income up to $118,500 only — these taxes are born disproportionately by the middle and working classes.

Misleading Emphasis on Entitlements

As noted above, about 40 percent of the federal budget is spent on

Medicare and Social Security, the two largest entitlement programs, which are paid for not with federal income taxes, but with payroll taxes. The wealthy do not pay a higher percentage of income than anybody else to provide these benefits. In fact, those who have an income above $118,500 actually pay a smaller proportion of their annual income to support these entitlement programs — the higher the income, the smaller the proportion.

Fairness is in the Eye of the Beholder

In fairness to the defenders of the 1 percent, we should acknowledge that there is no absolute standard of fairness in our society. To some, fairness comes down to "keeping what you've earned." To others it means paying the same proportion of your own earnings as everybody else. And to others it means giving back to the society that provided the opportunity for you to succeed. The argument is not so much about who is paying their fair share, but rather what constitutes a fair share in the first place. Liberals and conservatives have very different ideas of what fairness is. Some conservatives believe that the top 1 percent are entitled to their ownership of 70 percent of the society's wealth and that their obligation to the rest of society is fulfilled by shouldering a tax burden that is more or less equivalent to their share of national income, although they shoulder a tiny share of the burden of struggle, anxiety, and hardship that an increasing majority of their compatriots face every day.

PART 4

GOVERNMENT: POLICIES & PRIORITIES

THE G.O.P. IS THE PARTY OF SMALL GOVERNMENT

The era of big government is over.
— Democratic president Bill Clinton, State of the Union Address, January 23, 1996

CONSERVATIVES CLAIM...

Government is not the solution to our problems — it *is* the problem and should be limited as much as possible. Democrats — "tax and spend liberals" — use every opportunity to expand the size of government and waste tax-payer dollars on unnecessary and inefficient programs, whereas Republicans spend tax dollars more carefully and prefer to let citizens keep their money. Under Democrats, government always grows more than it does under Republicans.

THE REALITY

Whether you consider the size of the federal budget, the number of federal employees, or — if you're the literal minded type — the total amount of office space occupied by the federal government, you'll discover that the G.O.P. is the party of bigger government, while the Democrats prefer to keep things relatively lean.

"Relatively" is the key word. The United States is an enormous country with a population of more than 320 million. A government that could be accurately described as "small" is a practical impossibility, even if the public were willing to forego the major services that the government provides — from Social Security to education to national defense. But, of course, the public is not willing to forego these things.

The early 2000s provided an excellent opportunity for conservatives to put their supposed small-government philosophy into effect. George W. Bush was the first Republican president since Herbert Hoover to have G.O.P. majorities in the House and Senate for more than two years. (Dwight Eisenhower had G.O.P. majorities in both houses of congress from 1953 to 1955 — this was the only period of complete Republican control of government between Hoover and G.W. Bush.) The G.O.P. held the House for the first six years of Bush's presidency, and the Senate for four of those years. Let's consider the results.

Bush inherited a budget surplus and a declining national debt from his Democratic predecessor, Bill Clinton. Instead of continuing Clinton's fiscal policies, which had provided four straight balanced budgets, Bush, in collaboration with the Republican majorities in the House and Senate, enacted tax cuts and spending increases. The federal government was in deficit every year of his presidency. The national debt had grown by 90 percent by the time he left office. Two wars were financed with debt, rather than by tax increases, as every previous American war had been. What's more, the size of the federal government expanded, both in terms of spending and the number of employees on the government payroll. In other words, when the G.O.P. had the time and the opportunity and the power to enact their agenda, they presided over a big-government bonanza.

This shouldn't have surprised anyone. Over the past thirty years — since the election of Ronald Reagan — conservatives have contributed much more to the growth of government than liberals. If that sounds surprising, it's because Republicans have been very effective at claiming to favor limited government while acting in the opposite manner. But, unlike conservatives, the numbers don't lie.

Spending

If we look at federal spending increases per presidential term, it becomes instantly clear that Republicans are not the party of limited-government. Since 1980, Republicans have held the White House for five terms and Democrats for three. Under Republican presidents, spending has increased by an average of 6.9 percent per term, while under Democrats it has increased by 2.8 percent, less than half as much.[257] In fact, every Republican term saw greater spending increases than every Democratic term.

Here's how they stack up:

Reagan 1st term:	8.7 percent increase
G.W. Bush 2nd term:	8.1 percent increase
G.W. Bush 1st term:	7.3 percent increase
G.H.W. Bush:	5.4 percent increase
Reagan 2nd term:	4.9 percent increase
Clinton 2nd term:	3.9 percent increase
Clinton 1st term:	3.2 percent increase
Obama 1st term:	1.4 percent increase
Obama 2nd term:	5.6 percent *decrease*

As of the first quarter of 2016, federal spending actually had *declined* by 5.6 percent during Obama's second term, and by more than 13 percent since peaking (mostly as a result of mandatory expenditures associated with the economic crisis) in the Fall 2010.[258]

When measured as percentage of Gross Domestic Product — i.e., as a proportion of the economy as a whole — federal spending under Republicans has increased by an average of 1.24 percent per presidential term, while under Democrats it has actually *decreased* by 1.7 percent.[259]

Government Employees

Despite frequent conservative claims that government doesn't create jobs, there are actually millions of Americans who are employed by government at the federal, state, and local levels. Some of these are bureaucrats, some are public school teachers, some are firefighters, and some are cops. The point is that government jobs are very real, and, most would agree, pretty important to society, despite what conservatives say. But even though conservative rhetoric tends to be hostile towards government jobs, more of them are created and preserved under Republicans than under Democrats.

Since Barack Obama took office in January of 2009, total government employment in the U.S. had declined by about 600,000 as of September 1, 2012. Most of these losses came at the state and local levels, while federal employment remained roughly constant. So, in this most basic sense — i.e., in terms of the total number of people working in the public sector — the size of government in America has declined during the presidency of Barack Obama. By contrast, under his conservative predecessor, George W. Bush, total public sector employment increased by about 900,000 jobs *per term*, or 1.8 million in total. Indeed, had it not been for government jobs, total employment in the U.S. under Bush would have been negative.

Although the contrast between Obama and Bush seems surprising, it is actually typical of Democrats and Republicans in recent decades. Under Reagan, federal payrolls increased by an average of 24,625 jobs per year. Under Clinton, they decreased by an average of 42,375 per year. All in all, since 1980, federal payrolls have increased by an annual average of 8,750 employees under Republicans while they have *decreased* under Democrats by an average of 29,000.[260]

The Physical Size of Government

Even when it comes to office space, Republicans have been more responsible than Democrats for the expansion of government in America. In their two-year investigation for the Washington Post into the post 9/11 expansion of America's national security apparatus, "Top Secret America", Dana Priest and William Arkin revealed that, under the Republican administration of George W. Bush, the size of the federal government had exploded, even in the most literal and, if you will, concrete sense:

"In Washington and the surrounding area, 33 building complexes for top-secret intelligence work are under construction or have been built since September 2001. Together they occupy the equivalent of almost three Pentagons or 22 U.S. Capitol buildings - about 17 million square feet of space."[261]

Not That There's Anything Wrong with That

The problem with the G.O.P.'s attitude toward government is not so much their hostility as their hypocrisy. In a country of over 300 million citizens, the government is bound to be enormous; neither party could shrink the size of government without cutting services that a majority of citizens support and rely on. Conservatives may speak contemptuously about government, but when they're in the majority, they rarely cut spending or limit the power and influence of government. That's not necessarily a bad thing. Given that 60 percent of the federal budget goes to Social Security, Medicare/Medicaid and the military (three programs that huge majorities of citizens support) it seems that the citizens of this democratic republic don't especially favor limited government.

The problem isn't that conservatives preside over increases in the size of government; the problem is that they misrepresent reality and lie about their priorities.

REASONS FOR THE DISCONNECT?

Words Speak Louder than Actions

The truth is that the G.O.P. is not the party of small government — it's the party of *talking* about small government. Conservatives show very little commitment to or aptitude for cutting government spending, but they're very good at publicly demonizing government whenever there is a camera or a microphone around. If you say something loud enough and often enough, people will start to believe it.

Symbolism

Republicans get a lot of attention for insisting on symbolic cuts that don't add up to significant savings. Consider the well-publicized fiscal crusades that conservative deficit hawks have waged against foreign aid, public television, arts funding, and "pork barrel" spending, also known as "earmarks:" none of these programs amounts to even 1 percent of the federal budget. Republicans make a big show of demanding cuts that will not significantly control government spending, but when it comes to their own large scale spending, they keep silent.

Democrats Leave Government-Bashing to the Republicans

As the party of Social Security, Medicare, Civil Rights, and "Obamacare," Democrats aren't naturally hostile to government. On the contrary, they believe in using government to promote the general welfare as the Constitution demands and the public expects. Democrats also happen to have a superior record of keeping the budget under control when they're in power (for more on this, see Part 5, chapter 1, "The G.O.P. is the Party of Fiscal Responsibility"). They do not believe that government is "the problem" and they have no reason to pretend that it is in order to score political points.

REPUBLICANS REVERE THE CONSTITUTION MORE THAN DEMOCRATS DO

We the people are the rightful masters of both Congress and the courts, not to overthrow the Constitution but to overthrow the men who pervert the Constitution.
— Abraham Lincoln

CONSERVATIVES CLAIM...

The founding documents of the United States are virtually sacred — they must be respected and defended at all costs. Republicans revere the Constitution and are dedicated to upholding its principles. Liberals don't respect either the spirit or the letter of the Constitution, while conservatives always do.

THE REALITY

Conservatives speak reverentially about the Constitution but have repeatedly demonstrated their willingness to distort or disregard any part of the document that happens to conflict with their views or their agenda. Republican legislators routinely treat the Constitution's most essential principles with disregard and even, on occasion, with contempt.

For example, in recent years, conservatives have supported efforts to deprive prisoners of due process (in violation of the Fifth

Amendment), to subject detainees to torture (in violation of the Eighth Amendment), to monitor the telephone conversations and emails of U.S. citizens on U.S. soil (in violation of the Fourth Amendment), to limit access to the polls for eligible voters (in violation, variously, of no fewer than five constitutional amendments).

How do conservative views and policies actively defy the Constitution? Let us count the ways.

Voter Suppression

Voting is the essential mechanism of democracy — it is how we make our preferences known, and how we hold our elected officials accountable to the public will. The right to vote is the fundamental right, without which all other rights become vulnerable. No fewer than five constitutional amendments explicitly address the right of citizens to vote: the 14th, 15th, 19th, 24th, and 26th.

And yet, in recent years, conservatives have launched what amounts to a series of coordinated assaults on the ability of eligible citizens to participate in free and fair elections. Consider the spate of voter ID laws that were passed in Republican-dominated state legislatures around the country in 2012 — specifically, the use of voter ID laws to limit access to the polls (this subject is discussed at length in Part 6, Chapter 1, "Voter Fraud Poses a Serious Threat to American Democracy"). New voter ID laws disproportionately affect demographic groups who are inclined to vote for Democrats — namely the poor, the young, the elderly, African-Americans, and Latinos.

If these laws had been passed and implemented soon after an election, leaving ample time for the public to be informed and to adjust to the new laws before the next election, liberals would not necessarily object. But in state after state, Republican-controlled legislatures sought to pass these laws during an election year, in many cases within less than six months of the election, in an atmosphere of controversy and confusion. Moreover, these laws were designed to address only one kind of voter fraud — in-person voter fraud — which is so rare as to be statistically irrelevant.

In Pennsylvania, for instance, the government admitted that it was not aware of a single case of in-person voter fraud in the state, or, for that matter, in any other state. At the same time, nobody disputed that thousands of eligible citizens would be effectively disenfranchised by the law, given the limited time between passage of the law and the next election. In other words, the conservative supporters of the voter ID law considered it acceptable to disenfranchise thousands of eligible voters by passing a law that was designed to solve a non-existent problem.

This pattern has been repeated in Republican-dominated legislatures throughout America. In 2011 and 2012, 25 voter ID laws were passed in 19 states. Most of these were blocked, overturned, or modified by the Justice Department or the courts — because they were determined to be unconstitutional.[262]

Choice

In the 1973 Roe v. Wade decision, the U.S. Supreme Court ruled that a woman's right to an abortion is protected under the 14th Amendment to the Constitution. Accordingly, every American woman has a constitutionally protected right to obtain an abortion in the early stages of pregnancy — that is, before the fetus becomes "viable" (i.e., able to survive outside the womb), which normally occurs between twenty-four and twenty-seven weeks into a pregnancy. About 90 percent of all abortions occur during the first twelve weeks, well before the point of viability.

Unable to win the battle over abortion in the courts — in other words, on the basis of a legitimate constitutional argument — Republicans have sought to circumvent the Constitution by effectively restricting women's access to abortion. They have passed medically unnecessary, onerous, and sometimes humiliating laws at the state level, which are designed to make abortion prohibitively difficult to obtain. These state laws have included mandatory waiting periods, mandatory counseling, and even physically invasive and medically unnecessary procedures such as trans-vaginal ultrasound.

Twenty-four states have also passed so-called "TRAP" laws — Targeted Regulation of Abortion Providers. These are laws that are designed to place particular burdens on doctors who perform abortions and the operators of facilities where abortions are performed. Some of these laws require that doctors have admitting privileges at a hospital within a few miles of the abortion clinic. Some establish minimum size requirements for rooms and corridors of abortion facilities, causing existing facilities to have to either undertake expensive renovations or to close down. What all these laws have in common is that they are designed to make life difficult if not impossible for abortion providers.[263]

This conservative war on a constitutionally protected right has succeeded in restricting women's access to abortion. According to the Guttmacher Institute, by 2005 87 percent of all counties in the U.S., and 97 percent of non-metropolitan counties, had no abortion provider.[264]

Conservatives found the Constitution itself to be an impediment to their agenda, so they found ways around it.

The Debt Ceiling Controversy

In the summer of 2011, Republicans in Congress threatened to cause the U.S. Treasury to default on its debts for the first time in American history. Technically, they were refusing to authorize an increase in the national debt to cover commitments that had already been approved by congress.

That last part is worth restating carefully, since it is often obscured by all the technical language associated with parliamentary procedure and the budget process. By refusing to raise the debt ceiling, Republicans in Congress were refusing to raise the adequate funds to cover financial commitments that *the U.S. Congress itself had already authorized.* This was not a matter of denying new spending — it was a plain refusal to fulfill legally binding obligations that had already been made in the name of the American people. Or, to put it a bit less technically, the Republicans wanted to force the U.S. government into becoming a deadbeat.

Section 4 of the 14th Amendment asserts, "The validity of the public debt of the United States, authorized by law, including debts incurred for payments of pensions and bounties for services in suppressing insurrection or rebellion, shall not be questioned."[265] This provision of the 14th Amendment was passed in order to ensure that representatives from newly re-admitted Southern states could not prevent the U.S. government from paying the debts incurred during the Civil War. The essential principle is that of the continuity of the U.S. government. A new congressional majority may pursue its own policies in the present and into the future, but it may not refuse to uphold the obligations that the United States government has already entered into.

By threatening not to raise the debt ceiling, Republicans in Congress demonstrated that they were prepared to allow the U.S. to default on its debts for the first time in history. What's more, they rejected the constitutional principle of continuity.

Reading Christianity into the Constitution

Conservatives insist on reading Christianity into the Constitution, which fails to mention it even once. Nevertheless, they insist that the founders intended the United States to be a Christian nation, and that the Constitution itself is biblically inspired.

The Constitution mentions God precisely zero times. Jesus Christ is not mentioned anywhere in the document. The only mentions of religion in the Constitution are prohibitions against imposing any religious test for office (Article 6, paragraph 3), or establishing a state religion (the 1st Amendment), or preventing anyone from practicing his or her religion, whatever that religion may be (the 1st Amendment).

Conservative Christians, in other words, are not interested in what the Constitution actually has to say about religion, nor do they respect the Constitution's explicit separation of church and state.

Domestic Spying

Conservatives have allowed the fear of terrorism to override their commitment to civil rights.

Section 215 of the Patriot Act empowers the FBI to spy on people inside the United States, including U.S. citizens, without obtaining a warrant or even demonstrating probable cause. This is clearly in conflict with the 4th Amendment, which states: "The right of the people to be secure in their persons, houses, papers, and effects, against unreasonable searches and seizures, shall not be violated, and no warrants shall issue, but upon probable cause, supported by oath or affirmation, and particularly describing the place to be searched, and the persons or things to be seized."

The law also allows items to be seized based solely on the FBI's assertion that the seizure is part of an investigation "to protect against international terrorism or clandestine intelligence activities." Under the Patriot Act, this assertion is sufficient in itself; it does not have to be justified by any probable cause or reason for suspicion.[266] The idea that law enforcement officials can conduct searches or surveillance of citizens without obtaining a warrant, or even informing a judge, should be a cause of outrage to anyone who cares for the spirit and letter of the Constitution. And yet these provisions have enjoyed overwhelming support from Republicans whose fear of terrorism far outweighs their respect for the Constitution.

Of course, the Patriot Act has not been supported only by Republicans — support for the act has been unusually bi-partisan in a highly partisan era. But the fact that many Democrats have joined the G.O.P. in disregarding the Constitution in this particular case does not detract from the central argument of this chapter. Whereas there has been at least some dissent among Democrats in Congress, there has been virtually none among Republicans. When the original bill passed in the House of Representatives by a vote of 357 to 66 (with 9 abstentions), 62 of the 66 "nay" votes were Democratic.[267] When the act was re-authorized in 2011, by a vote of 275 to 144 (with 14 abstentions), 117 of 144 "nay" votes came from Democrats.[268]

Indefinite Detention

Article 1, Section 9 of the Constitution asserts that "the privilege of the writ of habeas corpus shall not be suspended, unless when in cases of rebellion or invasion, the public safety may require it." That means that anyone who is arrested must be brought before a judge so that the causes for arrest and detention can be assessed and determined to be either valid or invalid.

The Constitution states clearly that this right of detainees may be suspended only in times of "rebellion or invasion." The so-called "war on terror" is neither a rebellion nor an invasion, yet conservatives in the aftermath of 9/11 have consistently supported indefinite detention without arraignment or trial. Under the Patriot Act, the president has the right to order, without providing a reason, the indefinite detention of any individual, including American citizens on U.S. soil, in stark defiance of the letter and spirit of the Constitution.

Torture

In the aftermath of 9/11, the Bush administration developed a set of harsh interrogation techniques collectively referred to by the euphemism "enhanced interrogation." The most controversial and widely reported of these techniques, known as waterboarding, has been designated as a form of torture by most experts and governments — including the United States itself. Indeed, the U.S. executed Japanese prisoners of war who were found guilty of waterboarding American prisoners during World War II.[269]

Other "enhanced interrogation" procedures involve exposure to extreme temperatures, beating, sleep deprivation, slamming into walls, sexual humiliation, and "controlled fear," in which detainees are exposed to terrifying menaces, such as viciously barking dogs. These techniques were explicitly devised to inflict pain, humiliation, and terror on defenseless prisoners in U.S. custody. And although they were also designed so as to avoid the "intense pain and suffering" associated with "death, organ failure or permanent damage resulting in a loss of significant body functions" in practice they have resulted in precisely these results on numerous occasions.[270] More than 100 detainees have died in U.S. custody, with over twenty-five having been officially ruled homicides by the CIA and/or other internal investigators. Homicides.

This information came to light during the course of a hearing before the congressional subcommittee on the Constitution, Civil Rights and Civil Liberties on June 18, 2008. It was provided by Colonel Lawrence Wilkerson (a Republican), former chief of staff to Secretary of State Colin Powell (a Republican), whose prepared testimony read in part: "As I compiled my dossier for Secretary Powell, and as I did further research, and as my views grew firmer and firmer, I needed frequently to reread that memo; that is to say, the memorandum of February 7, 2002. I need to balance in my own mind the overwhelming evidence that my own government has sanctioned abuse and torture, which, at its worst, has led to the murder of 25 detainees and a total of at least 100 detainee deaths. We had murdered 25 or more people in detention."[271]

The 8th Amendment prohibits "cruel and unusual punishment." Even if one could argue that the so-called "enhanced interrogation techniques" did not technically constitute torture, it is very hard to argue that they are not cruel. The conservative defense is that these procedures were being conducted away from U.S. soil, which is true enough. But it is also a technicality. They have gone to great care to circumvent a moral principle enshrined in the Constitution because they find it inconvenient or frightening, to abide by it. Regardless of whether there may be any merit to the conservative approach to interrogation (and the preponderance of expert opinion worldwide says otherwise), it is certainly less respectful of the letter and spirit of the 8th Amendment than the liberal position, which opposes torture under any circumstances.

It should also be noted that President Ronald Reagan, in 1988, signed the United Nations Convention Against Torture, which prohibits any "cruel, inhuman or degrading treatment" of prisoners under any circumstances whatsoever.[272]

Grover Norquist's "Taxpayer Protection Pledge"

Article 1, Section 8 of the Constitution gives congress the power to raise taxes, which is one of the essential functions and responsibilities of the House of Representatives. Traditionally, Congress increases taxes during times of national emergency, especially war. Almost every Republican member of the federal government has abdicated this constitutional responsibility by signing a pledge never to raise taxes under any circumstances whatsoever. This "Taxpayer Protection Pledge" was written by a man named Grover Norquist, founder of Americans for Tax Reform. Norquist is a conservative activist who has never held elected office in the United States. His organization is an independent advocacy group that is not accountable to the public.

By the end of 2011, all but four Republican members of the House of Representatives (238 of 242) and all but six Republicans in the Senate (41 of 47) had signed Norquist's pledge, promising to "ONE, oppose any and all efforts to increase the marginal income tax rate for individuals and business; and TWO, oppose any net reduction or elimination of deductions and credits, unless matched dollar for dollar by further reducing tax rates."[273] By contrast, only two Democrats in the House and three in the Senate had signed the pledge.

The point is not that federal legislators should raise taxes, but that they should be free to do so, and prepared to do so if a crisis demands it. By committing never to allow taxes to rise under any circumstances, come what may, they reject a potentially important constitutional role in favor of a blind commitment to an organization that is not responsible, or accountable, for the general welfare.

Frivolous Constitutional Amendments

In recent decades, the Republican Party has adopted several constitutional amendment proposals into its platform, despite the fact that they have no chance of becoming the law of the land. In order to be adopted into the Constitution, a proposed amendment must pass by a two-thirds majority in each house of Congress and then be ratified by three-fourths of the states.

A constitutional amendment to ban same sex marriage will never be ratified in a country in which more than half of citizens support same-sex marriage. A constitutional amendment to ban abortion is not viable in a country in which 75 percent of the people support the right to abortion under at least some circumstances. A constitutional amendment to protect the right to pray in schools is totally redundant, given that all Americans have enjoyed this right continuously since 1791, when the 1st Amendment was adopted.

So why would the Republican Party repeatedly engage in such exercises in futility?

Because implausible constitutional amendments are anything but futile when it comes to generating controversy, attracting political support, and raising money. Constitutional amendments sound momentous. They provide politicians with opportunities to "take a stand" and to appear seriously engaged with issues of historical importance. They provide pretexts for the creation of national political organizations that become multi-million dollar fundraising enterprises.

In other words, Republicans routinely use the constitutional amendment process as a political and fundraising tool. This is hardly a reverential way to treat the Constitution.

The Constitution is not a puzzle or a cryptogram; it was not devised in order to hide its true meanings. By going to extreme lengths to distort the plain meaning of the Constitution, while pretending that they possess the hidden key to its true meaning, conservatives are doing the opposite of respecting it — they are using and abusing it as a tool to impose their views on society, in complete contradiction to the spirit and purpose of the Constitution itself. That is the very opposite of respect.

REASONS FOR THE DISCONNECT?

Confusing Words with Deeds

Republicans do speak and write reverentially about the Constitution. But words are cheap, and speaking reverentially is not the same as showing real respect. Conservatives readily disregard the letter and spirit of the Constitution whenever it comes into conflict with their agenda. They are quick to abandon any constitutional principles that would require them to alter or modify their policies, or to tolerate policies that they oppose.

Unchallenged Hypocrisy

Republicans mention the Constitution all the time, whereas Democrats tend to mention it less often. It is the same with patriotism, fiscal responsibility, and supporting the troops — Democrats actually have a better record, but Republicans talk about it more often, more consistently, and with more self-congratulation. Since neither the Democrats nor the media do much to expose conservative pretense and hypocrisy regarding the Constitution, Republican claims go unchallenged and are taken at face value. Republicans thus tend to get the credit they demand.

REPUBLICANS SUPPORT TROOPS AND VETERANS MORE THAN DEMOCRATS DO

Vets Job Corp Act was just defeated. 58-40. A huge disappointment. Today, politics won over helping vets.
— Tweet from @IAVA (Iraq and Afghanistan Veterans of America) reacting to a Republican filibuster of a jobs bill for veterans, September 19, 2012[274]

CONSERVATIVES CLAIM...

The G.O.P. is the party most closely aligned with the military and has the troops' back. Republicans have more respect and gratitude for military service than Democrats do. Because they are more patriotic and care more about the defense of our nation, conservatives make a greater priority of supporting active troops and veterans.

THE REALITY

If by "support" you mean hot air and empty gestures, then there is no question that the G.O.P. excels at supporting the military. But when it comes to providing practical support that actually benefits active-duty troops and veterans, Republicans as a group have a record that is at best no better than that of Democrats and in most respects is demonstrably inferior. Indeed, it is Democrats who have consistently

164

taken the lead in promoting the interests of service members.

Iraq and Afghanistan Veterans of America (IAVA) periodically assigns letter grades to all members of the House and Senate, based on their support for troops and veterans. The IAVA Congressional Report Card for 2010 assigned a total of 154 D and F grades — 142 went to Republicans and 12 to Democrats. Meanwhile, ninety-four congressmen received A or A+ grades, of whom ninety-one were Democrats and three were Republicans.[275] Overall, 97 percent of A grades went to Democrats while 92 percent of D and F grades went to Republicans.

In the Senate, all 9 Senators who received an A rating were Democrats. Among 33 Senators who received a rating of D or F, all were Republicans, except for one Democrat (Russell Feingold of Wisconsin).[276]

What accounts for such a disparity? In a word: money. While Republicans have shown little ambivalence about spending well over a trillion dollars on the wars in Iraq and Afghanistan (the most conservative estimate was actually about $1.5 trillion already spent as of December 2014), they have demonstrated a fierce reluctance to spend even a tiny fraction of this amount on the well-being of veterans returning from those same wars.[277]

In the Summer of 2012, Democrats introduced legislation — the Veterans Jobs Corp Act — to help provide jobs for veterans of Iraq and Afghanistan. The Congressional Budget Office determined that the act would have cost taxpayers $1 billion over five years, which is about a fifth of what we've been spending on the Afghanistan War alone *every month* since it began.[278]

The bill would have created job training programs for veterans, as well as career counseling and assistance in searching for jobs. It also would have provided jobs for veterans in national park conservation and preservation of historic sites, and would have given priority to veterans applying for jobs as firefighters, EMTs and police officers.[279] Given that the bill sought to create job opportunities primarily in the public sector, it's possible that Republicans opposed it out of ideological hostility to expanding the size of government rather than ideological hostility to spending. Either way, though, the G.O.P. placed their ideological commitments above the welfare of veterans.

Around the same time, the House Budget Committee, chaired by conservative fiscal vision-leader and soon-to-be-selected G.O.P. vice presidential candidate Paul Ryan, announced plans to cut $6 billion a year from the annual Veterans Affairs budget by changing eligibility requirements, which would make more than a million veterans ineligible to continue receiving benefits for which they had already qualified.

By contrast, when Democrats still held the majority in the House in 2009, they passed legislation to expand the number of veterans who could qualify to receive health coverage from the VA by more than a quarter million. They also voted to increase the VA budget by $350 million in order to cover more veterans and their families.[280]

In November of 2012, President Obama signed into law the "Returning Heroes Tax Credit," which provides tax incentives for employers who hire unemployed veterans, and the "Wounded Warrior Tax Credit," which provides more generous incentives for those who hire disabled veterans. These are tax credits that the president himself had proposed in 2011.[281]

This Democratic leadership in providing tangible support for troops and veterans is not a recent development. When we review the history of the United States since World War II, we see that even when support for troops and veterans has been uncontroversial and bipartisan, the Democrats have always been in the vanguard.

The G.I. Bill

The Servicemen's Readjustment Act of 1944, commonly known as the G.I. Bill, was a bi-partisan bill passed by large majorities in the House and Senate, which were both held by the Democrats at the time. It was signed into law by Democratic president Franklin D. Roosevelt.

The law provided educational grants, various forms of housing assistance, unemployment benefits, and low-cost loans to veterans returning from war. The G.I. Bill has been in effect ever since and has been supplemented and enhanced on numerous occasions, most notably in 1984 and 2008.

The Montgomery G.I. Bill was passed into law in 1984.[282] It provides thirty-six months of education and/or training benefits for veterans, and was named after its principle sponsor, Democratic congressman Gillespie "Sonny" Montgomery.

In 2008, congress passed the Post 9/11 G.I. Bill — officially known as the Veterans Educational Assistance Act — which provided further educational support, job-training, and housing assistance for veterans returning from war.[283] No such measures were passed while the G.O.P. controlled both houses of congress and the White House in the aftermath of 9/11. It was only after Democrats were elected to majorities in the House and Senate in 2006 — five years after the invasion of Afghanistan and three-and-a-half after the invasion of Iraq — that new legislation was proposed to support the veterans of America's latest wars.

The post 9/11 G.I. Bill, introduced in 2007 by Democratic Senator Jim Webb, was initially resisted by Republicans. President Bush threatened to veto it. The G.O.P. presidential candidate at the time, John McCain, himself a veteran, initially opposed the bill, but ultimately did not vote against it — he was one of only two senators who did not cast a vote either for or against the bill when it came before the senate for a final vote in late June of 2008 (the other was Ted Kennedy, who was recovering from surgery to remove a brain tumor). Then-senator and Democratic presidential candidate Barack Obama voted for it, as did a large majority of both Democrats and Republicans (the bill ultimately passed the Senate by a vote of 92-6 and the House by a vote of 416-12).[284]

Like its predecessors, the original G.I. Bill and the Montgomery G.I. Bill, the Post 9/11 G.I. Bill was a bipartisan effort that ultimately passed with overwhelming support in the House and the Senate. It should be noted, however, that it took Democratic leadership to initiate the process and then overcome Republican resistance in order to pass legislation that would provide actual — not merely verbal

— support for veterans returning from war.

Republicans based their initial opposition to this expansion on predictions that the bill would hurt retention levels (i.e., the number of service members who re-enlist once they have completed their period of service) since it would provide an incentive for service-members to leave the military at the earliest opportunity in order to take advantage of the new benefits. Democrats pointed out that the bill would boost recruitment at about the same rate as it would lower retention, since it would provide an additional incentive for people to join the military in the first place. But regardless of the relative merits of these arguments, here was a situation in which Democrats were proposing legislation to support veterans while Republicans opposed it. Moreover, the Republicans' argument was not supportive of the troops themselves — it was based on a desire to keep people in the military not for their own sake, but for everyone else's. Republicans, in other words, preferred to actually deprive troops of support so that they would not choose to leave the service.

Stress and Suicide

After more than ten years of war in Iraq and Afghanistan, suicide among active-duty troops and veterans has escalated to unprecedented levels. In recent years, the suicide rate among active duty troops in the Army and Marines has risen to more than twice the national average. Among veterans, the problem is even more alarming. Although only about 1 percent of Americans have served in the military since the beginning of the Afghanistan War, veterans account for 20 percent of suicides in the United States.[285]

In 2012, 349 active-duty U.S. troops killed themselves — more than died in combat.[286] According to the Center for Disease Control, the national suicide rate is about 12 per 100,000 people. About 1.44 million service members make up the active-duty U.S. military. A rate of suicide consistent with the national average would be 173 — less than half of what it actually is.

Of course it would be unfair to blame Republicans for the high suicide rate among active-duty troops and veterans. It is, however, entirely fair to hold them accountable for doing nothing about it, and even opposing the attempts of Democratic legislators to support those service members who are most in need of help. Democrats have regularly attempted to increase budgets for veterans' health and to make health services available to a greater number of veterans, whereas Republicans have moved to block Democratic efforts while providing no alternatives of their own. Democrats have also acted to help provide employment opportunities for veterans, which Republicans have also resisted, despite the fact that financial desperation and idleness are major causes of stress, depression, and suicide.

Unnecessary and Unjustified Wars

The war in Iraq cost the lives of 4,486 members of the U.S. Armed Services.

American troops are patriotic and loyal. They place themselves unquestioningly in the hands of their leaders. They sacrifice their own personal liberty and safety in the belief that they will be used to defend the Constitution and the American people. They trust that whenever they are sent into battle, it will always be in a worthy and just cause. They trust that they will only be used to fight the good fight.

The Iraq War was the deepest imaginable betrayal of this trust. A war that was "sold" to the American people, like soap or a new car, on the basis of lies by a Republican administration eager for war — which is to say, eager to send more than a hundred thousand Americans into harm's way, knowing that many would die and that many more would be physically injured or psychologically damaged and in many cases both, and that hundreds of thousands of American military families would be disrupted, traumatized, or even torn apart.

The Republicans who worked so hard to concoct a barely credible pretext for invading and occupying Iraq did not have to "sell" the war to the troops because the troops are loyal and devoted to duty. The promoters of the Iraq war took this unquestioning loyalty as given — which it was, in the most literal sense. They took it and used it and gave nothing in return. Except, of course, words of support. There have been plenty of those.

REASONS FOR THE DISCONNECT?

The Military Leans Right

Surveys of active duty troops and veterans have shown consistently higher levels of support for Republicans than Democrats, which is no doubt true.[287] But when we examine the results more closely, we learn that the military is hardly monolithic in its conservatism.

A definite majority of high-ranking officers identify themselves as politically conservative, but lower ranking military personnel express a range of political affiliations that is more consistent with society as a whole — in other words, most are self-identified moderates, while roughly equal numbers identify themselves as liberals and conservatives. Although officers account for only 14 percent of military personnel, they account for virtually 100 percent of military presence in the media. Nobody would pay much attention if five hundred enlisted troops signed a letter endorsing a presidential candidate; when five hundred retired generals did just that for Mitt Romney, it was news.[288] This creates the impression that the troops as a whole overwhelmingly support the G.O.P., which in turn suggests that they must feel that way because the G.O.P. supports the troops.

Money

Republicans do tend to support the military more strongly than Democrats do in one key respect: spending. Republicans oppose cuts to the military budget, and often seek to increase it even for no particular reason. 2012 G.O.P. presidential candidate Mitt Romney, for example, proposed increasing military spending by $2 trillion, though he was unable to explain what he would have spent it on, and despite the fact that the Pentagon didn't ask for, or even want, the money.

The unwillingness to cut the military budget would appear to represent support for the troops in a very concrete sense. But this money is not intended to increase salaries, or benefits, or care. As we've already seen, Republicans actually want to reduce financial support for troops and veterans and their families.

The real beneficiaries of massive military spending are the defense contractors who provide war materiel and services to the armed forces. These industries spend tens of millions of dollars every year on lobbying and exert enormous influence on lawmakers in Washington.[289]

So, it's certainly true that Republicans support the military industrial complex, just not the actual troops.

Jingoism

Republicans speak the language of patriotism more consistently and more loudly than do Democrats. They equate patriotism with toughness. Accordingly, they present a more deliberately aggressive — or "hard line" — front to the world, often expressing an open contempt for diplomacy. It often seems that more war is their answer to every foreign policy dilemma.

Readiness to use the military appears to be a vote of confidence, which is arguably a kind of support. But expressions of confidence and admiration don't constitute policies that actually benefit troops and veterans.

Words vs. Deeds

As we've already seen throughout this book, Republicans excel at proclaiming their support for causes and values that they don't actually support in any practical sense. Whether it's the Constitution

171

itself, or "limited government," or "family values," or "supporting the troops," Republicans say all the right things and get a lot of credit for "taking a stand." But they consistently fail to promote or even consent to policies that would translate their fine sentiments into deeds that actually promote the causes and values they claim to stand for.

Worse, the actual policies that Republicans support all-too-often accomplish the opposite of what their words express. They praise the Constitution while subverting it. They affirm their commitment to limited government while expanding it. They piously honor family values in the abstract while ignoring the needs of actual families and enacting policies that promote exactly the sorts of behavior they deplore. And so it is with the troops, of whom we as a nation have required so much, and to whom we have given so little in return. Conservatives are quick to wrap themselves in the flag and sing the troops' praises — but praise is all they have to offer.

"OBAMACARE" IS A GOVERNMENT TAKEOVER OF HEALTHCARE

This is, to my mind, the most blatantly obvious case of politics trumping policy I've ever seen in my life. Because this is an idea, that four or five years ago, Republicans were touting. A guy from the Heritage Foundation spoke at the bill signing in Massachusetts about how good this bill was...Basically, you know, it's the same bill. [Romney] can try to draw distinctions and stuff, but he's just lying.

— MIT professor Jonathan Gruber, principle architect of both Mitt Romney's Massachusetts healthcare plan and "Obamacare"[290]

CONSERVATIVES CLAIM...

The Patient Protection and Affordable Care Act, known as "Obamacare," is a major power grab by the federal government, which will now insert itself into the healthcare decisions of millions of Americans. Federal bureaucrats will decide what doctors you can see and what procedures you are eligible for. The government will establish "death panels" which will review cases and make life and death decisions about who may receive treatment, potentially denying life saving coverage to elderly patients.

J.P. BERNBACH

THE REALITY

The Patient Protection and Affordable Care Act is in no sense a government takeover of the healthcare system. The government will not take over hospitals, nor establish new government-run hospitals. The government will not take over private medical practices, nor establish new government-run practices. The government will not take over pharmaceutical companies, nor establish new government-run companies. Doctors will not become government employees, nor will they be required to consult with the government about treatment they can provide. The government will not compete against private health insurers by establishing a public alternative to private insurance.

"Obamacare" is based, almost exactly, on the healthcare law passed in Massachusetts under Republican governor Mitt Romney in 2006, which was based on a plan developed by the Heritage Foundation, a conservative think tank. The distinctive quality of both laws is that they rely primarily on the existing private sector, by helping citizens to afford private insurance rather than by providing a government-run alternative. In other words, the defining feature of "Obamacare" is precisely that it is *not* a government takeover, but rather a set of free-market solutions. That is why liberals have never liked the approach, while conservatives loved it until the very day that Democratic president Barack Obama embraced it.

In a nutshell, "Obamacare" makes private insurance cheaper and available to more people. The law achieves this in two ways which depend on one another in order to work: (1) by legally requiring for-profit insurance companies to cover more people than they did previously, such as those with "pre-existing conditions;" and (2) by requiring members of the public either to purchase insurance, or, if they chose not to, to pay a penalty.

The logic behind these two interdependent provisions is simple: the additional expense to insurance companies of covering people who are more likely to get sick (i.e., those with pre-existing conditions) is offset by the millions of new customers flooding into

174

the market. Since everyone — young and old, healthy and unhealthy alike — is required to participate in the newly-expanded market, health insurance companies receive plenty of healthy new customers who will pay regular premiums while demanding less in the way of reimbursements for treatment. This is a free-market solution designed to keep healthcare coverage in the private sector; it explicitly avoids the public insurance option (think "Medicare for everyone") that liberals would have preferred, and which is available to citizens of every other developed nation.

"Socialized Medicine" — Not

One thing "Obamacare" definitely *isn't* is "socialized medicine." Consider the U.K., by comparison, which has a genuinely socialist healthcare system — the National Health Service. The hospitals in the system are owned and operated by the government; the doctors and nurses in the system are employed by the government. The system is paid for by taxes and provides "free" healthcare to all citizens — i.e., at no charge beyond what they have already paid in taxes.

"Obamacare," on the other hand, helps citizens to purchase health-insurance from companies in the private sector. Under "Obamacare," most plans include deductibles and a variety of copays which require all but the poorest citizens to cover a portion of their health-care costs out of pocket. Among other things, "Obamacare" is a law that requires citizens to pay money to for-profit companies — that is nowhere close to socialism.

A Word About "Death Panels"

The claim that there are "death panels" in "Obamacare" was an outrageous lie and a vicious slander against a policy that was designed to provide real relief and care to tens of millions of Americans. There is nothing in the law to support that accusation, which is based on a complete distortion of a provision of the Act that covers consultations about "end of life" care — in other words, "Obamacare" will require insurance companies to reimburse you if you wish to meet with your doctor to discuss treatment options and make plans for how you will be cared for if you or a loved one should become incapacitated by old age, terminal illness, or a catastrophic accident. That is the closest thing to a "death panel" in the PPACA.

On the other hand, conservative critics of "Obamacare" have nothing to say about the actual death panels whose verdicts many millions of Americans have endured for decades: those departments within private health insurance companies whose sole purpose is to review claims in search of reasons to deny coverage. How many stories have we all heard of people who died because they could not get their insurers to pay for potentially life-saving treatments or operations? With the passage of "Obamacare," those "death panels" will have less power to refuse coverage to those who have the greatest need of it.

REASONS FOR THE DISCONNECT?

Ignorance

"Obamacare" is relatively simple in principle, but the law itself is hundreds of pages long and dauntingly complex in its details. As a result, few people have actually read it and there is a widespread failure to understand what the law actually does.

Fear

Healthcare is a life and death issue. It's natural to be worried about the potential effects of a new law that will affect the way many people in the U.S. receive their medical care. Although tens of millions of Americans were uninsured for years, and millions who had insurance were routinely denied coverage, the system before "Obamacare" was at least a known quantity — what if this controversial new system was even worse? With all the conservative talk about "death panels" and "socialized medicine" it's not surprising that many feared things would get even worse under the new healthcare law. The devil you know…

Cynicism

The passage of a universal healthcare law represents one of the major legislative achievements of the past fifty years, both in terms of the heavy parliamentary lift and the sweeping social impact of the law. Conservatives did not want to see a Democratic president, along with Democratic majorities in both the House and the Senate, get credit for a landmark success that will be remembered for generations to come.

John Gruber, who was the principle architect of both the Romney plan in Massachusetts and President Obama's national plan, put it this way: "Look, if this succeeds, then Obama becomes F.D.R. This is the most important social policy accomplishment since the 1960s. And if this succeeds, this could be the kind of benefit to the Democratic Party that Social Security was. So if I was the Republicans, I'd be screaming and kicking and scratching to kill it too, on purely political grounds…On politics, this is your Waterloo. You've got to fight this tooth and nail. And so they're fighting it tooth and nail. "

That makes political sense. But it is vile to pursue partisan political advantage at the expense of the well-being of tens of millions of citizens.

THE EVIDENCE FOR CLIMATE CHANGE IS INCONCLUSIVE

The risk of climate change is clear and the risk warrants action. Increasing carbon emissions in the atmosphere are having a warming effect. There is a broad scientific and policy consensus that action must be taken to further quantify and assess the risks.
— The website of ExxonMobil, the world's largest producer of fossil fuels[291]

The future is now. And it is hot.
— James E. Hansen, director of NASA's Goddard Institute for Space Studies[292]

CONSERVATIVES CLAIM...

There is no consensus in the scientific community about whether the Earth's climate is getting warmer. Even among those who believe the Earth is getting warmer, there is widespread disagreement about whether it's caused by humans.[293] Global warming may even be a hoax, cooked up by radical environmentalists.

THE REALITY

In November of 2012, the National Climatic Data Center issued a report that included these observations: "Including this November, the ten warmest Novembers have occurred in the past twelve years. The ten coolest Novembers on record all occurred prior to 1920. November 2012 also marks the 36th consecutive November and 333rd consecutive month with global temperature higher than the long-term average. The last month with a below average temperature was February 1985, nearly twenty-eight years ago."[294] 333 consecutive months is twenty-seven years and nine months.

2013, 2014, and 2015 were all warmer. 2015 was in fact the warmest year since average global temperatures have been recorded (beginning in 1880).

The 2000s are the hottest decade on record, and the 2010s are on pace to be even hotter. Ice caps are melting. Sea levels are rising. More than 97 percent of climate scientists agree that the Earth's atmosphere is heating up at an unprecedented rate and that carbon dioxide emissions from human activity are the major cause.

CO_2

Although the science is complex, the basics of global warming are not difficult to grasp. Human activity causes excessive global warming, because human activity causes large amounts of carbon dioxide to be emitted into the atmosphere. Carbon dioxide traps heat. This particular property of CO_2 was proved by a British scientist named John Tyndall in the 19th century and is not a matter of dispute.[295] All other things being equal, a system that contains more carbon dioxide will be hotter than it would be with less carbon dioxide.

For the past 650,000 years — which is more than three times as long as human beings have existed on planet Earth — the level of carbon dioxide in the atmosphere has ranged between 180 and 300 parts per million. At no point in all that time did the level of CO_2 ever rise above 300 parts per million — that is, until around 1950. Since then, it has been rising steadily, in precisely the same sense that a rocket ship rises steadily from the ground towards the sky. Today the concentration of CO_2 in the atmosphere is above 400 parts per million and rising fast.[296] This is also not a matter of dispute.

What is different about the world since 1950? Lots and lots of cars. And lots of airplanes. And plenty of new coal-fired power plants. And more cars. Human activity generally introduces a great deal of CO_2 into the atmosphere through the burning of fossil fuels, and this number has been increasing exponentially over the course of the past century.

There were roughly twelve million cars on the planet in 1922.[297] Today, human beings produce about eighty million new cars and trucks *every year*.[298] The total number of motor vehicles surpassed one billion in 2010.[299] That represents an increase of more than 8,000 percent in less than a century. And, of course, this exponential growth in CO_2-producing human activity isn't limited to cars. Airplanes crisscross the globe. Coal fired power plants supply most of the world's electricity. In all, total annual global emission of CO_2 from fossil fuels has almost doubled over the past thirty years, from about 18.5 billion metric tons in 1980 to more than 32 billion in 2012.[300] None of these statistics is a matter of dispute.

It shouldn't be hard to accept that all of this might have some kind of impact on the environment. Given that carbon dioxide is a heat-trapping gas, it simply isn't possible that the Earth's atmosphere could experience a 33 percent increase in concentration of CO_2 (from 300 to 400 parts per million) without simultaneously getting warmer, just as it isn't possible for you to put on a goose-down jacket without getting warmer.

So, it is not a matter of dispute that burning fossil fuels produces CO_2. And it is not a matter of dispute that human beings burn great quantities of fossil fuels, thus introducing great quantities of CO_2 into the atmosphere. And it is not a matter of dispute that in the middle of the last century the concentration of CO_2 in the atmosphere surpassed the highest levels that the planet has seen in more than half-a-million years, and that this level continues to skyrocket. And it is not a matter of dispute that CO_2 traps heat. And it is not a matter of dispute that the average temperature of the globe has been steadily increasing and that the first two decades of the 21st century are the hottest ever recorded.

But somehow, when you put all of these things together, it produces grounds for skepticism?

Experts Agree

The Intergovernmental Panel on Climate Change (IPCC) is the leading international organization dedicated to the study of climate change.[301] It was established in 1988 by the World Meteorological Association and the United Nations Environmental Programme for the purpose of reviewing and assessing scientific research into climate change. They conduct comprehensive reviews of the published work of thousands of scientists around the world and issue periodic assessment reports. In 2001 they reported for the first time that there was a scientific consensus about the reality of human-caused climate change. In 2007, they reaffirmed this conclusion, with a probability of 90 percent.[302]

The IPCC's conclusions have been reaffirmed by the most important and authoritative scientific bodies in America, including the American Meteorological Society, the American Geophysical Union, the American Association for the Advancement of Science, and the National Academy of Sciences.[303]

In 2008 scholars in the Department of Earth and Environmental Sciences at the University of Illinois at Chicago conducted a survey of 3,146 experts, representing "a large and broad group of Earth scientists," to determine their views on global warming. They found that a large majority — 82 percent — agreed that "human activity is a significant contributing factor in changing mean global temperatures." When the sample was restricted to include only actively publishing climate scientists, that percentage increased to 97.4. The authors of a report on the survey observed, "it seems that the debate on the authenticity of global warming and the role played by human activity is largely nonexistent among those who understand the nuances and scientific basis of long-term climate processes."[304]

181

A 2010 review of the published works of 1,372 climate scientists appeared in the official journal of the National Academy of Sciences. It noted "striking agreement among climate scientists on the tenets of anthropogenic [i.e., caused by human beings] climate change (ACC)" and concluded that "97- 98 percent of climate researchers most actively publishing in the field support the tenets of ACC as outlined by the Intergovernmental Panel on Climate Change."[305]

In fact, 97 percent may actually be a conservative figure (if you'll pardon the irony). A review of all available peer-reviewed articles by scientists relating to "climate change" and/or "global warming" published between 1991 and 2012 determined that out of a total of 13,950, only 24 explicitly rejected the hypothesis that global warming is caused by human activity.[306] That's 1 out of every 581, or 0.17 percent, which suggests that the scientific consensus in favor of human-caused climate change is all but unanimous. The study was conducted by James L. Powell, executive director of the National Physical Science Consortium who served twelve years on the National Science Board, having been appointed by two Republican presidents, Ronald Reagan and George H. W. Bush. Hardly the prototype of a tree hugger.

A leading climate change skeptic — Richard A. Muller, who is a professor of physics at the University of California and director of the Berkeley Earth Surface Temperature project — reversed course and announced, in July 2008, that he had come to accept the reality of human-caused global warming. In a prominent op-ed in the New York Times, entitled *"The Conversion of a Climate-Change Skeptic"* he described his change of views as a "total turnaround."[307]

Big Business Agrees

The Carbon Disclosure Project conducts an annual survey of "Global 500" companies. The "Global 500" comprises the 500 largest companies (by market capitalization) included in the FTSE Global Equity Index Series. In 2012, 405 out of the 500 corporations participated in the survey, whose results revealed that the great majority of major global corporations accept the reality of global warming and have taken steps to address it.

81 percent of companies that responded to the survey identified climate change as an immediate physical danger. 78 percent of companies (up from 68 percent in 2011) had already integrated policies to address climate change into their overall business strategy. 96 percent of respondents reported that they have a board member or senior executive dedicated to overseeing climate change issues.[308]

Consensus

All of this goes to show that there is certainly a consensus about the reality of climate change, especially among those who actually know something about it. That doesn't mean that the consensus is infallible, or that there can be no serious questions or objections.[309] It is possible, though not likely, that the scientific consensus about climate change is incorrect. It is possible, though not likely, that the tiny minority of scientists who reject the consensus will be vindicated in years to come. Time, as they say, will tell.

But even if the reality of human-caused climate change can conceivably be denied by serious people, there is no question that the consensus among experts today is overwhelming. If you found yourself in an unfamiliar place and asked directions of a crowd of 100 locals, and 97 of them told you to go North, while one told you to go South, and two said they weren't sure, what would you do? While it's certainly possible that one is right and 97 are wrong, you'd probably be unwise to presume that this is the case.

And Even If, Despite All the Evidence and the Consensus of Experts, You're Still Not Convinced...

Try the following thought experiment, inspired by Blaise Pascal, the 17th century French mathematician and philosopher.

Pascal wrote that a rational person who has no proof of God's existence should nevertheless live as though God exists, since there is nothing to lose by doing so, even if God turns out not to exist. On the other hand, to live without faith carries an immense risk if it turns out that God actually does exist — i.e., eternal damnation. To put it another way, if you wager that God exists, you will lose nothing if you turn out to be wrong, but gain everything if you turn out to be right. If you wager that God does not exist, you gain nothing if you turn out to be right, but lose everything if you turn out to be wrong.

Be that as it may, a similar (identical, in fact) logic applies to climate change.

Developing clean and sustainable energy sources carries no downside for society and plenty of upsides. It increases energy independence, is good for the environment, enhances national security and economic stability, and will ultimately save people money. It also opens up a new set of industries in which American ingenuity and enterprise can lead the world.

All these benefits accrue even if there turns out to be no man-made impact on global climate. And if climate change is real, then we gain the enormous additional benefit of slowing it down, possibly reversing it, and at least ceasing to aggravate it.

On the other hand, if we fail to modify our consumption habits and develop cleaner, more sustainable energies, the best case scenario is that we continue to pollute our air and water, continue to depend at least partially on foreign oil, continue to be subject to volatile energy prices, and ultimately find ourselves poorly prepared for the time when fossil fuels start to run out.

That's the best case scenario. On the other hand, if it turns out that the scientific consensus is accurate, then we will have allowed climate change to worsen, while providing no alternatives to switch to before it becomes too late, and may actually cause - *cause*, mind you — a global catastrophe.

This should be a no brainer for a rational person.

REASONS FOR THE DISCONNECT?

Climate Change is a Bummer

Nobody wants to think of a huge global catastrophe, especially when there doesn't seem to be an easy, or at least clear, solution. The problem is messy and the range of potential solutions is complex. What's more, addressing climate change demands a long-term strategy that will pose considerable inconvenience and expense in the short term in exchange for long-term benefits that are vague and uncertain. It's not surprising that people don't want to think about it.

Environmentalists are a Bummer

Not all of them, to be sure. But many environmentalists, who are legitimately alarmed by the prospect of global environmental catastrophe, come across as...well, alarmist. What's more, they often make their appeals through negative emotions, like fear and guilt ("haven't you thought about your carbon footprint!?"), which turn people off and drive them away.

Misinformation, Disinformation, and Propaganda

Companies that produce fossil fuels are among the world's biggest and richest. Indeed, ExxonMobil is not just the world's largest oil company — it's the world's largest company, period. Their products are the principle causes of climate change, which means that any serious attempt to reduce carbon emissions constitutes an attempt to reduce their profits. They have everything to gain by promoting the idea that global warming is just a controversial theory. The tens of millions of dollars they spend on lobbying and public information (or, rather, misinformation) campaigns is tiny in comparison with the billions they stand to lose if serious policies are enacted to address global warming.

The Media's "Balance" Fetish

As mentioned above, the great preponderance of peer-reviewed scientific studies confirms the reality of human-caused climate change while only a tiny percentage dispute the consensus. But relatively few people ever read any of these studies, and even fewer read enough to know that experts are virtually unanimous. Most people get their information from the media where, more often than not, the authors or TV hosts strive to be even-handed by presenting "both sides" of the issue. Even though (at least) 97 percent of experts fall on one side and only (at most) 3 percent on the other, when representatives of each side appear on a television segment or magazine article, they are evenly matched, which can suggest that both points of view are more or less equally valid.

Tiny Little Numbers

Global temperature increases of 1 or 2 degrees don't sound like such a big deal, when the temperature in most places varies by ten times as much every twenty-four hours. Vast oceans — miles deep and thousands of miles wide, containing literally billions of billions of gallons of water — rise by a few centimeters. It's hard to imagine how this could be a big deal, even though it actually is.

Huge Enormous Numbers

Some of the numbers involved in discussions of climate change are so enormous that they become abstract and almost impossible to grasp. How do you conceive of billions of tons of gas? It certainly sounds like a lot, but...who knows? Millions of square miles of ice melt sounds pretty alarming, but...is it really? The magnitude of the quantities involved can boggle the mind and leave one feeling baffled, numb, and unable to know how to think about it.

Mumbo Jumbo

Climate change is a technical subject that depends on science that most of us don't understand. Most people are simply not qualified to judge the various arguments on their merits, so they have to rely on experts, activists, and public officials for guidance. Conservative politicians and pundits abuse the good faith of their followers and supporters by feeding them misinformation that they are not equipped to doubt.

When challenged about their opposition to any attempts to address climate change, conservative politicians have recently started to adopt a know-nothing approach, saying "I'm not a scientist." Apparently this is intended to absolve them of having to take a position. But they don't seem to realize the implication of their own words — if non-scientists aren't in a position to offer a valid opinion, presumably it's the scientists who actually know what they're talking about. And 98 percent of them agree that human-caused climate change is happening.

PART 5

GOVERNMENT: SPENDING

THE G.O.P. IS THE PARTY OF FISCAL RESPONSIBILITY

Reagan proved deficits don't matter.
— Vice President Dick Cheney[310]

This debt explosion has resulted not from big spending by the Democrats, but instead the Republican Party's embrace, about three decades ago, of the insidious doctrine that deficits don't matter if they result from tax cuts.
— David Stockman, former Reagan Administration Budget Director[311]

CONSERVATIVES CLAIM...

Republicans are "fiscally responsible" — they care about balancing budgets and keeping spending under control. Democrats, on the other hand, are reckless spendthrifts who waste taxpayer dollars on expensive programs, heaping up a horrible burden of debt for future generations.

THE REALITY

The reality — and the irony — is that Democrats have been consistently more conscientious in managing budgets than Republicans. As we've already seen in a previous chapter (Part 4, Chapter 1 "The G.O.P. is the Party of Small Government"),

government spending is typically higher when a Republican is in the White House. It should hardly come as a surprise, then, that by the standard measures of fiscal responsibility — balanced budgets, annual deficits, and the overall accumulation of debt — Republican performance is consistently inferior to that of Democrats.

Balanced Budgets

The federal budget has been balanced twelve times since the end of World War II. Nine of these balanced budgets have occurred under Democratic presidents. Three have occurred under Republican presidents, and each of those Republican presidents was named Dwight Eisenhower. No Republican president has balanced the federal budget since fiscal year 1960. Since then, Democratic presidents have done it five times, most recently in fiscal year 2001.

Democrats don't talk much about balanced budgets because they are not especially concerned about them. A reasonable deficit is entirely consistent with a sound fiscal policy and a thriving economy. The key word, of course, is "reasonable."

Annual Deficits

Democrats have a long record of running lower deficits than Republicans. Indeed, a running theme in the fiscal history of the presidency is that of Democrats reducing deficits inherited from their Republican predecessors.

Since the end of World War II, every Republican president except Eisenhower has presided over an increase in the size of the deficit in relation to GDP, while every Democrat has presided over a decline. Republican presidents have left office with an average deficit to GDP ratio of 3.32 percent, while Democrats have left with an average of 1.02 percent. That means that during the average Republican administration, the annual deficit tends to grow three times as fast in relation to the economy as it does under Democrats.

Two Democratic presidents, Lyndon Johnson and Bill Clinton, left surpluses to their successors. No Republican president has. Three Democrats, Johnson, Clinton, and Obama, have presided over a decline of the annual deficit in real terms — in other words, the actual dollar amount of debt being accumulated every year has been lower at the end of their administration than at the beginning (under Obama, who has yet to complete his second term, this was true for fiscal year 2015 and is projected to hold true for 2016 and 2017.)

Under Clinton, the deficit declined by 90 percent in his first term and was eliminated entirely in his second — he presided over four straight surpluses. Under Obama, the deficit declined by 50 percent in his first term and by an additional 35 percent during the first two years of his second term.

Under every Republican president since World War II, the annual deficit has increased over the course of his term in office. Reagan famously doubled the deficit (and doubled the debt — more on that below). Under George H.W. Bush it increased by two-thirds. George W. Bush, who inherited a surplus from his fiscally responsible predecessor, left his successor an annual deficit of over a trillion dollars, the largest in American history in nominal terms and the highest as a percentage of GDP since the height of World War II.[312]

Federal Debt

And then there's the matter of the national debt, which fiscal conservatives claim to care about above all things. Once again, there is a drastic disconnect between conservatives' stated priorities and the actual performance of Republicans in office.

Over the course of all Republican presidencies since World War II, the national debt has increased by an average of 6.97 percent of GDP. Under Democrats it has *decreased* by an average of 8.5 percent — and that includes the precipitous rise in debt which occurred during Obama's first term owing the Great Recession. (Pre-Obama, the debt to GDP ratio declined by an average 12.6 percent under Democrats.)

Using the long historical time-frame is actually a favor to Republicans, who, once upon a time, really did have a legitimate claim to being fiscally responsible. G.O.P. performance in fiscal matters has been much worse during the latter half of the period we've been considering. As we've seen, Eisenhower presided over three balanced budgets. Some forty years later, as we've also seen, George W. Bush actually inherited a surplus, which he immediately squandered. In the interval between Ike and "Dubya," G.O.P. fiscal policy had discarded prudence in favor of recklessness.

The turning point was 1981, when Ronald Reagan became president and brought about his fiscal revolution, which involved cutting taxes drastically, increasing military spending, and not offsetting the resulting revenue losses with any substantial cuts to existing government programs. The pretext for all of this was that tax cuts would supercharge the economy to such an extent that revenues would actually rise, despite the lower rates at which Americans and American businesses were taxed. As we've seen (in Part 1, Chapter 3 "Tax Cuts Increase Revenue") this is, to put it politely, hogwash.

Before and After Reagan

During the thirty years prior to Reagan's assumption of the presidency, the national debt of the U.S. was basically constant — though it fluctuated from year to year, it remained remarkably stable. Between 1950 and 1980, the debt increased nominally from $257 billion to $908 billion, but when adjusted for inflation the values are more or less the same. In 2015 dollars, the debt in 1950 stood at the equivalent of $2.52 trillion; in 1980 it stood at the equivalent of $2.61 trillion. That represents an increase of 3.5 percent over thirty years.[313]

What's more, while the debt remained constant in real terms, it declined precipitously in relation to the size of the economy — while the debt remained the same, the economy grew. In 1950, the national debt amounted to 92 percent of GDP; by 1980 this ratio had declined to 32.5 percent.[314]

Ronald Reagan replaced a long-standing bipartisan policy of fiscal conservatism with a radical new policy of "Fiscal Conservatism." He increased the national debt by more than 100 percent over the eight years of his presidency. On the day he left office, the debt stood at $2.87 trillion, which is the equivalent of $5.5 trillion in 2015 dollars. (He is often accused of actually tripling the debt, which is true in nominal terms, but not when the numbers have been adjusted to account for inflation.) As a proportion of GDP, the debt also rose under Reagan, from 32.5 percent to 51.5 percent.

Yes: for thirty years, the federal debt stayed more or less the same, and then, over a period of eight years, Ronald Reagan doubled it. Under his successor, George H.W. Bush, the debt continued to rise — when he left office in 1993, the debt stood at $4.35 trillion (equivalent to $7.14 trillion in 2015 dollars) and had increased to 64 percent of GDP. All in all, during twelve years of G.O.P. stewardship of the economy under Reagan and the first President Bush, the national debt had almost tripled in real terms, and doubled in relation to the size of the economy.

Democratic president Bill Clinton showed considerably more budgetary restraint, presiding over the smallest increase in the national debt since the presidency of another Democrat, Jimmy Carter. Mid-way through Clinton's second term, the debt actually started to shrink — the annual budget went into surplus for the first time since the presidency of Lyndon Johnson, another Democrat. When Clinton left office, the national debt had risen nominally by $1.42 trillion (from $4.35 trillion to $5.77 trillion) but in inflation-adjusted terms it had risen by only 8.25 percent. Moreover, the debt had declined by 8.4 percent relative to the economy, from 64 percent of GDP in 1993 to 54.6 percent in 2001. As to the deficit — there was no deficit anymore. Clinton presided over four straight balanced budgets and left his successor with an annual surplus that exceeded $100 billion.

The inheritor of this surplus, Republican George W. Bush, immediately canceled it by enacting tax cuts during his first year in office, and then again in his third year. The first fiscal year for which he was responsible, 2002, saw the return of deficits, which have been with us ever since. The Bush tax cuts led to a decline in revenues which are estimated to have sacrificed upwards of $5 trillion in revenue. The wars in Afghanistan and Iraq led to a drastic increase in expenditures. An expansion of Medicare led to another increase in expenditures. This was post-Reagan Fiscal Conservatism in action, and it led to Reagan-like levels of debt.

By the end of 2008, the national debt had ballooned by 70 percent in real terms (when adjusted for inflation) and by 27.8 percent relative to GDP. The debt to GDP ratio was now 82.4 percent — the highest level since 1950. Bush also saddled his successor, Barack Obama, with the largest annual budget deficit — more than $1.2 trillion — in the history of the United States. (The final deficit for fiscal year 2009 was $1.41 trillion, but about $200 billion of that was owing to parts of Obama's economic stimulus program that went into effect almost immediately.) That deficit amounted to about 10 percent of GDP, by far the highest since World War II.

Under Obama, the continued to rise, from $11.88 trillion in 2009 to $18.12 trillion in 2015. Adjusted for inflation, that represents an increase of 38 percent — considerable but not astronomical. The debt to GDP ratio has surpassed 100 percent for the first time since World War II (when it exceeded 120 percent). Deficits, however, have declined. By the end of his first term, Obama had cut the annual deficit in half; by the end of 2015 he had cut it by two thirds, and by three quarters in terms of GDP.

This is a mixed record — the national debt is certainly very high, but that's because it was already very high and rising rapidly before Obama even took office. Since inheriting a crashing economy, Obama has presided over a relatively moderate increase in the debt (by post-Reagan standards) while reducing the size of the annual deficit from 10 percent to 2.5 percent of GDP, which is lower than under any Republican president since Richard Nixon.

REASONS FOR THE DISCONNECT?

Republicans Talk a Big Game

They talk incessantly about balanced budgets and spending cuts without ever doing anything about it. And they have derided Democrats as "Tax and Spend Liberals" so consistently, for so long, and with so little coordinated pushback from Democrats, that the name has stuck, despite the fact that Democrats have a much better record of fiscal responsibility than Republicans. The last time federal expenditures actually decreased from one year to the next was in 1965, when Democrats controlled the White House and both houses of congress.

We're often told that actions speak louder than words, but the G.O.P. has proven that that's not always the case — all too often, the opposite is true. Democrats actually reduce the deficit and occasionally even balance budgets, while Republicans only talk about doing these things. But who gets the credit for being fiscally serious?

Tax-Cut Mania Does Not Equal Fiscal Responsibility

Republicans confuse anti-tax ideology with fiscal responsibility, as though the two things are one and the same. They are actually distinct and, in many respects, mutually exclusive.

By railing against taxes at every opportunity, Republicans create the impression that they are concerned with budgets — but this does not logically follow. All it means is that they're concerned with low taxes. But, if you cut taxes without cutting spending, you are not being fiscally responsible — you're actually being the opposite.

When you fund new programs — or wars — without raising taxes or cutting existing levels of spending, you unavoidably create deficits and increase the debt burden on future generations. That's exactly what Republicans have been doing consistently for the past thirty-five years.

197

Republicans are Hawkish About Cutting Things that Cost Virtually Nothing, While Ignoring Real Expenses

Republicans have consistently refused to be serious about cutting spending in any fiscally significant measures. They rail against foreign aid, arts funding, earmarks, "waste and fraud," creating the impression that they are spending hawks. The problem is that even if you cut 100 percent of these things, it would amount to little more than one or two percent of the annual federal budget and have no impact at all on the ever-increasing national debt.

Democrats don't just believe in government; they believe in paying for it. They seek reasonable and equitable tax policies to fund programs that benefit Americans, and which Americans largely support, without building up unsustainable levels of debt. Over 80 percent of the federal budget is non-discretionary: Defense (about 20 percent), Medicare and Medicaid (about 20 percent), and Social Security (about 20 percent), other mandatory spending (about 17 percent) and interest on the debt (about 5 percent).[315]

Republicans have demonstrated that they are dedicated above all to short-term political gain by proposing lower taxes without controlling spending in any meaningful way. They use accounting tricks and distracting, deceptive rhetoric ("Eliminate earmarks!" "Cut foreign aid!") to obscure their consistent record of fiscal delusion, hypocrisy and recklessness.

THE DEFICIT IS OUT OF CONTROL

The debt and the deficit is just getting out of control, and the administration is still pumping through billions upon trillions of new spending. That does not grow the economy.
— 2012 G.O.P. vice presidential candidate Paul Ryan

CONSERVATIVES CLAIM...

The federal deficit is out of control. President Obama's policies are responsible for the current high levels of deficit spending, which are hurting the recovery. The economy will recover more quickly if government spending is cut and the budget is balanced.

THE REALITY

The deficit refers to the difference between annual tax revenues and government spending, or "outlays." When the government raises less money in taxes than it spends in a given year, which is usually the case, there is a budget deficit. Deficits are normal, under both Republicans and Democrats — there have only been twelve years since the end of World War II when the government has produced a balanced budget or a surplus; all the other years have produced deficits. The national debt is the cumulative total of all annual deficits.

The deficit reached a post World War II peak of 9.8 percent of GDP during the height of the financial crisis, in fiscal year 2009 (which began October 1, 2008, before Barack Obama was elected president). But even then, it was not in any sense out of control, nor was it unprecedented. During World War II, the annual budget deficit exceeded 30 percent of GDP, more than three times higher than the highest level of the Great Recession.

After remaining high for a couple of years, the deficit has declined each year since 2011, as the economy has recovered.[316] In dollar terms, the deficit has fallen by almost a trillion dollars during the Obama presidency, from an all-time high of $1.4 trillion at the peak of the recession in 2009 to $438.4 billion in 2015. Moreover, the 2015 deficit amounted to 2.5 percent of GDP, which is around the post-World War II average, and lower than the average over the past forty years.

The expression "out of control" implies something not only volatile, but unpredictable. In fact, the deficit is entirely predictable, because government spending and tax revenues can both be estimated in advance with reasonable accuracy. Most government expenses are actually automatic — in other words, most expenditures are implemented according to law, and thus can't be changed except by an act of congress. In 2015, non-defense related discretionary spending accounted for less than 20 percent of the federal budget.

The deficit was very high for a few years because of the financial crisis. High levels of unemployment and underemployment meant that the federal government took in less tax revenue than it would have in a healthier economy. At the same time, more people were drawing on government-provided relief, such as unemployment benefits and food stamps. Lower revenues and higher outlays produce higher deficits.

A president — any president — does not have unilateral power to change this. It's really congress that would have to pass legislation to cut spending enough to lower the deficit. But that would almost certainly mean cutting services to those who were hardest hit by the economic crisis, which would have had an even more depressing effect on the economy, while it was straining to recover.

When the government puts money into the pockets of the

unemployed or the working poor, the money doesn't actually remain in their pockets. They tend to spend it right away on the necessities of life — food, clothing, rent, gasoline, electricity bills. In other words, that money flows quickly back into the economy, helping to sustain local businesses which would suffer if their customers, hard hit by the recession, were to stop spending money.

In addition to these automatic factors contributing to the deficit, the Obama administration took several steps to shore up the recovery by helping working Americans who were struggling. Unemployment benefits were extended several times, and payroll taxes — i.e., for Social Security and Medicare — were temporarily reduced because of the economic crisis.[317] This added to the deficit by lowering tax revenues and increasing spending.

The point is that the deficit, while certainly high, is not out of control in any literal sense. The size of the deficit is the direct and predictable result of decisions made by congress and the president during the early 2000s. President Obama inherited the largest budget deficit in history and opted not to cut spending during an economic crisis, based on the historically sound principle that austerity — i.e., severe spending cuts — during a recession will tend to inhibit recovery because it withdraws money from an already struggling economy.

REASONS FOR THE DISCONNECT?

Semantics

While it is fair to point out that the deficit is very large, it isn't at all accurate to say that it is out of control, or even that it is excessive simply because it is large. As we've seen, relative to the size of the economy as a whole (GDP) the 2015 deficit was actually average by post World War II standards, and low by post 1980 standards.

The expression "out of control" is often used to imply something unpredictable and dangerous, which is misleading. Many politicians and pundits use the specter of an out of control deficit to provoke a kind of budget hysteria, either for political gain — "vote for us because the other guys are destroying the country!" — or to keep people reading/watching — "stay tuned for on-going disaster coverage!" Either way, it confuses rather than clarifies the discussion about the national debt, which is a serious issue but not a catastrophic problem.

Context

The deficit is certainly high, but it isn't anywhere near its all-time high. During World War II it reached over 30 percent of GDP, more than triple the highest rate during the Great Recession, and more than ten times the current rate. Out of context, the trillion dollar deficits that occurred in 2009, 2010, and 2011 sound huge and scary, but they were never unmanageably high relative to the size of the overall economy. And then, as we've seen, within a few years the deficit had been cut by half in dollar terms and by three quarters relative to GDP.

One can make a legitimate case that the national debt is too high and that we should be striving to cut the deficit even further — there are fair points to be made on either side of the argument. But it is not legitimate to say that the deficit is out of control, or even excessive compared to previous years. In 1985, the half-way point in the Reagan presidency, the deficit stood at $212.3 billion, the equivalent of $467.7 billion in 2015 dollars, and amounted to 5 percent of GDP.[318] The budget deficit for 2015 was $438.4 billion, and amounted to only 2.5 percent of GDP.

SOCIAL SECURITY IS ON THE VERGE OF BANKRUPTCY

The Social Security trust fund...is already facing imminent bankruptcy.
— House Speaker John Boehner, December 1, 2011

CONSERVATIVES CLAIM...

The Social Security system is about to go broke. If it is not fixed in the near future, it will either have to stop paying benefits or cause an enormous drain on public finances, massively increasing the debt and deficit. Some sort of radical reform will be required in order to save Social Security.

THE REALITY

Social Security is not even close to going bankrupt. What's more, it is actually impossible for the system to go bankrupt because of the way that it's designed.

Contrary to what many people believe, Social Security is not a set of individual retirement accounts. It's more like a giant pool of money which is constantly being drained and replenished at the same time — drained in the form of benefits paid out to today's retirees and replenished in the form of annual payroll taxes paid into the system by today's workers. As long as there are tens of millions of Americans working and paying payroll taxes, the Social Security system will be funded. There are currently over 150 million workers contributing to the system every year.[319]

You pay into the system each year of your working life in exchange for the guarantee that when you retire you will receive annual benefits, based on your lifetime contribution into the system. The money you pay into the system each year is not set aside for you — it goes into the pool of money used to pay current beneficiaries. When the time comes for you to retire, your Social Security benefits will be provided by those who are still in the workforce.

So what's the problem?

Problems arise when payments into the system fall below the amount owed to current beneficiaries, resulting in an annual shortfall. This started occurring 2010, for the first time since 1983, and is projected to continue indefinitely unless the funding process is updated to ensure that revenues and benefits are brought into balance. This is what constitutes the so-called "crisis."

The worst case scenario — i.e., if the government takes no action at all — is that the system will continue to pay full benefits through approximately 2035, when the trust fund will have been depleted. After that, benefit payments will drop by roughly 23 percent. In other words, if Social Security funding is not adjusted, recipients from around 2035 onwards would receive about 77 percent of the benefits that they have coming to them. That's bad, and it would cause significant hardship to millions of Americans, but it's not a catastrophe. And it certainly isn't bankruptcy.

This isn't because the system is poorly designed or obsolete — it's because of the baby-boom population bulge, because more people are living longer after retirement, and because workers today are receiving an increasingly large portion of their compensation in forms other than wages — such as bonuses, healthcare coverage, and other benefits which are not subject to social security tax.

The government anticipated these problems back in the 1980's. In 1983 Ronald Reagan appointed a commission, headed by Alan Greenspan, to come up with a way to keep Social Security financially sound. The commission accomplished this by adjusting revenues in order to accumulate a surplus in the years leading up to the anticipated shortfall. [320]

The total accumulated surplus currently amounts to about $2.5 trillion and is projected to increase through 2023 to about $3.5 trillion. This surplus will serve to cover the annual revenue shortfalls up to sometime in the early or middle 2030's, ensuring full payment of promised benefits even if nothing is done to further reform the system in the meantime.[321]

As Alan Greenspan remarked in 2010: "Even if the trust fund level goes down, there's no action required, until the level of the trust fund gets to zero," he said. "At that point, you have to cut benefits, because benefits have to equal receipts."[322] Alternatively, full benefits can be preserved by making certain adjustments, such as means testing the program, raising the retirement age, increasing the payroll tax, and/or raising the cap on the portion of income subject to the payroll tax (which stood at 118,500 as of 2015).

The Social Security program's annual trustees report lays out the situation clearly: "Annual cost exceeded non-interest income in 2010 and is projected to continue to be larger throughout the remainder of the 75-year valuation period. Nevertheless, from 2010 through 2022, total trust fund income, including interest income, is more than is necessary to cover costs, so trust fund assets will continue to grow during that time period. Beginning in 2023, trust fund assets will diminish until they become exhausted in 2036. Non-interest income is projected to be sufficient to support expenditures at a level of 77 percent of scheduled benefits after trust fund exhaustion in 2036, and then to decline to 74 percent of scheduled benefits in 2085."[323]

So, even in the unlikely event that nothing is done in the next twenty years to address Social Security's long-term funding problem, three generations from now the system will still be providing retirees with annual benefits that amount to three quarters of today's guaranteed levels. That's not ideal, but it certainly isn't bankruptcy.

REASONS FOR THE DISCONNECT?

Right-Wing Propaganda

Right-wingers have a major problem when it comes to Social Security: They hate it, but most Americans love it. Social Security enjoys the support of a huge majority of Americans, who would never vote for candidates who declared their intention to dismantle or even modify the program. In other words, there is no straightforwardly democratic way for opponents of Social Security to get what they want, so they have to resort to non-democratic means — i.e., tricks.

One trick is to convince the public that there is a crisis that requires immediate action, otherwise the whole system will fail. In effect, they are trying to make people believe that if something isn't done right away to "fix" Social Security, then the whole thing may go down the tubes. Hence the talk of "bankruptcy" and "going broke" or the latest fetish of the far right: That Social Security is a Ponzi scheme, which suggests that it is both fragile and fraudulent, neither of which is true.

If right wing extremists succeed in convincing enough people that the system is in danger of going out of business, they may be able to gain support for legislation to dismantle it under the pretense of "saving" it.

Confusing Conservative Criticism

Social Security is required by law to invest its annual surplus in government bonds. This accumulated surplus — the trust fund — therefore actually constitutes a debt owed by the Federal Government to the Social Security program. In other words, Social Security surpluses have the paradoxical effect of actually adding to the national debt. The fact that one part of the government can be indebted to another part of the government is confusing to many people and is easily construed as some sort of accounting gimmick, which lends credibility to some of the exaggerated conservative complaints about the system's legitimacy and solvency.

People Don't Understand How the System Works

If this weren't the case, then the right-wing propaganda would be ineffective, since most Americans would understand that it is literally impossible for Social Security to go broke.

Given that the system is actually very simple to understand this shouldn't be a problem, and yet it is — probably because Social Security has been so popular and so successful for so long that there hasn't been a need for people to know much about the ins and outs of how the system functions. All people needed to know was that their money would be available to them when the time came to retire. That's how it has worked for generations - and that's how it will continue to work in the generations to come, so long as a few relatively minor and easy fixes are made to ensure that the system can handle the Baby Boom generation without having to reduce benefits.

The reality is that Social Security is one of the most successful and most popular government programs in the history of the United States. It has operated with a surplus for most of its existence and has never run a deficit. And all the while it has reliably provided retirement benefits to well over 100 million Americans and will continue to do so for generations to come.

EARMARKS ARE A MAJOR CONTRIBUTOR TO THE DEFICIT

Earmarks, as an issue, were created by John McCain...The reason John McCain created the earmark controversy is because he needed to say he was tough on spending. He wanted to run as a conservative, so he created an issue that had very little to do with the deficit.

— G.O.P. presidential candidate and former Senator Rick Santorum, January 12, 2012[324]

CONSERVATIVES CLAIM...

Earmarks are a form of wasteful, "pork barrel" spending that allow members of congress to funnel money to pet projects — they serve no legitimate purpose and are a huge drain on the public purse. Eliminating earmarks would be a big step towards balancing the federal budget.

THE REALITY

Earmarks are provisions attached to congressional legislation, which allocate specific quantities of money for particular programs or projects. Altogether, they typically amount to less than $20 billion per year. That may seem like an awful lot of money until you compare it to the annual federal budget of the United States, which was just under $3.7 trillion in 2015.[325]

Some earmarks are actually used for worthy purposes, such as building libraries or schools, while some are indeed used for "pork barrel" spending, which many consider to be wasteful or frivolous, such as the notorious "bridge to nowhere" in Alaska. But even if we threw out the good with the bad and did away with all earmarks, we'd be trimming a grand total of 0.5 percent (that's one half of one percent) off the federal budget. Trimming earmarks is not an effective way to control spending.

Consider, for example, the December 2010 Senate omnibus spending bill, which included (according to Senator John McCain, a relentless crusader against earmarks) 6,488 earmarks totaling $8 billion. This sounds outrageous. And it may well have been outrageous. But as a portion of the entire $1.25 trillion spending bill, these thousands of earmarks accounted for less than two thirds of one percent of the total — 0.64 percent, to be precise. Earmarks may be obnoxious, but when it comes to out-of-control government spending, they are not the problem.

The Democratic controlled 110th Congress instituted significant reforms to the process, including a ban on all earmarks to for-profit corporations and a requirement that all earmark requests be disclosed publicly. The White House now provides a data base of earmarks and their congressional sponsors.[326]

Those reforms seem to have worked. From 2009 to 2010, the total number of earmarks fell by 10 percent, from 10,160 to 9,129, while the total cost dropped by over 15 percent, from $19.6 billion to $16.5 billion[327].

In 2010, the Republican conference in the House of Representatives went even further by banning earmarks altogether.[328] This may make for excellent symbolism and attract support from conservative constituents, but it simply does not represent a serious attempt to address, let alone reduce, government spending.

Indeed, in the years since earmarks have been limited, the U.S. has continued to post the some of the largest deficits in its history.

REASONS FOR THE DISCONNECT?

Mistaking Molehills for Mountains

Yes, many (but not all) earmarks are silly and some of them are even scandalous, but they just don't amount to a hill of beans relative to the entire federal budget. Even if you were to eradicate earmarks altogether, the savings would account for less than 1 percent of the budget and have a minimal impact on the deficit.

The Principle of the Thing

Many earmarks do in fact constitute pork barrel spending and it's certainly true that the process has been abused over the years, costing taxpayers billions of dollars. As a matter of principle, the desire to reform the abuse of earmarks is justifiable and even admirable — but as a practical matter, it just won't help to control spending in any meaningful way.

Ideological Posturing

Many earmarks are easy to ridicule (e.g., fruit fly research or the notorious "bridge to nowhere" in Alaska) regardless of whether they are actually beneficial. And even though the sums involved are miniscule as a portion of the overall deficit, they sound enormous to most of us. Harping on outrageous sounding earmarks is an easy way for politicians to get credit for being fiscally hawkish, while avoiding taking stands on the politically unpopular tax increases or spending cuts — such as cuts to entitlements and the military — which would be required in order to actually reduce the deficit and the debt.

PART 6

LAW & ORDER

VOTER FRAUD IS A SERIOUS THREAT TO AMERICAN DEMOCRACY

The parties are not aware of any incidents of in-person voter fraud in Pennsylvania and do not have any direct personal knowledge of in-person voter fraud elsewhere.
— From a stipulation filed in the case of Viviette Applewhite v. Commonwealth of Pennsylvania, July 12, 2012[329]

CONSERVATIVE CLAIM...

Voter fraud is a pervasive phenomenon in America, which poses a serious threat to our democratic system. Voter ID laws are necessary to ensure the integrity of the electoral process and to protect the fundamental right of all citizens to have their votes freely and fairly counted.

THE REALITY

Voter fraud in the United States is only slightly less rare than unicorns.

To be precise, in the last 15 years no state in the Union has documented levels of fraud exceeding 0.004 percent of the vote in a statewide or federal election.[330] That's one vote in twenty-five thousand, or less than four one-thousandths of a percent. The many investigations into the matter of voter fraud are unanimous: it is always rare, usually accidental, and never decisive in determining the outcome of an election.

No American should need reminding that our national electoral process is a many-splendored confusion of variable procedures and inconsistent standards, which vary not only from state to state, but also from county to county, and sometimes even precinct to precinct. This system is barely a system at all — it is, rather, a predicament, an embarrassment, a fiasco, and a hot mess. There are plenty of reasons to lack confidence in the electoral process and to doubt the reported results of closely contested elections, but deliberate fraud at the ballot box is simply not one of them.

A five-year investigation by the Justice Department, during the George W. Bush presidency, resulted in a total of 120 charges and 86 convictions nationwide, although prosecutors acknowledged that many of the cases resulted from confusion about eligibility rather than deliberate fraud.[331] Indeed, it is common for cases of alleged voter fraud to result from errors (deliberate or otherwise) by clerks or poll workers — not voters — such as the time when voters in Ohio were directed to the wrong polling station by a poll worker who didn't understand the difference between even and odd numbers. (I'm not making this up.[332])

Academic studies yield entirely consistent results: Barnard College professor Lorraine Minnite determined that since 2002, the incidence of voter fraud at the federal level has averaged 8 cases per year nationwide.[333] The Brennan Center for Justice, which has looked exhaustively into the matter at both the state and federal levels, determines voter fraud to be "both irrational and extremely rare" over the same period. It is irrational because penalties are high for each individual case (up to five years in prison and $10,000 in fines[334]), and because you would need to get hundreds, if not thousands, of individuals to show up in person to cast illegal votes in order to sway an election decisively — a highly inefficient enterprise that would be pretty hard to keep secret.

"Because voter fraud is essentially irrational, it is not surprising that no credible evidence suggests a voter fraud epidemic. There is no documented wave or trend of individuals voting multiple times, voting as someone else, or voting despite knowing that they are ineligible. Indeed, evidence from the microscopically scrutinized 2004 gubernatorial election in Washington State actually reveals just the opposite: though voter fraud does happen, it happens approximately 0.0009 percent of the time. The similarly closely-analyzed 2004 election in Ohio revealed a voter fraud rate of 0.00004 percent."[335]

Even right-wing organizations dedicated to proving that voter fraud is a common menace to democracy have trouble turning up actual cases. Consider, for instance, the recent bundle of convictions in Minnesota for intentional voter fraud in the 2008 election. These cases were investigated and brought to the attention of the authorities by Minnesota Majority, a self-described "state legislative watchdog group" committed to uncovering voter fraud. In their report, they proudly proclaim: "we believe this is the highest number of voter fraud convictions obtained in any state for a single election cycle since 1936."[336] That sounds pretty impressive. So, how many subversives did they find? 113.

A total of 2,921,147 votes were cast in Minnesota on November 4th, 2008, of which 113 have been proved fraudulent. That's 0.0039 percent, or, if you prefer words, thirty nine out of every million votes.[337] What's more, all 113 perpetrators were felons who cast ballots although they were legally ineligible to vote. Fair enough — those felons did indeed technically commit voter fraud. But they certainly weren't participating in any kind of organized attempt to steal an election.

So Why Are Conservatives Obsessed with This Issue?

Conservatives' obsession with voter fraud makes very little sense if they are legitimately concerned with the integrity of the voting process and the reliability of electoral results. Indeed, it is as irrational as voter fraud itself. But it makes total sense if they are using the specter of fraud as a pretext for enacting legislation aimed at suppressing the participation of voters who are likely to vote Democratic.

Republican efforts to address the non-existent problem of voter fraud involve passing voter ID laws that address only one type of fraud: voter impersonation at the polls. In the already miniscule arena of criminal voter wrongdoing, this accounts for less than one out of every two hundred cases. The other one hundred and ninety nine cases involve tampering with absentee ballots, falsifying vote tallies, and a variety of other more effective ways of influencing election results — none of which is addressed by voter ID laws. These laws do, however, create obstacles to voting for millions of mainly minority and poor Americans who do not happen to have any of the requisite forms of government-issued ID and for whom obtaining one would be difficult. Even Republicans acknowledge this:

> "Among Republicans it is an 'article of religious faith that voter fraud is causing us to lose elections,' [Royal] Masset [former political director of the Republican Party of Texas] said. He doesn't agree with that, but does believe that requiring photo IDs could cause enough of a drop-off in legitimate Democratic voting to add 3 percent to the Republican vote."
> — Houston *Chronicle*, May 18, 2007[338]

There hasn't been a single Republican proposal to combat the types of voter fraud that can't be prevented with a photo ID, despite the fact that they occur 200 times more frequently than in-person voter fraud.[339]

REASONS FOR THE DISCONNECT?

They See Dead People

Voter rolls throughout the country continue to carry the names of people who are no longer eligible to vote. There is nothing sinister in this — people die, or move away; some may even go to jail. If the board of elections is not explicitly notified, then the name of a

no-longer-eligible voter will remain registered. However, for fraud to occur, someone must show up at the polls on election day, identify himself or herself as the individual listed in the voter registry, and then cast a fraudulent vote. This hardly ever happens.

The System Seems Vulnerable

There are actually few ironclad safeguards protecting us against voter fraud. But that doesn't mean that there are millions, thousands, or even dozens of Americans who are therefore committing it. The record consistently shows that a statistically insignificant number of people commit voter fraud, and that most of the handful of cases that do occur are mistakes. There aren't many safeguards against indecent exposure or assaulting random people on the street either, but, even so, these acts rarely occur (although not as rarely as voter fraud) because most people just aren't inclined to commit them, and because there are serious legal penalties in store for those who do.

They Can't Believe They're Losing

Many conservatives believe that America is a "center-right" nation (see Part 1, Chapter 1 "The U.S. Is a Center-Right Nation") and that their own views, values, and priorities are naturally those of the majority, or, as they often put it, "real Americans." But if that's the case, how could someone with a name like Barack Hussein Obama have won a majority of the popular vote, twice, unless he somehow stole the elections? A dystopian fantasy of massive voter fraud at the polls is easier for many right-wingers to accept than the simple truth that a majority of Americans are actually not very conservative, and so prefer not to vote for Republicans.

The G.O.P. Wants to Suppress Democratic Votes, Not to Mention Democracy Itself

As we've seen, most measures to combat the non-existent problem of

217

voter fraud have been enacted by Republicans, and consist of laws requiring voters to present a legally approved form of identification before they can vote. These laws disproportionately affect groups that traditionally vote Democratic, such as the elderly, the young, African Americans and Latinos, many of whom do not currently have any of the required forms of ID. What's more, voter ID laws only address one kind of fraud: voter impersonation, which accounts for less than 0.5 percent of all cases of voter fraud.[340] In other words, they have decided to devote all of their efforts at eradicating the rarest form of an extremely rare phenomenon.

At best, this is an ineffective solution to a non-existent problem - like erecting a fence to keep out dragons, which a) don't actually exist, and b) even if they did, could fly anyway. But, of course, this isn't just a well-meaning but pointless precaution that happens to disenfranchise eligible voters unintentionally. The disenfranchisement is the point, and the precaution just a pretext.

In 2000, 14 states had some form of voter ID laws. As of 2016, 34 states have them. All but five (Washington, Hawaii, Delaware, Connecticut, and Rhode Island) are states that had Republican governors and/or Republican majorities in their state legislatures at the time the laws were passed. Although Voter ID laws have been around in a few states since the 1950s, "strict" voter ID laws were not introduced until 2006 (the law is considered "strict" if it denies citizens the right to vote unless they present an approved form of ID). All eleven states with "strict" Voter ID laws are G.O.P. controlled states.[341]

If Republican legislatures were genuinely concerned with maintaining the integrity of the voting process, as they claim, they would focus on absentee ballot fraud and other types of fraud that, while still rare, are far more prevalent than voter impersonation. Instead, they have chosen an approach that addresses a non-existent problem in a manner that explicitly allows them to disenfranchise hundreds of thousands, possibly millions of eligible voters. And that — not voter fraud -- is the actual threat to democracy in America today.

DEMOCRATS WANT TO TAKE AWAY
PEOPLE'S GUNS

The Democratic National Committee is virtually 100 percent anti-firearms ownership, and the Republican National Committee stands on the side of the freedom.
—Wayne LaPierre, CEO and Executive Vice President of the National Rifle Association[342]

CONSERVATIVES CLAIM...

Democrats want to repeal the 2nd Amendment and ban guns in America.

THE REALITY

No, they don't.

It is certainly true that Democrats have consistently supported regulation of guns to ensure public safety — but so did the National Rifle Association until the 1970s. These regulations have included background checks and waiting periods for gun purchasers, registration and licensing for gun owners, and bans on certain types of weapons, such as semi-automatic assault rifles, which are designed specifically for the purpose of killing human beings. None of these regulations was designed to take guns away from law-abiding citizens, or to prevent them from using guns for hunting or recreation or defending their property.

Democrats tend to favor tougher limitations on who can purchase guns, what types of guns they can own, how and where they may carry and use them, and how they must be stored and maintained. But it is not at all true that Democrats favor anything approaching a ban. Indeed, if they wanted to prohibit the ownership of guns, why would they pay so much attention to regulating them?

If Democrats are motivated to eliminate guns from America's streets and homes, as conservatives claim, then they have been remarkably ineffectual. When they controlled both houses of congress and the White House from 2009-2011, the only gun-related legislation that passed the president's desk — and which he signed into law — were expansions of existing rights. In 2010, President Obama signed bills allowing people to carry loaded, concealed weapons on their persons in national parks, and in their checked baggage on Amtrak trains.[343]

That's right: gun owners enjoy more rights under Barack Obama than under George W. Bush, or any other recent president, for that matter.

Accordingly, in 2009 President Obama received an "F" grade from the Brady Campaign to Prevent Gun Violence, which is America's largest and most influential (which isn't saying much) gun-control advocacy organization.[344] The group's president, Dan Gross declared, "I can tell you we're very disappointed with his lack of leadership on this issue."[345]

The truth is that Democrats are not motivated by a desire to deprive law-abiding citizens of their right to own guns. They are motivated by the desire to make America a safer place, which they have succeeded in doing in those places where they've been able to enact reasonable gun-control laws. In recent years, owing largely to conservative rhetoric, Democrats at the federal level have done very little to promote gun-safety, as the example of President Obama and the Democratic congressional majorities of 2009-2011 demonstrates.

At the state and local levels, however, Democrats have been able to make a difference. The highest levels of gun violence in the U.S.

occur in those predominantly conservative states with the fewest restrictions on gun ownership. In predominantly liberal states where strong gun laws are in place, such as New York, New Jersey, and Massachusetts, the average number of gun-related deaths is 5 per 100,000 — less than half the national average of 10.2 per 100,000. In every red state, with the exception of Nebraska and the Dakotas, the rate of gun death is higher than the national average.[346] [347]

REASONS FOR THE DISCONNECT?

Confusing Regulation with Prohibition

Gun safety laws are not first steps towards banning all guns any more than seatbelt laws and speed limits were first steps towards banning automobiles.

Democrats have never expressed a desire to ban all guns, or take them away from law-abiding citizens, but they do favor regulation to ensure public safety. That would seem to be a reasonable position in a country whose levels of gun violence are dozens of times higher than those of any other developed nation on Earth. Nevertheless, conservatives have consistently confused regulation with prohibition. By stoking fears of prohibition, they make resistance to any and all regulation seem like a reasonable — indeed, virtuous — stand in defense of liberty.

The Exaggerated Influence of the National Rifle Association

The NRA is the country's largest, wealthiest, and most prominent gun advocacy organization. As such, they command a great deal of media attention and wield a great deal of influence in Washington. But their visibility and influence has more to do with the amount of noise they make and the amount of money they spend than with the proportion of Americans whose interests they actually represent.

The NRA has over four million members. In a country of more

221

than 300 million people, that amounts to only about 1.5 percent of the population. What's more, it amounts to only about 4.5 percent of gun owners, of whom there are about ninety million in the U.S. So it's hardly surprising that the NRA doesn't represent the views of most Americans, or even most American gun owners. It may, however, come as some surprise to learn that the NRA doesn't even represent the views of most of its own members.

For instance, the NRA vehemently opposes mandatory background checks for all gun purchasers, whereas 74 percent of NRA members support them, not to mention 87 percent of gun owners who are not NRA members, and 92 percent of all Americans.[348] [349]

The NRA spent almost $3 million on lobbying in 2012.[350] They stay in the news by making provocative statements in the aftermaths of tragic massacres that command national attention. They claim to represent the interests of 30 to 40 percent of the population — i.e., all gun owners — while actually representing the interests of a tiny minority. In a world in which influence is a matter of perception, all of this combines to make them seem bigger and more mainstream than they actually are.

The Paranoia Business

If the NRA doesn't represent the majority of its own members, let alone gun owners in general, who does it represent? Two distinct constituencies whose interests overlap: gun extremists and the gun manufacturing industry. Both constituencies are prepared to pay large amounts of money to the NRA, which has evolved into an enormous enterprise in its own right, with over $200 million in annual revenues, less than half of which come from membership dues.[351]

The industry wants to sell as many guns as possible so as to maintain profits in a market with fewer and fewer individual buyers. Extremists are a genuinely paranoid minority of Americans who, though few, are willing to accumulate large numbers of weapons, and to spend an inordinate amount of energy and money to support an organization that advocates for them. The NRA has a financial interest in stoking this paranoia in order to ensure that donations from these hysterical precincts continue to flow.

When Barack Obama was elected, gun purchases soared because of fears that he would pass legislation to ban firearms altogether, making the sale of guns illegal and confiscating them from gun-owners throughout the country. Although candidate Obama did support a renewal of the ban on assault weapons, which expired in 2004, he had at no time suggested banning guns in general. And even if he had wanted to do so, conservatives, who credit themselves with being on especially intimate terms with the Constitution of the United States of America, ought to have rested easily in the knowledge that no ban on firearms would get past the courts so long as the Second Amendment remained in place.

But that is beside the point. Gun sales have skyrocketed under Obama, because of the baseless fear that he and the Democrats want to "take away your guns." As gun sales soar, so does the apocalyptic rhetoric.

In case you think that "apocalyptic" is too strong a word, consider these quotes from a recent editorial by Wayne LaPierre, the NRA's main spokesperson:

> "Hurricanes. Tornadoes. Riots. Terrorists. Gangs. Lone criminals. These are perils we are sure to face—not just maybe. It's not paranoia to buy a gun. It's survival...We, the American people, clearly see the daunting forces we will undoubtedly face: terrorists, crime, drug gangs, the possibility of Euro-style debt riots, civil unrest or natural disaster. Gun owners are not buying firearms because they anticipate a confrontation with the government. Rather, we anticipate confrontations where the government isn't there—or simply doesn't show up in time."[352]

Describing the NRA's vision as "apocalyptic" may actually be an understatement.

By fanning the flames of paranoia, the NRA enhances its own

stature, not to mention its revenues, while helping to drive up gun sales. And that is ultimately the point, since rising gun sales benefit the NRA's principle constituency — gun manufacturers. When it comes to firearms in America, paranoia is very good for business.

GUN CONTROL LAWS ARE UNCONSTITUTIONAL BECAUSE THEY VIOLATE THE SECOND AMENDMENT

The National Rifle Association has been in support of workable, enforceable gun control legislation since its very inception in 1871.
— NRA Executive Vice President Franklin L. Orth, NRA's *American Rifleman* Magazine, March 1968

CONSERVATIVES CLAIM...

The Second Amendment to the Constitution provides all Americans with an unconditional right "to keep and bear arms." Any attempt to modify or restrict gun ownership is therefore unconstitutional.

THE REALITY

The right to keep and bear arms is not at all unconditional. The Constitution plainly asserts that gun ownership is subject to regulation by the U.S. House of Representatives — i.e., the Federal Government.

It is only since the 1970's that this has been a matter of controversy at all. Until that time, the nation's largest and most influential gun-rights organization, the National Rifle Association, consistently supported a variety of gun control laws, including registration, waiting periods, and outright bans on certain types of fire-arms.[353]

The framers of the Constitution predicated the right of citizens to keep and bear arms on the necessity of having a citizen army ready to defend the country in case of insurrection or foreign invasion. These militias were to be organized by the individual states, but very definitely under the authority of congress. A plain reading of the Second Amendment makes this abundantly clear, so let's take a look at the complete text of the Second Amendment:

> A well regulated militia being necessary to the security of a free state, the right of the people to keep and bear arms shall not be infringed.

Note the words "well regulated." It would be surprising if the founders had used the phrase "well regulated" in a sentence that was actually intended to prohibit regulation. But, of course, the second amendment does not prohibit regulation — it does the very opposite, by establishing the principle of federal regulation of state militias as the essential basis for granting citizens the right to keep and bear arms.

We should note that the word "state" in the text of the second amendment refers to the nation as a whole, rather than the individual states of the union. The words "state" and "country" are interchangeable, as James Madison actually demonstrated in an earlier draft of the Second Amendment: *"The right of the people to keep and bear arms shall not be infringed; a well armed and well regulated militia being the best security of a free country..."* [emphasis mine].

Most public discussions about gun rights begin and end with the Second Amendment, but to fully understand the original intent of the framers, one also has to read the main body of the Constitution, which unambiguously asserts that state militias are subordinate to the Federal Government. Specifically, Article 1, Section 8, Clause 16 states:

"The Congress shall have the power...

To provide for calling forth the Militia to execute the Laws of
the Union, suppress Insurrections and repel Invasions;
To provide for organizing, arming, and disciplining, the
Militia, and for governing such part of them as may be
employed in the Service of the United States, reserving to the
States respectively, the Appointment of the Officers, and the
Authority of training the militia according to the discipline
prescribed by Congress..."[354]

Note the words, "well regulated," "organizing," "disciplining,"
"governing," "in the Service of the United States," and "according to
the discipline prescribed by Congress." These words and phrases
don't exactly suggest a paramount concern with limiting the
regulatory powers of the Federal Government.

And indeed, at the time the Constitution was being written and
debated, Anti-Federalists, who opposed the Constitution, fretted over
exactly this point. They objected to a constitution that would grant
the federal government too much power over the individual states.
Their objections against federal control of state militias demonstrate
the fact that the militias were never intended by the founders to be
state-controlled, but were, on the contrary, intended to be subject to
the Federal Government.

Consider, for example, Anti-Federalist Patrick Henry's objections:

"Let me here call your attention to that part which gives the
Congress power 'to provide for organizing, arming, and
disciplining the militia, and for governing such part of them as
may be employed in the service of the United States—reserving
to the states, respectively, the appointment of the officers, and
the authority of training the militia according to the discipline
prescribed by Congress.' By this, sir, you see that their control
over our last and best defence is unlimited. If they neglect or
refuse to discipline or arm our militia, they will be useless: the
states can do neither—this power being exclusively given to
Congress. The power of appointing officers over men not

disciplined or armed is ridiculous; so that this pretended little remains of power left to the states may, at the pleasure of Congress, be rendered nugatory."[355]

Henry's words make absolutely no sense unless we recognize, as he did, that the framers of the constitution intended gun ownership to be tightly regulated by the Federal Government. Patrick Henry may well have agreed with today's gun rights advocates, but he was speaking against the Constitution and not in favor of it. In other words, today's radical pro-gun position is so far from being constitutional that it perfectly aligns with the views of those who vehemently opposed the Constitution and the Bill of Rights itself.

There is no discussion anywhere in the Constitution of a right to keep and bear arms except in the context of well-regulated militias. Therefore, regardless of any and all disputes about the extent to which state militias are subject to regulation by the Federal Government, there is simply and clearly no basis in the Constitution from which to infer an unconditional right of individual citizens to possess any weapons for any purpose.

REASONS FOR THE DISCONNECT?

Simplistic Thinking

Regulation is a question of degree. Nobody is trying to outlaw guns or take them away from law-abiding citizens. But in a political environment in which every issue is reduced to a "pro" and a "con" position, proponents of gun rights often see no distinction between regulation and prohibition — they imagine that any restrictions on gun ownership are somehow tantamount to banning them altogether, which isn't the case.

Relentless Lobbying

The NRA is one of the most powerful lobbies in Washington and has spent tens of millions of dollars to influence lawmaking at both the state and federal levels. The organization claimed credit for unseating nineteen members of congress in the pivotal 1994 mid-term election, including the Democratic Speaker of the House, Tom Foley. They could thus claim to have played a major part in delivering to Republicans their first House majority in thirty-eight years. Having established their influence at the ballot box, they gained all the more influence in the halls of Congress, which has only increased over the succeeding years.

Paranoia

There has always been a paranoid fringe of the American right that is hostile to government and constantly fearful that their rights are about to be taken away from them. In the late 50s, this fringe was best represented by the extremist John Birch Society, which considered it reasonable to accuse the Republican president, Dwight Eisenhower (of all people), of being a Communist agent. The Civil Rights movement and the social upheavals of the 1960s only increased their paranoia and swelled their numbers.

The rise of the gun-rights movement occurred in the aftermath of these social upheavals. Many conservatives were hostile to and fearful of a changing society in which they sensed their own views and values becoming marginalized by a new Liberalism. Increasing numbers of these conservatives identified with the extreme right wing's growing hostility to and suspicion of the government that had passed Civil Rights legislation and the sweeping Gun Control Act of 1968.

The mid-1970s saw the emergence of new hardline anti-gun-control organizations. In 1974 the Second Amendment Foundation and in 1975 the GOA — Gun Owners of America — were founded by hardliners who felt that even the NRA was too weak in its defense of gun owners' rights. This drove the NRA to take increasingly hardline positions in order to maintain its credibility with conservatives and its dominance as America's major gun advocacy organization.

Politics

Conservative advocacy groups and politicos understand that scaring people or making them feel that their rights are at risk is a great way to get them to support you with money and/or votes — that is, if you present yourself as their defender. By establishing, for the first time in American history, the idea that unrestricted gun ownership is a civil right, conservatives were able to portray any and all gun control measures as attempts to deprive American citizens of their constitutional rights, attempts to "take away your freedoms." The votes and the money have been rolling in ever since.

UNDOCUMENTED IMMIGRANTS
INCREASE CRIME RATES

They're bringing drugs. They're bringing crime. They're rapists. And some, I suppose, are good people.
— Donald Trump, announcing his candidacy for the presidency, June 16, 2015

CONSERVATIVES CLAIM...

Having entered the country illegally, undocumented immigrants are predisposed to engage in criminal behavior, making Americans less safe.

THE REALITY

There is no evidence to suggest that illegal immigration increases crime — in fact, all of the evidence points to the contrary. Crime rates among undocumented immigrants are actually lower than among the population as a whole. This is true across the board. Drugs, theft, assault, rape, murder — in each of these areas, crime rates are actually lower among undocumented residents nationwide.[356]

Tim Wadsworth, a professor of sociology at the University of Colorado, who studied the impact of immigration on crime rates in cities with populations greater than 50,000, determined that "the cities that experience the greatest growth in immigration were the same ones that were experiencing the greatest declines in violent crime."[357] Far from being unusual, these findings are entirely consistent with statistics gathered by the FBI and the U.S. prison system.

According to the FBI, states on the Mexican border, which have the highest levels of illegal immigration, actually have comparatively low rates of violent crime — in fact, the four big cities (i.e., with populations over 500,000) with the lowest crime rates in the entire nation are all in border states: San Diego, Phoenix, El Paso and Austin.[358] One of those cities — El Paso — is literally on the border.

These findings are corroborated by the Bureau of Justice Statistics, which shows that levels of violent crime through 2008 were lower for all five states with the highest number of undocumented immigrants per capita. Arizona had its lowest per capita violent crime rate since 1971 (447 per 100,000); California its lowest rate since 1970 (503 per 100,000); Illinois its lowest rate since 1973 (525 per 100,000); and Texas its lowest rate since 1984 (507 per 100,000).[359]

Another way of determining the relative crime rate among undocumented immigrants is to look at prison statistics, which reveal that the incarceration rate for native-born U.S. citizens is five times higher than that of immigrants, illegal and legal combined.[360]

Throughout the state and federal prison systems, non-citizens accounted for 94,498 out of a total population 1,613,656 (i.e., just over 4 percent) in 2009. Illegal immigrants represent a fraction of this "non-citizen" population, which also includes legal immigrants and foreign visitors to the U.S.[361] The exact number is unclear, but whatever it is, it must be considerably less than 4 percent. By comparison, roughly 7 percent of the total United States population are non-citizens.[362] In other words, immigrants are underrepresented in the prison population.

The truth is that the great majority of undocumented immigrants are here for work. They want to stay in the U.S. for as long as possible. They are not interested in making trouble and don't want to draw attention to themselves because they don't want to be deported.

Many immigrants, illegal and otherwise, come from regions (such as Europe, East Asia and North Africa) with lower rates of violent crime than the U.S., which has among the highest in the developed world and higher than many in the developing world.[363]

Undocumented immigrants most likely contribute to lower crime rates in the U.S., even — perhaps especially — in those places where they are perceived to increase crime.

REASONS FOR THE DISCONNECT?

The Fallacy that One Crime Necessarily Leads to Another

Many assume that people who have committed one crime (in this case, illegally entering or remaining in the U.S.) are predisposed to commit more. But this just isn't the case. Does the fact that you cheat on your taxes mean that you're more likely to commit burglary? Does the fact that you disregard traffic laws mean that you're more likely to commit assault and battery? Of course not. In fact, as immigration rates rose throughout the 1990s (they have been declining since the early 2000s), crime rates simultaneously fell — in other words, peak levels of illegal immigration to the U.S. coincided with record low levels of crime.[364]

Xenophobia

The majority of undocumented immigrants to the U.S. are Mexicans and Latinos from other countries. There is a widespread — and incorrect — belief among Americans that Latinos are more disposed to crime than the general population. In fact, crime rates among Latinos are lower in all categories than among the population as a whole, and are equivalent to or lower than White crime rates in most categories.[365]

Association of immigrants with the Drug Trade

Conservatives frequently associate immigrants with the illegal drug trade. This is a popular tactic because people associated with the drug business are by definition criminals, and are much more likely to engage in violent crime. However, a comparatively tiny proportion of undocumented immigrants are engaged in the drug trade. In a few isolated areas where there is a regular flow of drug traffic, crime associated with the drug trade is a serious problem. The national media primarily focus on these areas, and by highlighting the involvement of any immigrants, create the illusion that the problem is more widespread among all immigrants than it actually is.

THE DEATH PENALTY DETERS VIOLENT CRIME

I don't think you should support the death penalty to seek revenge. I don't think that's right. I think the reason to support the death penalty is because it saves other people's lives.
— George W. Bush

The death penalty actually hinders the fight against crime.
— Robert M. Morgenthau, Manhattan District Attorney

CONSERVATIVES CLAIM...

The death penalty protects the lives of the innocent by providing a deterrent to violent criminals who would otherwise act on their murderous impulses. If the possibility of execution were removed, violent crime rates would rise and more innocent people would die.

THE REALITY

There are no data that clearly support the deterrent effect of the death penalty — in fact, the weight of historical evidence and expert opinion decisively contradicts the proposition that executions deter violent crime.

Although the number of Americans who believe that the death penalty serves as a deterrent has declined over the years, the deterrence argument continues to be promoted by death penalty advocates in order to create a general impression that it is a matter of serious debate among crime and law enforcement experts, which it is not.

Death penalty states have consistently higher murder rates than states without the death penalty. In 2010 the ten states with the highest murder rates all had the death penalty. Of the top twenty, all except one — Michigan (11th highest) — had the death penalty.[366]

And that's not just a recent trend, nor is it a slight difference — in the years since 1995, death-penalty states have experienced an average of 38 percent higher rates of homicide than states that lack this so-called "deterrent." In 2007, for example, the homicide rate was 42 percent higher in death penalty states than in non-death-penalty states. Even in 2010, when the national murder rate hit a twenty year low, it was still 25 percent higher in death penalty states.[367]

In 2008, all fourteen states without the death penalty had murder rates below the national average.[368] Think about that for a moment. The overall homicide rate nationwide is actually higher than the rate in states where the threat of execution does not exist. For this to be true, the incidence of murder has to be higher in the states that do threaten to put murderers to death. If every state in the union adopted the death penalty, the national murder rate would be more likely to rise than to fall.

That last point is not just an ironic observation — about 20 percent of professional criminologists believe that the death penalty not only fails to deter murder, but actually encourages it.[369] This theory is known as the "brutalization effect." When the state puts an individual to death, it legitimizes the act of killing as a form of vengeance and promotes the idea that killing is acceptable — even moral — under certain conditions. It also undermines the idea that every human life is sacred, while promoting the idea that some lives are less valuable than others, and that some people actually deserve to die. All of this may serve to desensitize the public to the feeling that killing is unacceptable and immoral under any and all circumstances.

While there is no definitive study to support the existence of a brutalization effect, there are plenty of studies that demonstrate a definite correlation between the death penalty and high rates of murder. The FBI, for example, has found that police officers are safest in states with no death penalty and least safe in death penalty states:

"According to statistics from the latest FBI Uniform Crime Report, regions of the country that use the death penalty the least are the safest for police officers. Police are most in danger in the South, which accounts for 80 percent of all executions (90 percent in 2000). From 1989-1998, 292 law enforcement officers were feloniously killed in the South, 125 in the West, 121 in the Midwest, and 80 in the Northeast, the region with the fewest executions - less than 1 percent. The three leading states where law enforcement officers were feloniously killed in 1998 were California, the state with the highest death row population; Texas, the state with the most executions since 1976; and Florida, the state that is third highest in executions and in death row population."[370]

Law enforcement professionals themselves express very little faith in the death penalty as a deterrent. In a 2008 national survey, police chiefs ranked the death penalty dead last when asked what factors were "most important for reducing violent crime." They also considered it the least efficient use of taxpayer money for that purpose.[371]

REASONS FOR THE DISCONNECT?

The Truth is Counterintuitive

At first, common sense seems to dictate that the harsher the penalty, the more powerful the deterrent — but in this case, common sense is

237

at odds with reality. The fact is that most violent crimes are not planned in advance. According to the FBI, about two-thirds of all murders happen spontaneously, either during the course of a lesser crime, or because of an argument that escalates into violence. [372] Most murders are not committed by reasonable actors who take the time to consider the potential consequences of their actions.

Criminals Don't Plan on Getting Caught

People who commit pre-meditated crimes usually expect to get away with it. They don't intend to be caught and punished. Since they expect to escape justice altogether, they're not likely to be deterred by a method of punishment which they believe they'll never have to face.

Revenge is Sweet, but Not Entirely Respectable

Serious and reputable scientific studies have demonstrated that the desire to see people punished for bad behavior is actually a deep, primal urge within the human brain.[373] Many people derive emotional satisfaction from seeing wrongdoers suffer "the ultimate penalty." To them, it just seems right that the punishment should fit the crime. Nevertheless, the death penalty is rarely defended — at least in public — on the basis of pure retribution. Why is this?

Perhaps because people feel that there is something problematic about craving emotional satisfaction from the extinction of another human life, even a guilty one. The argument that the death penalty serves as a deterrent sounds respectable and reasonable, even though it is neither — and it does make for a powerful deterrent against any feelings of guilt associated with deriving satisfaction from seeing a fellow human being put to death.

PART 7

THE WORLD

TERRORISM POSES THE GREATEST THREAT TO AMERICAN LIVES

At what point then is the approach of danger to be expected? I answer, if it ever reach us, it must spring up amongst us. It cannot come from abroad. If destruction be our lot, we must ourselves be its author and finisher. As a nation of freemen, we must live through all time, or die by suicide.
— Abraham Lincoln, January 27, 1838

The only thing we have to fear is fear itself— nameless, unreasoning, unjustified terror which paralyzes needed efforts to convert retreat into advance.
— President Franklin D. Roosevelt, 4 March 1932

We cannot wait for the final proof — the smoking gun that could come in the form of a mushroom cloud.
— President George W. Bush, 7 October 2002

CONSERVATIVES CLAIM...

Terrorism is a major and constant threat to the lives of all Americans. Terrorists could strike at any moment and there is a real possibility that they'll get their hands on a nuclear device and detonate it in a highly populated area in the U.S. We must, therefore, allocate hundreds of billions of dollars to defend Americans from this threat.

THE REALITY

If you are a U.S. citizen, you have a much greater chance of being elected to Congress than of being involved in a terrorist incident. Congratulations.

There is, of course, no perfect way to quantify the likelihood of future terrorist incidents occurring on U.S. soil. The most accurate approach is to extrapolate from historical data, which demonstrate that with the exception of a series of coordinated events on a single horrible day — September 11th, 2001 — terrorism is an exceedingly rare occurrence in the United States.

According to the Global Terrorism Database, there were a total of fifty-three terrorist-caused deaths on U.S. soil between 9/11 and the end of 2014 (the last year for which they have comprehensive data).[374] The New America Foundation puts the total number of post 9/11 deaths resulting specifically from terrorist attacks by Jihadist Muslims at forty-five, less than the forty-eight deaths from extreme right-wing attacks during the same period — from just after 9/11 through the end of 2015.[375] Depending on which data set you use, that works out to an average of between three and four terrorism-related deaths per year.

If you are an American civilian abroad, chances of being killed by terrorism are higher, but only slightly. According to the National Counterterrorism Center, for example, the total number of fatal terrorist attacks in 2011 involving U.S. private citizens abroad was seventeen. Fifteen of these occurred in a single country, Afghanistan. "Overall, U.S. private citizen deaths constituted only 0.13 percent of the total number of deaths worldwide (12,533) caused by terrorism in 2011."[376] The more comprehensive and up-to-date Global Terrorism Database records a total of 105 Americans killed in terrorism-related deaths outside the U.S. between 9/11 and the end of 2014.

Returning to American soil, if we exclude the unique catastrophe of 9/11, there is an average of three to four terrorism-related deaths per year. In a population of almost 320 million, that makes your chances of being killed by terrorism less than one in eighty million, in any one year. Given an average life expectancy of 79 years, your lifetime odds of dying in a terrorist incident are less than one in a million.

To put that into perspective, your lifetime odds of being struck by lightning are 1 in 84,000 — about twelve times more likely than being killed by terrorism. Your odds of dying in a motor vehicle accident? 1 in 88 — about 11,500 times more likely. Dying of a gunshot wound? 1 in 306 — 3,200 times more likely. Drowning in the bathtub? 1 in 10,500 — 95 times more likely. [377]

At least twenty people a year die from being crushed by televisions, other appliances or furniture — more than five times as many as die from terrorism.[378]

Putting Money Where Our Fear Is

Another way to put this into perspective is to look at the amount of money we spend on terrorism prevention - about $1 trillion dollars in the years since 9/11. This enormous figure includes only expenditures on homeland security; it does not include the cost of the wars in Iraq and Afghanistan. [379]

Using anti-terrorism spending as a benchmark, if we allocated resources to preventing threats in direct proportion to their actual likelihood of occurring, every ten years we'd spend $14.5 quadrillion on preventing car accidents. That's about 750 times the annual Gross Domestic Product of the United States. We'd spend $3.5 quadrillion (about 185 times GDP) on preventing cancer; $122 trillion (about 6.5 times GDP) on preventing bathtub drownings; and $4 trillion (20 percent of GDP) on preventing venomous bee, wasp, and hornet stings.

In other words, if we reacted to every potential danger in proportion to the actual level of threat it poses, using our fear of terrorism as the standard, our society would come to a fearful halt. We would all live in mortal dread of lightning strikes and snakebites. No one would ever get on a plane, or get in the car, or leave the house, or even take a bath.

As to the threat of a nuclear terrorist attack — as terrifying and destructive as such an incident would be, it is far less likely to occur than a conventional incident. Even sovereign nations with billions of dollars at their disposal have great difficulty developing a nuclear device. And although there is a handful of so-called "loose nukes" unaccounted for in the former Soviet Republics, the challenge of transporting such a device half-way around the world and successfully detonating it is so great as to make it much more unlikely than an already unlikely conventional attack.

None of this is to say that terrorism is a trivial matter or that we shouldn't be vigilant about preventing it. But there are many hazards that are far more prevalent, and much more destructive to American lives, which we manage to accept as simply the regrettable but normal hazards of living human lives in an occasionally dangerous world.

REASONS FOR THE DISCONNECT?

Terrorists Want to Scare You

That, after all, is the point of terrorism. A single incident is devastating for the dozens or hundreds or, in the unique case of 9/11, thousands of people involved, but for the vast majority of people it is a remote event that has no direct effect on their lives. But when transmitted via the news media into millions of households and car radios, it can be amplified into a national catastrophe. The real way to "let the terrorists win" is to be scared of terrorism.

The Media Wants to Scare you

That's one of the most effective ways to get ratings. News programs are full of natural disasters, home invasions, abductions, fires, and floods — not to mention a whole range of epidemics (from ebola to bird flu) that seem always to be just around the corner, but never actually arrive. Scary stories grab your attention in a way that nothing else does, and terrorism is about as scary as it gets.

Politicians Want to Scare You

That's how many of them manage to "scare up" votes. By exaggerating the threat of terrorism and by taking a strong "anti-terror" position, they can appeal to voters by presenting themselves as vigilant guardians of national security — and who doesn't support that?

People Like Being Scared

Young people pay good money to see horror movies on the big screen. Older people stay at home and get their horror from the TV news. Either way, the effects are the same — people are actually attracted to experiences that stir up their fears and anxieties. At least horror movies don't pretend to be reality. The exaggerated peril and sensationalism of TV news pretends to be the truth. And people believe it. That's what's really scary.

IRAN POSES AN EXISTENTIAL THREAT TO THE U.S.

We are of the opinion that Iran is a rational actor...We also know, or we believe we know that Iran has not decided to make a nuclear weapon.
— Chairman of the Joint Chiefs of Staff, General Martin Dempsey, February 19, 2012 [380]

CONSERVATIVES CLAIM...

Iran is an unpredictable, malevolent rogue state that poses a grave and immediate danger to U.S. national security. They are on the verge of acquiring nuclear weapons, which they intend use against Israel and possibly the U.S. as well. They must be stopped by whatever means necessary, even if that requires bombing or even invading Iran.

THE REALITY

Iran has very little capacity to inflict physical harm on the United States, whose military force is at least thirty times the size of Iran's and probably much bigger than that. The Iranian army does not have the ability to invade the United States, nor can the Iranian navy besiege, blockade, or effectively attack the U.S. Even if it had nuclear weapons, which it doesn't, Iran could not seriously threaten the U.S.

since it lacks missiles with sufficient range to reach North America.[381]

Iran has not been associated with a terrorist attack on U.S. soil. What's more, the Iranian regime understands that any attack that could be traced back to them would likely provoke a massive U.S. military retaliation. While the wars in the neighboring states of Iraq and Afghanistan have turned out to be long, messy, and tragic affairs for the United States, the initial phases of each war — i.e., the invasion and removal of Saddam Hussein's government in Iraq, and Mullah Omar's Taliban in Afghanistan — were accomplished easily and within a matter of weeks. The leaders of Iran are well aware of what the U.S. military can do to effect regime change.

Iran has long claimed that they have no plans to develop nuclear weapons. This claim was affirmed as recently as 2012 by no lesser an authority than the Chairman of the Joint Chiefs of Staff. Nevertheless, many experts have suspected Iran of harboring long-term ambitions to develop a nuclear

The Iranians do not currently have the ability to produce a nuclear weapon and have agreed not to pursue one. In July 2015, Iran reached a deal, known as the Joint Comprehensive Plan of Action, with the United States, along with France, Germany, the U.K., Russia, and China. The agreement requires Iran to give up 98 percent of their Uranium stockpiles (which they claimed they had never intended to use for other than peaceful purposes) and not to enrich their remaining uranium to a level above 3.67 percent, which is well below weapons-grade (90 percent). The agreement is in effect for fifteen years, and includes strict regime of inspections as well as constant surveillance of Iranian nuclear facilities. The U.S. may at any time unilaterally declare Iran to be in breach of the terms of the agreement, in which case a range of U.N. sanctions will "snap back" into place immediately.[382]

Even if Iran were to somehow manage to pursue a nuclear weapon in secret, it would still take them at least another year to actually build a single device. The United States currently has over 2,000 active nuclear warheads and Israel is estimated to have between 100 and 200.[383] While it is certainly true that the Iranian regime is odious

247

in many ways, they are not suicidal.

This last point is critical when discussing Iran. Current and former heads of military and intelligence services in both the U.S. and Israel have asserted that Iran's leadership are "rational actors" who are not about to launch an attack that would provoke a catastrophic military response from either Israel or the United States.

Conservative alarm over Iran's potential to develop a nuclear weapon is based on the assumption that the leaders of the Iranian regime, most notably Grand Ayatollah Khamenei, are basically crazy — that they are willing to court certain doom in order to inflict a single grievous blow on Israel or the "the Great Satan," the United States. But at least two ex-Mossad chiefs,[384] [385] a former defense minister of Israel,[386] and the last Chairman of the Joint Chiefs of Staff,[387] have all asserted that, contrary to what right-wing hawks believe, the leaders of Iran are rational strategists who may engage in brinkmanship but do not pose an existential threat.

Israel Defense Minister, Ehud Barak, declared in February 2010, "I don't think the Iranians, even if they got the bomb, (would) drop it in the neighborhood...They fully understand what might follow. They are radical but not totally crazy. They have a quite sophisticated decision-making process, and they understand reality." [388]

In the Spring of 2015, General Stanley McChrystal — former commander of the Joint Special Operations Command and one of the principle architects of America's counter-insurgency strategy in the Middle East — stated that Iran was "obviously a rational actor and they're a democracy."[389]

It's certainly true that Iran is a dangerous country that has the power to make serious mischief in its own neighborhood. But Iran would simply not be capable of seriously threatening U.S. national security, even if it wanted to.

The View From Tehran

One doesn't have to sympathize with Iran's odious regime to recognize that it is reasonable for them to conclude that they are surrounded by hostile forces bent on removing them from power. Within the last decade, the U.S. has invaded and occupied Iran's eastern and western neighbors, Afghanistan and Iraq, toppling their governments and replacing them with regimes more friendly toward America. The top five recipients of U.S. foreign aid are immediate neighbors of Iran, and three of them - Iraq, Afghanistan and Pakistan - dominate Iran's borders to the west and east.

Iran's fear of U.S. action to change its leadership is not unjustified, even leaving aside the calls for regime change that emanate from the halls of Congress on a more or less weekly basis. In 1953, the CIA developed and implemented a plan (codenamed "Operation Ajax") to remove Mohammed Mossadegh Iran's democratically elected prime minister, from power and replace him with a successor more amenable to U.S. and British interests — the Shah. This coup overturned a democratically elected constitutional government and replaced it with an authoritarian monarch who ruled the country for a quarter-century until he himself was ousted in a coup in 1979.

In 1988, a U.S. naval vessel shot down an Iranian passenger airliner, killing all 290 civilians on board. The incident occurred during peace-time, in Iranian airspace and over Iranian territorial waters. The U.S. admitted responsibility, expressed regret (but did not formally apologize), and paid more than $60 million to compensate the families of the victims. Although it was most likely a genuine tragic error, it was also literally an attack by U.S. military forces on Iranian citizens in Iranian territory.

The U.S. has little reason to fear Iran. Iran, on the other hand, has plenty of reasons to fear the U.S.

REASONS FOR THE DISCONNECT?

Credulity

Iran's president from 2005 to 2013, Mahmoud Ahmedinejad, made numerous vile and provocative remarks about Jews and the state of

Israel. He denied Israel's right to exist and made numerous other statements that were interpreted as direct threats against Israel. Although these remarks were genuinely offensive and alarming, they were only remarks. Ahmedinejad never took any action consistent with his rhetoric.

Iran has a relatively weak presidency — the president is subordinate to the Supreme Leader, i.e., the Grand Ayatollah; he does not control foreign policy; he is not the Commander in Chief of the military; he must have his cabinet appointments approved by parliament. While Ahmedinejad did have the ability to make incendiary remarks on the international stage, he lacked the power to put them into effect or to make war unilaterally.

It's paradoxical that right-wingers entirely mistrust the leaders of Iran, but are prepared to take them at their word when it comes to threats, many of which are designed for domestic consumption.

Opportunism

By inflating the Iranian threat, conservative hawks create an opportunity to demonstrate how "tough" and serious they are about defending the U.S. They also establish a pretext for beefing up the military-industrial complex, justifying potential spending levels above what the Pentagon has said it wants or needs.

Confusion

For many conservatives, the whole region from North Africa to South Asia via the Middle East is an area of undifferentiated menace. They have a tendency to conflate all the antagonists of that region into a monolithic threat to the U.S. Many fail — or refuse — to recognize the distinctions between the various actors throughout the region and simply don't understand that the government of Iran has an agenda distinct from those of Al Qaeda and/or ISIS and/or the Taliban, which are ideological movements that don't have to concern themselves with the day to day management of a sophisticated nation state.

Islamophobia

Conservatives promote the image of turbaned Islamists as cartoon villains motivated purely by the desire to destroy the U.S. and its allies, regardless of the consequences to themselves. As a result, many Americans actually believe that the Iranian regime is so unhinged and malevolent that it would spend billions of dollars to develop a nuclear weapon in order to attack Israel or the United States without provocation, even though that would mean suicide for the themselves and their country.

CHINA OWNS MOST OF AMERICA'S DEBT

The threat of borrowing from China is greater than the threat of an armed conflict with China.
— Senator Tom Coburn (R — Oklahoma), July 18, 2011[390]

CONSERVATIVES CLAIM...

We are up to our ears in debt to China. The U.S. government has borrowed an excessive amount of money from the Chinese, which gives them a dangerous amount of influence over America's affairs and our economic destiny.

THE REALITY

As of February 2016, China owns just over $1.25 trillion worth of U.S. Treasury securities, which amounts to 6.5 percent of the national debt, which then stood at $19.126 trillion. Please note the decimal point between the 6 and the 5 — it's very important. The total portion of U.S. debt that China owns currently amounts to 6.5 percent. Not sixty-five. Six point five. Big difference.[391]

The fact is that most of the U.S. national debt — about 70 percent - is held by Americans. That includes individuals and entities such as banks, pension funds, and the U.S. government itself (i.e., the people of the United States).[392] The remaining 30 percent of the debt is owned by foreign individuals, financial institutions, and governments. About 20 percent of this foreign-owned debt is owned by the Chinese government. So, even thought China accounts for the largest single share of the foreign-owned portion of America's debt, it still amounts to a fraction of a fraction.[393]

China's share of U.S. debt fluctuates on a monthly basis. Over the course of the year from February 2015 to February 2016, it ranged between $1.223 trillion and $1.270 trillion. By comparison, Japan's holdings during the same period ranged between $1.224 trillion and $1.122 billion. Japan actually held more U.S. debt in February of 2015 than did China. Nobody expressed relief (or even noticed) when our ally Japan surpassed China to become the largest foreign holder of U.S. debt.

If China's goal was to undermine the U.S. economy by accumulating massive amounts of debt, it's unlikely that they would allow the source of their influence to diminish from time to time, especially when they have plenty of cash on hand and could easily increase their purchases of U.S. treasury securities if they wanted to.

The U.S. Doesn't "Borrow" Money — It Sells Bonds

It is also highly misleading to say that America "borrows" money from China. This is about as accurate as saying that your bank borrows money from you when you decide to deposit money in a savings account that earns modest annual returns. The U.S. government doesn't ask China for a loan. Rather, China unilaterally decides to invest its money in U.S. Treasury securities because these provide a safe, reliable, and liquid place to keep their savings. China has the world's highest foreign currency reserves, amounting to $3.2 trillion as of April 2016 and they need a place to put some of that surplus cash. There is no global equivalent of a savings bank for countries — but the closest equivalent is U.S. Treasury bonds.[394]

Another useful analogy is the stock-market. Imagine that you decide to pursue a low-risk investment strategy by purchasing highly rated stock in a stable, well-managed company that is likely to maintain its value over time while producing modest returns. In a technical sense, you are lending money to the company whose stocks you're buying. But that's not really what you're doing — you're investing your money sensibly, with the expectation that it will maintain its value and grow modestly over time. One of the advantages of stocks is that they are highly liquid — you can sell them at any time and retrieve your cash. While Treasury bonds can't be cashed in before they're due, they can be easily traded with third parties or sold in exchange for cash.

The U.S. Treasury doesn't decide who to sell its bonds to — it places them on an open market so that they are available for purchase by anyone who wants to buy them. It so happens that the Chinese are active purchasers of U.S. bonds, as are the Japanese, because they find them to be a desirable investment, since their value is stable, they are backed by the full faith and credit of the U.S. government, and they can be resold, which means that they can function as a kind of currency.

U.S. Treasury securities are liquid assets that are easily traded on a global market. They are in essence the most reliable and universal unit of exchange between countries. The fact that China and other countries continue to invest heavily in U.S. bonds reflects confidence in America's stability, prosperity, and solvency. These are strengths, not weaknesses.

While there is certainly a debate to be had over whether America's current and projected debt levels are sustainable, that has very little to do with China specifically, or any other country besides the United States. The issue is debt in itself, not who happens to own it.

REASONS FOR THE DISCONNECT?

Accounting Error

As we've seen, the portion of U.S. debt in foreign hands amounts to about 30 percent of the total. Of this 30 percent, China owns the single largest portion — roughly $1.25 trillion, or 6.5 percent of all U.S. debt. If you look at a list of foreign owners of U.S. debt, you'll see China at the top. So it is correct to say that China owns the largest quantity of *foreign-owned* U.S. debt. Out of context, that may sound to some people (millions, in fact) as though China owns most of America's debt — especially given that many Americans don't realize that almost three quarters of all U.S. debt is actually held by Americans.

Scare Tactics

Politicians are well versed in the art of misleading the public (and, for that matter, one another) by saying things that aren't technically false to imply things that are absolutely false. Conservative politicians use the claim that the United States "borrows" money from China in order to justify cuts to programs that they oppose but many Americans support, such as Planned Parenthood.[395] This is a particularly insidious tactic in a time when tens of millions of Americans are struggling with immense levels of personal debt. By mischaracterizing the nature of China's investment in U.S. bonds, politicians and pundits evoke the anxieties that Americans feel about their own debts. By stirring up these anxieties, conservatives create the false impression that the United States is close to broke and thus needs to slash benefits and programs, which most Americans would never go along with unless they felt it was an emergency.

Xenophobia

China has seen a dramatic rise in its fortunes, its prestige, and its global influence over the past two decades. It is the world's most populous nation and has one of the world's most dynamic economies. No country on Earth besides China can credibly rival the United States in terms of wealth and power. For Americans who believe that the U.S. is entitled to a position of unchallenged dominance in world affairs, any indication of China's growing wealth and power is cause for alarm.

DOMESTIC OIL PRODUCTION
PROMOTES ENERGY INDEPENDENCE

Drill, baby, drill!
— Republican chant

CONSERVATIVES CLAIM...

There's plenty of oil left in the ground within U.S. territory. If we eliminate restrictions on domestic oil drilling, especially environmental regulations, we can free up enough oil to meet our energy needs and minimize our dependence on foreign oil. Liberals and environmentalists are preventing us from achieving energy independence.

THE REALITY

The phrase "energy independence" suggests that we will be able to fulfill all our energy needs with fuel derived from within our own borders — the more oil we produce, the less we will import, until we are producing so much oil domestically that we don't need to import any. But the phrase is misleading because it doesn't reflect how things actually work.

The United States has recently surpassed Saudi Arabia and Russia to become the world's largest producer of petroleum products, including oil and natural gas. In 2015, the U.S. exported 1.733 billion barrels of petroleum products (including crude oil, gasoline, kerosene, and heating oil). In the same year, we imported 3.431 billion barrels, almost exactly twice as much. Why didn't we take a giant step towards energy independence by just keeping all the oil we produced and importing only 1.7 billion? [396]

The reason is very simple: oil extracted from the ground by private companies, such as Exxon-Mobil and BP, does not necessarily remain in America (some does; some doesn't) — most of it ends up on the world market. Oil prices in the U.S. rise and fall along with prices everywhere else, according to global supply and demand.

The government has very little to do with this. Given that the oil is extracted by for-profit corporations operating in a capitalist economy, the government does not have the power to tell the companies where they can and can't sell their petroleum products or how much they can sell it for. If we were a socialist country, that might be possible, but we're not, so it isn't.

A Crude Exception

There was actually one very important government limitation on the free market for oil products. Starting with the oil crisis in the early 1970s, U.S. crude oil was listed as a commodity "in short supply," which meant that exports were restricted by the Department of Commerce. Crude oil could not be exported without a special license, which was very hard to obtain. In practice, this system functioned as a virtual ban on crude oil exports. Refined petroleum products, such as gasoline, were not subject to this restriction.

The export ban, in place since 1973, was lifted in December 2015. The reason? Much of the new oil being extracted in the U.S. today is of a lighter grade than U.S. refineries are currently equipped to handle, so oil producers want to be able to export more of this oil to other countries as domestic production continues to rise. In other words, higher domestic oil production, which is supposedly the road to energy independence, is actually driving a rise in *exports*.[397]

"Energy Independence" Isn't Energy Independence

The Energy Information Agency's "Annual Energy Outlook" for 2015 predicts that the U.S. will become a "net oil exporter" sometime between 2019 and 2040.[398] In other words, as a nation, we will be selling more oil than we buy; we will be, in the technical sense, "energy independent." But that doesn't mean we will no longer be importing foreign oil — only that we'll be exporting more oil than we import. We'll still be importing hundreds of millions of barrels from other countries.

And who, exactly, is "we" anyway?

When we talk about the fact that "we" are producing record amounts of oil, who are we actually talking about? It's not really the U.S.A., as in the American people or its government. "We" refers to the oil companies — both domestic and foreign — who extract the oil from U.S. territory, in order to sell it wherever they choose, whether in the U.S. or abroad.

As long as the oil is in the ground, it belongs to the people of the United States, or to whoever owns the land under which the oil lies. As soon as it is extracted, it belongs to the company that extracted it. This is true regardless of whether it is an American company such as Exxon-Mobil or Texaco, or a foreign-owned company such as BP or Shell. As noted above, the U.S. government has little say in what oil companies do with the oil once they've extracted it from the ground. According to the rules of the free market, oil companies are free to sell their petroleum products here in the U.S. or ship them abroad to sell elsewhere. As we've already seen, they chose to export more than a billion-and-a-half barrels of the stuff in 2015 alone.

The point is that more drilling in the U.S. does not lead inevitably to anything resembling national energy self-sufficiency. It leads, rather, wherever the oil companies decide to go. If you'd prefer to have a system in which oil extracted from U.S. territory must remain within the U.S. and can be sold only on the domestic market, then you will need to get Congress to pass a series of major new laws regulating the industry. And, by the way, that makes you a socialist.

We Do Not Control Our Own Destiny

Given that the U.S. is now the world's leading producer of petroleum products, it seems reasonable to assume that we can play a decisive role in establishing the price of oil. But it's not so. The U.S. currently produces about 15 percent of the world's oil, which is nothing to sneeze at, but not enough to influence the price per barrel in any decisive way. If the past is any indication, there is little correlation between rising and falling production levels in the U.S. and the global price of oil.

Over the past ten years, the price of a barrel of oil has climbed to $150 (June 2008), then crashed precipitously to $50 (December 2008), climbed gradually back up to $120 (April 2012), held more or less steady for two years at an average price of about $100 (hitting $105 in June 2014), then plummeted to below $50 (January 2015), then rallied slightly before crashing down to $28 in January 2016, and then rising to just over $45 (May 2016).[399] During this period of almost nauseating volatility, U.S. domestic oil production rose steadily year after year, increasing by a total of about 50 percent between 2008 and 2016. Even if U.S. domestic oil production has some small impact on the global price of oil, it is so diluted by a host of other factors that it is totally indiscernible.

Consider, for instance, the three years from 2009 to 2012, during which time U.S. oil production rose by 15 percent. During the same period, gas prices jumped from about $2.00 to $3.50 per gallon — an increase of 75 percent.[400] If you're thinking "but that's just a three year period during a major economic crisis — hardly representative of normal conditions" (or something along those lines) you should know that the Associated Press analyzed 36 years worth of data on U.S. gas prices and domestic oil production and came up with no statistically valid correlation between the two. That's right — none.

Here's an excerpt of their report: "Seasonally adjusted U.S. oil production dropped steadily from February 1986 until three years ago [i.e., 2009]. But starting in March 1986, inflation-adjusted gas prices fell below the $2-a-gallon mark and stayed there for most of the rest of the 1980s and 1990s. Production between 1986 and 1999 dropped by nearly one-third. If the drill-now theory were correct, prices should have soared. Instead they went down by nearly a dollar."[401] And as we've already noted, although domestic oil production increased from 2011 to 2012, so did the cost of gasoline at the pump.

In other words, when it comes to petroleum prices, we do not control our own destiny.

Ultimately, the problem is not dependence on foreign oil; the problem is dependence on oil, no matter where it comes from. Even if we were somehow generating all our oil at home and keeping it within our own borders to be sold on an exclusively American market (thus realizing the unwittingly socialistic dreams of the "drill baby drill!" crowd), it would still continue to become an increasingly expensive and scarce commodity. The entire economy depends on energy. As oil becomes scarcer and more expensive, every aspect of the economy becomes increasingly burdened by the rising cost of doing business and the rising cost of living. In other words, we will all be getting poorer and poorer, year after year. This is not a path to any sort of independence worthy of the name.

I'll let the non-partisan Congressional Budget Office have the last word:

"Even if the United States increased production and became a net exporter of oil, U.S. consumers would still be exposed to gasoline prices that rose and fell in response to disruptions around the world."[402]

Actually, on second thought, I'll add one more observation. In order to become truly independent of foreign sources of oil, we need to do more than just be a net exporter — we need to be supplying 100 percent of the energy we consume. That is not going to happen so long as most of our energy comes from a global market for fossil fuels.

There is only one path to full energy independence: renewable energy, from increasingly efficient and affordable technologies that convert free and unlimited sources of energy such as wave, wind, and sunlight into increasingly cheap, usable, locally-generated power. (If you've read Part 2, Chaper 5 "Renewable Energy Isn't a Viable Alternative to Fossil Fuels." then you already know all about this.)

REASONS FOR THE DISCONNECT?

Apples and Oranges

It seems obvious that more domestic oil production should lead directly to cheaper and more plentiful fuel at home. But producing as much as we consume doesn't mean that we consume only what we have produced within our own borders — oil is sold in a global marketplace. We produce a lot of apples and oranges in this country, too, but that doesn't stop us from importing apples from New Zealand and oranges from Brazil, while exporting apples to Mexico and oranges to China.

"We" Isn't Us

As we've seen, American oil doesn't actually belong to the American people — that would be socialism. It belongs instead to global, for-profit corporations that have no legal obligation to function in a manner that serves the public interest. That's their right. What's more, they have a responsibility to operate in the best financial interests of their shareholders — i.e., to maximize profits. In the era of increasing global demand, dwindling supply and harder-to-access oil, that means ever-rising prices, regardless of how much is being produced here at home.

Political Opportunism

Everybody suffers when the price of oil goes up. It's tempting for politicians to appeal to voters by claiming to offer solutions that will provide easy and permanent relief. Since the economics of the oil business are complicated and mysterious to most people, it's all too easy for opportunistic politicians to mislead the public by pretending that they have simple and effective policies that will increase "energy independence" and lower fuel prices.

Patriotism

"Energy independence" sounds like a kind of freedom, and the U.S. is, after all, the land of the free. Americans don't like the idea of having to depend on others — self-sufficiency is one of the great American virtues. The notion that we "depend" on foreign countries for vital resources is distasteful to many Americans, who prefer to think that we can take care of all of our own needs.

THE US SPENDS TOO MUCH ON FOREIGN AID

Foreign aid suffers from a lack of domestic constituency, in large part because the results of the programs are often not immediately visible and self-evident. Properly conceived and efficiently administered, however, security assistance programs, an essential complement to our defense effort, directly enhance the security of the United States.
— Ronald Reagan[403]

Foreign aid is not something the vast majority of Americans support, but definitely not conservatives.
— Rand Paul

CONSERVATIVES CLAIM...

Foreign aid is a waste of tax dollars that contributes hugely to the deficit while gaining us little in return. We should stop giving away money to countries that hate us and instead use the money in ways that benefit us directly. Cutting foreign aid could help us to lower the deficit and balance the budget.

THE REALITY

The United States spends less than one percent of its budget on foreign aid.

The total foreign assistance budget for 2015 was $32 billion, which accounted for 0.82 percent of the $3.9 trillion federal budget.[404] If we stopped spending any money on foreign aid, we would reduce the annual budget deficit (which was $486 billion in 2015) by about 6.5 percent, and the national debt (which was $18.15 trillion in 2015) by less than one fifth of one percent.[405]

We spend much less on foreign assistance than most Americans think we do. But we also spend much less than Americans think we *should*.

A 2010 survey asked Americans to estimate the share of the federal budget allocated to foreign assistance. The average answer was 27 percent, which the respondents considered to be excessive — they would have preferred to see the amount cut in half. In other words, Americans believed that the appropriate portion of the federal budget to be spent on foreign aid is about 13 percent.[406]

As we've already seen, the U.S. actually spends less than 1 percent on foreign aid. Does this mean that Americans would like to see the foreign aid budget increased by more than 1,300 percent? Of course not. But it does mean that Americans have a drastically distorted view of how many of our tax dollars go to foreign assistance. A 2015 survey by the Kaiser Family Foundation found that 95 percent of Americans overestimated the amount the U.S. spends on foreign aid.[407]

Most Foreign Aid Dollars are Spent in the U.S.

Not only do people misunderstand how much we spend; they misunderstand *how* we spend it. While it's true that a many tax dollars are distributed to foreign governments and international aid agencies, most of the money allocated to foreign assistance never leaves the United States.

When we "give" money to a foreign government, often what we're really doing is providing cash on condition that it be used to purchase American products, from grain to military hardware to consulting services.[408]

Consider, for example, one of the countries that receives the highest amount of U.S. foreign aid money: Egypt. Every year, we give them about $1.5 billion, almost all of which they are required to spend on American-made military equipment. NPR reporter Julia Simon looked into this and discovered that "every year, the U.S. Congress appropriates more than $1 billion in military aid to Egypt. But that money never gets to Egypt. It goes to the Federal Reserve Bank of New York, then to a trust fund at the Treasury and, finally, out to U.S. military contractors that make the tanks and fighter jets that ultimately get sent to Egypt."[409]

In this way, the Egyptian air force has acquired the fourth largest fleet of F-16 fighter jets in the world — more than two hundred planes, all purchased from the U.S.-based contractor, General Dynamics with U.S. foreign aid money.

How much does an F-16 cost? According to the Air Force's official website, somewhere between $15 and $20 million, depending on the model. However, if you read the fine print, you'll discover that those cost estimates are presented in 1998 constant dollars, which are worth about $1.50 in today's money.[410] Unless you're a functionary of the armed services trying to deceive people as to the true amount of tax-payer money that you're spending, you'll want to bump those figures up to $22.5 to $30 million per plane.

So that's around 5.5 billion tax dollars worth of foreign aid that have never left U.S. soil, but instead been pumped straight back in to the U.S. economy. Regardless of whether you think this is a wise use of tax dollars, you can't credibly bash the program on the grounds that it's a mere "giveaway" to foreigners.

Foreign Aid Really Does Help People

It's not an exaggeration to say that U.S. foreign assistance has saved the lives of millions of people on this planet. Foreign aid money has been used to build roads and sewage systems, to bring clean water and electricity to poor communities, and to fight the spread of infectious diseases with vaccines, medicines, and insecticide-treated mosquito nets.[411]

One major example of the efficacy of foreign aid spending is PEPFAR — the President's Emergency Plan for AIDS Relief. According to its own website, it is "the largest and most diverse HIV and AIDS prevention, care and treatment initiative in the world." The program has directly touched the lives of tens of millions of people around the world, predominantly throughout Africa, having provided antiretroviral treatment to more than 9.5 million people, HIV counseling and testing to more than 68.2 million people, including more than 14.7 million expectant mothers.[412]

A study by doctors at Stanford concluded that, where it has been implemented, PEPFAR had reduced the rate of deaths from AIDS by 10 percent, saving over a million lives as of 2009.[413] The total cost to U.S. tax payers over the twelve years since the program's inception has been a little less than $66 billion, which amounts to an average annual cost of about $5.5 billion — less that 0.15 percent of the federal budget.[414] Compared to what most Americans think we spend, that has to count as some kind of a bargain.

REASONS FOR THE DISCONNECT?

Economic Anxiety

As we've seen, most Americans have a greatly exaggerated idea of the amount we spend on foreign assistance. During times of real economic hardship, it pains people to think that the government is spending a large share of tax dollars on people in other countries.

Xenophobia

Painful as it is to acknowledge, there are millions of Americans who are fearful and suspicious of foreigners. In times of economic insecurity, the fear and suspicion spread and become more intense. Xenophobes aren't close to being a majority, but they do represent a large enough portion of the electorate to merit some severe pandering from politicians.

Pandering

Fear and outrage are powerful political tools — you can't expect Republican politicians to resist using these to their advantage, can you? Playing on people's exaggerated idea of what we spend on foreign aid is an easy way for politicians to get credit for being on the side of taxpayers, while avoiding the kinds of politically risky spending cuts — such as cuts to entitlements and the military — that would actually save tax payers money.

NOTES

1 Jan Crawford , "Adviser: Romney 'shellshocked' by loss,"
CBS News, November 8, 2012, http://www.cbsnews.com/8301-
250_162-57547239/adviser-romney-shellshocked-by-loss/

2 Ron Suskind, "Faith, Certainty and the Presidency of George
W. Bush," *New York Times Magazine*, October 17, 2004, http://
www.nytimes.com/2004/10/17/magazine/17BUSH.html

3, The O'Reilly Factor, Fox News, April 5, 2011

4 Federal Election Commission report: "Federal Elections 2008:
Election Results for the U.S. President, the U.S. Senate and the U.S.
House of Representatives,*"* July 2009, http://www.fec.gov/pubrec/
fe2008/federalelections2008.pdf

5 "Federal Elections 2012: Election Results for the U.S.
President, the U.S. Senate and the U.S. House of Representatives,"
Federal Election Commission, July 2013, http://www.fec.gov/
pubrec/fe2012/federalelections2012.pdf

6 "Party Affiliation," *Gallup* (accessed May 4, 2016), available at
http://www.gallup.com/poll/15370/party-affiliation.aspx

7 "Party Identification Trends, 1992-2014," Pew Research Center,
April 7, 2015, http://people-press.org/party-identification-trend

8 "Public Wants Changes in Entitlements, Not Changes in
Benefits," *Pew Research Center for the People & the Press*, July 7,
2011, http://www.people-press.org/2011/07/07/public-wants-
changes-in-entitlements-not-change-in-benefits/

9 "Majority of Americans say they support same-sex marriage,
adoption by gay and lesbian couples," *Public Religion Research
Institute*, May 19, 2011, http://publicreligion.org/research/2011/05/
majority-of-americans-say-they-support-same-sex-marriage-

adoption-by-gay-and-lesbian-couples/#.VyqAo2P4PjQ

10 According to a July 2010 CNN poll, 81% percent of Americans support a "path to citizenship" for illegal residents. (This represents a consistent trend: Gallup records 60+ percent support over the past several years — 2006 to present.)

11 Ali Frick, "Fearful Conservatives Push New Talking Point: 'This Is A Center-Right Country'," *ThinkProgress.org*, November 4, 2008, http://thinkprogress.org/politics/2008/11/04/31794/center-right-watch/

12 NBC News/Wall Street Journal Survey, conducted February 24-28, 2011, available at http://online.wsj.com/public/resources/documents/wsj-nbcpoll03022011.pdf

13 USA Today/Gallup poll conducted January 14-16, 2011, available at http://www.gallup.com/poll/145790/americans-oppose-cuts-education-social-security-defense.aspx

14 Neil King, Jr. and Scott Greenberg, "Poll Shows Budget-Cuts Dilemma," *Wall Street Journal*, March 3, 2011, http://www.wsj.com/articles/SB10001424052748704728004576176741120691736

15 Pete Kasperowicz, "Rep. Paul Ryan's budget passed by the House with 10 Republican defections," *The Hill*, March 19, 2012, http://thehill.com/blogs/floor-action/house/219093-paul-ryan-budget-passes-house-with-ten-republican-defections

16 Steven Thomma, "Poll: Best way to fight deficits: Raise taxes on the rich," *McLatchy Newspapers*, April 8, 2011, http://www.mcclatchydc.com/2011/04/18/112386/poll-best-way-to-fight-deficits.html

17 "Abortion," *Gallup* (accessed May 7, 2016), available at http://www.gallup.com/poll/1576/Abortion.aspx

18 "Abortion and Birth Control," *Pew Research Center* survey conducted April 4-15, 2012, via http://www.pollingreport.com/abortion.htm

19 Fox News Poll conducted by Anderson Robbins Research (D) and Shaw & Company Research (R). Dec. 5-7, 2011, available at http://www.foxnews.com/politics/2011/12/09/fox-news-poll-voters-back-plan-to-citizenship-for-illegal-immigrants/

20 Fox News Poll conducted by Anderson Robbins Research (D) and Shaw & Company Research (R). June 24-26, 2012, available at http://www.foxnews.com/politics/interactive/2012/06/27/poll-voters-say-neither-candidate-has-plan-for-economy/

21 Quinnipiac University Poll conducted July 1-8, 2012, available at http://www.quinnipiac.edu/institutes-and-centers/polling-institute/national/release-detail?ReleaseID=1774

22 Gallup poll conducted May 3-6, 2012, available at http://www.gallup.com/poll/154529/Half-Americans-Support-Legal-Gay-Marriage.aspx

23 "Election Statistics, 1920 to Present," *U.S. House of Representatives*, http://history.house.gov/Institution/Election-Statistics/Election-Statistics/

24 FairVote report: "Monopoly Politics", May 2014, http://www.fairvote.org/monopoly_politics#download_monopoly_politics

25 Dwight Eisenhower, "The Chance for Peace" address, delivered before the American Society of Newspaper Editors, April 16th, 1953 — http://www.eisenhower.archives.gov/all_about_ike/speeches/chance_for_peace.pdf

26 Source: Death Penalty Information Center — http://www.deathpenaltyinfo.org/death-penalty-international-perspective#interexec

27 Source: Death Penalty Information Center, chart: "Abolitionist and Retentionist Countries" — http://www.deathpenaltyinfo.org/abolitionist-and-retentionist-countries

28 Source: Pew Research Center survey conducted March 25-29, 2015, http://www.people-press.org/2015/04/16/less-support-for-death-penalty-especially-among-democrats/

29 Source: Death Penalty Information Center, table: "Number of Executions by State and Region Since 1976" — http://www.deathpenaltyinfo.org/number-executions-state-and-region-1976

30 Adam Liptak, "Court Extends Curbs on the Death Penalty in a Florida Ruling", *New York Times*, May 27, 2014 — http://www.nytimes.com/2014/05/28/us/court-rules-against-florida-iq-rule-in-death-cases.html

31 Garrett Epps, "Out of Spite: The Governor of Nebraska's Threat to Execute Prisoners", theatlantic.com, June 6, 2015 — http://www.theatlantic.com/politics/archive/2015/06/a-governor-threatens-to-execute-prisoners-out-of-spite/394949/

32 "It's official: Firing squads in Utah allowed," *Associated Press*, March 24, 2015 — http://www.usatoday.com/story/news/nation-now/2015/03/24/official-firing-squads-utah-allowed/70366174/

33 Source: Death Penalty Information Center, "State By State Lethal Injection" - http://www.deathpenaltyinfo.org/state-lethal-injection

34 Source: Death Penalty Information Center, "Financial Facts About the Death Penalty" - http://www.deathpenaltyinfo.org/costs-death-penalty

35 Judge Arthur L. Alarcón and Paula M. Mitchell, "Costs of Capital Punishment in California: Will Voters Choose Reform this November?", *Loyola of Los Angeles Law Review, vol. 46, S1 (2012)*. Available at: http://digitalcommons.lmu.edu/llr/vol46/iss0/1

36 Source: Small Arms Survey and UNODC (United Nations Office of Drugs and Crime) date, via *The Washington Post*, "Gun homicides and gun ownership by country" — http://www.washingtonpost.com/wp-srv/special/nation/gun-homicides-ownership/table/

37 Source: Harvard Injury Control Research Center, http://www.hsph.harvard.edu/hicrc/firearms-research/

38 Matthew Miller, David Hemenway, and Deborah Azrael, "State-level homicide victimization rates in the US in relation to survey measures of household firearm ownership, 2001—2003", *Social Science & Medicine, Volume 64, Issue 3*, February 2007, Pages 656—664 — http://www.sciencedirect.com/science/article/pii/S0277953606004898

39 Matthew Miller, Deborah Azrael, and Catherine Barber, "Suicide Mortality in the United States: The Importance of Attending to Method in Understanding Population-Level

Disparities in the Burden of Suicide", *Annual Review of Public Health Vol. 33: 393-408* (Volume publication date April 2012) — http://www.annualreviews.org/doi/abs/10.1146/annurev-publhealth-031811-124636

40 Nils Duquet & Maarten Van Alstein, "Firearms and Violent Deaths in Europe", *Flemish Peace Institute*, http://www.vlaamsvredesinstituut.eu/sites/vlaamsvredesinstituut.eu/files/files/reports/firearms_and_violent_deaths_in_europe_web.pdf

41 Source: Violence Policy Center, chart "State Firearm Death Rates, Ranked by Rate, 2011" (based on statistics from Centers for Disease Control and Prevention, National Center for Injury Control and Prevention) - http://www.vpc.org/fadeathchart14.htm

42 from the study "Does Strengthening Self-Defense Law Deter Crime or Escalate Violence? Evidence from Expansions to Castle Doctrine" by Cheng Cheng and Mark Hoekstra, both of Texas A & M university, *Journal of Human Resources, Summer 2013 vol. 48 no. 3 821-854* — http://jhr.uwpress.org/content/48/3/821.short

43 Source: Children's Defense Fund report, "Protect Children Not Guns 2013" — http://www.childrensdefense.org/library/protect-children-not-guns/protect-children-not-guns-2013.html

44 Source: Violence Policy Center, chart "State Firearm Death Rates, Ranked by Rate, 2011" (based on statistics from Centers for Disease Control and Prevention, National Center for Injury Control and Prevention) - http://www.vpc.org/fadeathchart14.htm

45 Source: Iraq Body Count Project — https://www.iraqbodycount.org/

46 Andrew Dugan, "On 10th Anniversary, 53% percent in U.S. See Iraq War as Mistake - Republicans most likely to say conflict was not a mistake" *Gallup*, March 18, 2013, http://www.gallup.com/poll/161399/10th-anniversary-iraq-war-mistake.aspx

47 John Tozzi, "Under Obamacare, 17 Million People Have Gained Health Insurance, RAND Finds", *BloombergBusiness*, May 6, 2015 — http://www.bloomberg.com/news/articles/2015-05-06/health-how-17-million-people-got-insurance-under-obamacare

48 "Health Insurance and Mortality in US Adults" by Andrew P.

Wilper, MD, MPH, Steffie Woolhandler, MD, Karen E. Lasser, MD, MPH, Danny McCormick, MD, MPH, David H. Bor, MD, and David U. Himmelstein, MD, in *American Journal of Public Health*, December 2009, Vol 99, No. 12 — http://www.ncpa.org/pdfs/2009_harvard_health_study.pdf

49 "Deaths: Final Data for 2013 — Table 10. Number of deaths from 113 selected causes", *National Vital Statistics Reports Volume 64, Number 2,* February 16, 2016, http://www.cdc.gov/nchs/data/nvsr/nvsr64/nvsr64_02.pdf

50 Source: Kaiser Family Foundation, table: "Status of State Action on the Medicaid Expansion Decision" - http://kff.org/health-reform/state-indicator/state-activity-around-expanding-medicaid-under-the-affordable-care-act/

51 Source: Kaiser Family Foundation, Health Tracking poll August 2015 - http://kff.org/health-costs/poll-finding/kaiser-health-tracking-poll-august-2015/

52 Source: Organization for Economic Cooperation and Development — "OECD Health Data 2014 - Frequently Requested Data" (accessed May 16, 2016), http://www.oecd.org/els/health-systems/oecd-health-statistics-2014-frequently-requested-data.htm

53 "Public's Policy Priorities Reflect Changing Conditions at Home and Abroad", *Pew Research Center*, January 15, 2015, http://www.people-press.org/2015/01/15/publics-policy-priorities-reflect-changing-conditions-at-home-and-abroad/#views-of-importance-of-environmental-protection-global-warming

54 Source: World Health Organization, Fact sheet N°266: *Climate change and health* - http://www.who.int/mediacentre/factsheets/fs266/en/

55 DARA International Foundation report: *Climate Vulnerability Monitor, 2nd edition — A Guide to the Cold Calculus of a Hot Planet* — http://daraint.org/wp-content/uploads/2012/09/CVM2ndEd-FrontMatter.pdf

56 Pew Research Center survey conducted November 6-9, 2014 — http://www.pewresearch.org/fact-tank/2015/08/03/partisans-differ-sharply-on-power-plant-emissions-limits-climate-change/

57 Source: U.S. Department of Energy, annual data on installed wind capacity available at: http://apps2.eere.energy.gov/wind/windexchange/wind_installed_capacity.asp

58 Source: Solar Energy industries Association, Solar Market Insight Report 2014 Q4 - http://www.seia.org/research-resources/solar-market-insight-report-2014-q4

59 "Air pollution causes 200,000 early deaths each year in the U.S." *MIT Laboratory for Aviation and the Environment*, http://lae.mit.edu/air-pollution-causes-200000-early-deaths-each-year-in-the-u-s/

60 "The Toll From Coal - An Updated Assessment of Death and Disease from America's Dirtiest Energy Source", *Clean Air Task Force*, September 2010, http://www.catf.us/fossil/problems/power_plants/

61 Senate Vote #262 in 2015, Cloture on S. 1881: "A bill to prohibit Federal funding of Planned Parenthood Federation of America" — https://www.govtrack.us/congress/votes/114-2015/s262

62 House Vote #505 in 2015, H.R. 3134: "Defund Planned Parenthood Act of 2015" — https://www.govtrack.us/congress/votes/114-2015/h505

63 Rebecca Kaplan, "Can Congress defund Planned Parenhood?", *cbsnews.com,* posted July 30, 2015 - http://www.cbsnews.com/news/can-congress-defund-planned-parenthood/

64 Source: *Planned Parenthood 2013-2014 Annual Report —* http://plannedparenthood.org/about-us/annual-report

65 Karen Pazol, PhD; Andreea A. Creanga, MD; PhD, Suzanne B. Zane, DVM; Kim D. Burley; Denise J. Jamieson, MD "Abortion Surveillance — United States, 2009", *Division of Reproductive Health, National Center for Chronic Disease Prevention and Health Promotion, CDC,* November 23, 2012, http://www.cdc.gov/mmwr/preview/mmwrhtml/ss6108a1.htm?s_cid=ss6108a1_w

66 National Center for Biotechnology Information report: "Abortion surveillance - United States, 2010" by Pazol K, Creanga AA, Burley KD, Hayes B, Jamieson DJ — Division of Reproductive Health, National Center for Chronic Disease

Prevention and Health Promotion, CDC, http://www.ncbi.nlm.nih. gov/pubmed/24280963

67 Gold RB, Sonfield A, Richards CL and Frost JJ, "Next Steps for America's Family Planning Program: Leveraging the Potential of Medicaid and Title X in an Evolving Health Care System", *Guttmacher Institute*, 2009, http://www.guttmacher.org/pubs/ NextSteps.pdf

68 Source: Gallup, *Historical Trends: Abortion* — http://www. gallup.com/poll/1576/abortion.aspx

69 Family Research Council website, http://www.frc.org/get. cfm?c=ISSUES&issue=MF

70 Family Research Council website, http://www.frc.org/mission-statement

71 "Teen Birth Rate per 1,000 Population Ages 15-19, 2010", *Kaiser Fmaily Foundation*, http://www.statehealthfacts.org/ comparemaptable.jsp?ind=37&cat=2&sub=11

72 Sarah Fass, "Paid Leave in the States A Critical Support for Low-wage Workers and Their Families" *National Center for Children in Poverty,*, March 2009, http://www.nccp.org/ publications/pub_864.html

73 Source: U.S. Social Security Administration - Social Security Programs Throughout the World — Europe, 2012: http://www.ssa. gov/policy/docs/progdesc/ssptw/2012-2013/europe/united_kingdom. html

74 Source: U.S. Social Security Administration - Social Security Programs Throughout the World — Europe, 2012: http://www.ssa. gov/policy/docs/progdesc/ssptw/2012-2013/europe/france.html

75 Source: U.S. Social Security Administration - Social Security Programs Throughout the World — Europe, 2012: http://www.ssa. gov/policy/docs/progdesc/ssptw/2012-2013/europe/germany.html

76 Source: U.S. Social Security Administration - Social Security Programs Throughout the World — Europe, 2012: http://www.ssa. gov/policy/docs/progdesc/ssptw/2012-2013/europe/russia.html

77 Source: U.S. Social Security Administration - Social Security Programs Throughout the World — Asia and the Pacific, 2010:

http://www.ssa.gov/policy/docs/progdesc/ssptw/2010-2011/asia/
china.html

78 Source: U.S. Social Security Administration - Social Security
Programs Throughout the World — Asia and the Pacific, 2010:
http://www.ssa.gov/policy/docs/progdesc/ssptw/2010-2011/asia/
india.html

79 Source: U.S. Social Security Administration - Social Security
Programs Throughout the World — Asia and the Pacific, 2010:
http://www.ssa.gov/policy/docs/progdesc/ssptw/2010-2011/asia/iran.
html

80 Source: U.S. Social Security Administration - Social Security
Programs Throughout the World — Asia and the Pacific, 2010:
http://www.ssa.gov/policy/docs/progdesc/ssptw/2010-2011/asia/
israel.html

81 Federal Employees Paid Parental Leave Act of 2009 (H.R.
626), Introduced by Democratic Representative Carolyn Maloney
and co-sponsored by 52 Democrats and Republicans. http://www.
govtrack.us/congress/bills/111/hr626

82 Family Leave Insurance Act of 2007 (S. 1681). Introduced by
Democratic Senator Chris Dodd, cosponsored by four Democrats
and one Republican. http://www.govtrack.us/congress/bills/110/
s1681

83 Family Leave Insurance Act of 2009 (H.R. 1723). Introduced
by Democratic Representative Pete Stark with 36 Democratic and
zero Republican cosponsors. http://www.govtrack.us/congress/
bills/111/hr1723

84 Pew Forum on Religion & Public Life / U.S. Religious
Landscape Survey: table "Marital Status by Protestant
Denomination", http://religions.pewforum.org/pdf/table-status-by-
denomination.pdf

85 Pew Forum on Religion & Public Life / U.S. Religious
Landscape Survey: table "Marital Status by Religious Tradition",
http://religions.pewforum.org/pdf/table-status-by-tradition.pdf

86 U.S. Census Bureau, American Community Survey Report:
"Marital Events of Americans: 2009", August 2011, Figures 3 and

4, "Divorce Rates for Men and Women by State: 2009" http://www.
census.gov/prod/2011pubs/acs-13.pdf

87 Census Bureau, Table 133. Marriages and Divorces—Number
and Rate by State: 1990 to 2009, http://www.census.gov/compendia/
statab/2012/tables/12s0133.pdf

88 Final Vote Results For Roll Call 151, House Resolution 112
" Establishing the budget for the United States Government for fiscal
year 2013 and setting forth appropriate budgetary levels for fiscal
years 2014 through 2022", http://clerk.house.gov/evs/2012/roll151.
xml

89 Center for Budget and Policy Priorities: "Statement of Robert
Greenstein, President, on Chairman Ryan's Budget Plan," March
21, 2012, http://www.cbpp.org/cms/index.cfm?fa=view&id=3712

90 Source: U.S. Census Bureau, "Current Population Survey,
2009 to 2011 Annual Social and Economic Supplements. Three-
Year-Average Median Household Income by State: 2009-2011 and
Two-Year-Average Median Household Income by State: 2010 to
2011", available at http://www.census.gov/hhes/www/income/data/
statemedian/index.html

91 Source: Henry J. Kaiser Family Foundation, Table: "Measures
of State Economic Distress: Housing Foreclosures and Changes in
Unemployment and Food Stamp Participation", (accessed May 19,
2016), http://www.statehealthfacts.org/comparetable.jsp?typ=5&ind
=649&cat=1&sub=151&sortc=7&o=a

92 Source: U.S. Census Bureau, Income, Poverty and Health
Insurance in the United States: 2011, Figure 5. "Poverty Rates by
Age: 1959 to 2011" http://www.census.gov/hhes/www/poverty/data/
incpovhlth/2011/figure5.pdf

93 source: Center for Disease Control, "Deaths: Final Data for
2010, table 18" http://www.cdc.gov/nchs/data/dvs/deaths_2010_
release.pdf

94 Centers for Disease Control and Prevention, Injury Prevention
& Control: Data & Statistics, charts: "10 Leading Causes of Death
by Age Group, United States — 2010" http://www.cdc.gov/injury/
wisqars/pdf/10LCID_All_Deaths_By_Age_Group_2010-a.pdf, and

"10 Leading Causes of Injury Deaths by Age Group Highlighting Violence-Related Injury Deaths, United States — 2010" http://www.cdc.gov/injury/wisqars/pdf/10LCID_Violence_Related_Injury_Deaths_2010-a.pdf

95 Children's Defense Fund report: "PROTECT CHILDREN NOT GUNS 2012", http://www.childrensdefense.org/child-research-data-publications/data/protect-children-not-guns-2012.pdf

96 Source: Harvard Injury Control Research Center at the Harvard School of Public Health, http://www.hsph.harvard.edu/research/hicrc/firearms-research/guns-and-death/index.html

97 Source: Behavioral Risk Factor Surveillance System (BRFSS) Survey Results 2001 for Nationwide Firearms, http://www.schs.state.nc.us/SCHS/brfss/2001/us/firearm3.html

98 "Number of Deaths Due to Injury by Firearms per 100,000 Population, 2009" Kaiser Family Foundation, http://www.statehealthfacts.org/comparemaptable.jsp?ind=113&cat=2

99 "Six facts about guns, violence, and gun control" by Ezra Klein, The Washington Post, July 23, 2012, http://www.washingtonpost.com/blogs/ezra-klein/wp/2012/07/23/six-facts-about-guns-violence-and-gun-control/

100 "Leaked: Conservative Group Plans Anti-Climate Education Program" by Stephanie Pappas, Scientific American, February 15, 2012, http://www.scientificamerican.com/article.cfm?id=leaked-conservative-group

101 "Treaty of Peace and Friendship between the United States of America and the Bey and Subjects of Tripoli of Barbary", available via *The Avalon Project — Documents in Law, History and Diplomacy,* http://avalon.law.yale.edu/18th_century/bar1796t.asp

102 Remarks to Members of the Congregation of Temple Hillel and Jewish Community Leaders in Valley Stream, New York, available via *The Ronald Reagan Presidential Library and Museum*, http://www.reagan.utexas.edu/archives/speeches/1984/102684a.htm

103 Source: Pew Research Center, *2014 Religious Landscape Study*, http://www.pewforum.org/religious-landscape-study/

104 Source: American Red Cross: http://www.redcrossblood.org/

learn-about-blood/blood-types

105 Source: Pew Research Center, *2014 Religious Landscape Study*, http://www.pewforum.org/religious-landscape-study/

106 *Annals of Congress. The Debates and Proceedings in the Congress of the United States.* "History of Congress." 42 vols. Washington, D.C.: Gales & Seaton, 1834—56, via The Founders Constitution, Volume 5, Amendment I (Religion), Document 53, http://press-pubs.uchicago.edu/founders/documents/amendI_religions53.html

107 James Madison, *A Memorial and Remonstrance Against Religious Assessments,* presented in the Virginia General Assembly on June 20, 1785, http://press-pubs.uchicago.edu/founders/documents/amendI_religions43.html

108 Kathrin Brandmeir, Dr. Michaela Grimm, Dr. Michael Heise, Dr. Arne Holzhausen, *Allianz Global Wealth Report 2015*, https://www.allianz.com/v_1443702256000/media/economic_research/publications/specials/en/AGWR2015_ENG.pdf

109 Source: Organization for Economic Cooperation and Development chart, "OECD Income Distribution Database (IDD): Gini, poverty, income, Methods and Concepts", (accessed May 2016) http://www.oecd.org/social/income-distribution-database.htm

110 Source: Death Penalty Information Center — http://www.deathpenaltyinfo.org/death-penalty-international-perspective#interexec

111 Source: Stockholm International Peace Research Institute, *SIPRI Yearbook 2015 - Armaments, Disarmament and International Security*, http://www.sipri.org/yearbook/2015

112 Jeffrey Owen Jones, "The Man Who Wrote the Pledge of Allegiance", *Smithsonian Magazine*, November 2003, http://www.smithsonianmag.com/history/the-man-who-wrote-the-pledge-of-allegiance-93907224/

113 Source: U.S. Department of the Treasury, https://www.treasury.gov/about/education/Pages/in-god-we-trust.aspx

114 Source: Pew Research Center, *2014 U.S. Religious Landscape Study*, http://www.pewforum.org/religious-landscape-

study/christians/christian/

115 Rick Perry for President 2012 Ad - "Strong" available at https://www.youtube.com/watch?v=kxzONeK1OwQ&feature=relat ed

116 Pew Forum on Religion & Public Life / U.S. Religious Landscape Survey (2007), http://religions.pewforum.org/pdf/table-party-affiliation-by-religious-tradition.pdf

117 Final Vote Results for Roll Call 1143 "Recognizing the importance of Christmas and the Christian faith", http://clerk.house. gov/evs/2007/roll1143.xml

118 Donovan Slack, "The Obamas go to church", *Politico*, January 15, 2012, http://www.politico.com/politico44/2012/01/ obamas-go-to-church-110919.html

119 The 2012 Democratic National Platform, http://www. democrats.org/democratic-national-platform#american-community

120 "Christmas Celebration Outlawed, December 25, 1659", *MassMoments.org*, http://massmoments.org/moment.cfm?mid=369

121 Stephen W. Stathis, Specialist in American National Government Government Division,"Federal Holidays: Evolution and Application", *Congressional Research Service*, February 8, 1999, http://www.senate.gov/reference/resources/pdf/Federal_ Holidays.pdf

122 National Christmas Tree Lighting 2015 - Event History & Timeline, http://thenationaltree.org/event-history/

123 President Barack Obama, remarks made at the National Christmas Tree Lighting Ceremony, December 01, 2011, *The White House*,http://www.whitehouse.gov/photos-and-video/ video/2011/12/01/national-christmas-tree-lighting-ceremony#transcript

124 President Barack Obama, remarks made at the National Prayer Breakfast, February 2, 2012, *The White House*, http://www. whitehouse.gov/the-press-office/2012/02/02/remarks-president-national-prayer-breakfast

125 Rockefeller Center New York Christmas Tree Lighting, http://www.rockefellercenter.com/events/2011/11/30/2011-

rockefeller-center-christmas-tree-lighting/

126 Ben Dimiero, Rob Savillo, & Jeremy Schulman, "Bill O'Reilly Covers The 'War On Christmas' More Than Actual Wars," *Media Matters for America*, December 22, 2011, http://mediamatters.org/blog/2011/12/22/bill-oreilly-covers-the-war-on-christmas-more-t/185683

127 "Operation Enduring Freedom – Fatalities by Year and Month", *iCasualties.org*, http://icasualties.org/oef/ByMonth.aspx

128 "America's Changing Religious Landscape", *Pew Research Center*, May 12, 2015 http://religions.pewforum.org/reports

129 "Freedom in the World — 2016," *Freedom House*, https://freedomhouse.org/sites/default/files/FH_FITW_Report_2016.pdf

130 Source: *The Economist Intelligence Unit* report: "Democracy Index 2015 — Democracy in an age of anxiety", http://www.eiu.com/public/thankyou_download.aspx?activity=download&campaignid=DemocracyIndex2015

131 Ian Vasquez and Tanja Porčnik, "The Human Freedom Index: A Global Measurement of Personal, Civil, and Economic Freedom," *The Cato Institute*, 2015, http://object.cato.org/sites/cato.org/files/human-freedom-index-files/human-freedom-index-2015.pdf

132 Martin Gilens and Benjamin I. Page, "Testing Theories of American Politics: Elites, Interest Groups, and Average Citizens," *Perspectives on Politics*, Vol. 12 No. 3, September 2014, 564-581, http://journals.cambridge.org/action/displayAbstract?fromPage=online&aid=9354310

133 Sahil Kapur, "Scholar Behind Viral 'Oligarchy' Study Tells You What It Means," *Talking Points Memo*, April 22, 2014, http://talkingpointsmemo.com/dc/princeton-scholar-demise-of-democracy-america-tpm-interview

134 Carl Bialik, "Most Americans Agree With Obama That More Gun Buyers Should Get Background Checks," *FiveThirtyEight*, Jan 5, 2016, http://fivethirtyeight.com/features/most-americans-agree-with-obama-that-more-gun-buyers-should-get-background-checks/#fn-1

135 Source: *The CIA World Factbook*, "Political Parties and Leaders," retrieved March 30, 2016, https://www.cia.gov/library/publications/the-world-factbook/fields/2118.html

136 *National Conference of State Legislatures*, "Voter Identification Requirements / Voter ID Laws," retrieved March 31, 2016, http://www.ncsl.org/research/elections-and-campaigns/voter-id.aspx

137 Source: *United States Census Bureau*, "Voting Age Population by Citizenship and Race (CVAP)," https://www.census.gov/rdo/data/voting_age_population_by_citizenship_and_race_cvap.html

138 Source: *The Sentencing Project*, "Felony Disenfranshisement," retrieved March 30, 2016, http://sentencingproject.org/template/page.cfm?id=133

139 Source: *World Prison Brief / Institute for Criminal Policy Research*, "Highest to Lowest — Prison Population Total," data retrieved March 29, 2016, http://www.prisonstudies.org/highest-to-lowest/prison-population-total?field_region_taxonomy_tid=All

140 "Finding Direction: Expanding Criminal Justice Options by Considering Policies of Other Nations," *Justice Policy Institute*, April 2011, http://www.justicepolicy.org/uploads/justicepolicy/documents/finding_direction-full_report.pdf

141 "Democracy Index 2015 — Democracy in an age of anxiety", *The Economist Intelligence Unit*, http://www.eiu.com/public/thankyou_download.aspx?activity=download&campaignid=DemocracyIndex2015

142 "CNN Late Edition with Wolf Blitzer — Interview With Donald Trump," CNN, Aired March 21, 2004, http://www.cnn.com/TRANSCRIPTS/0403/21/le.00.html

143 Source: *Bureau of Labor Statistics*, http://data.bls.gov/

144 Rick Newman, "Bill Clinton Is Right: The Economy Really Does Do Better Under Democrats", *U.S.News & World Report*, Sep 6, 2012, http://finance.yahoo.com/news/bill-clinton-economy-really-does-180730819.html

145 Ibid.

146 Source: *Bureau of Economic Analysis*, "Table 1.1.1. Percent Change From Preceding Period in Real Gross Domestic Product", http://www.bea.gov/iTable/index_nipa.cfm

147 Alan S. Blinder and Mark W. Watson, Woodrow Wilson School and Department of Economics Princeton University, "Presidents and the U.S. Economy: An Econometric Exploration," July 2014, http://www.princeton.edu/~mwatson/papers/Presidents_Blinder_Watson_July2014.pdf

148 Susan Fleck, John Glaser, and Shawn Sprague, "The compensation-productivity gap: a visual essay" *Monthly Labor Review*, January 2011, http://www.bls.gov/opub/mlr/2011/01/art3full.pdf

149 Lawrence Mishel and Heidi Shierholz, "The Sad But True Story of Wages in America", *Economic Policy Institute Issue Brief #247*, March 14, 2011, http://epi.3cdn.net/3b7a1c34747d141327_4dm6bx8ni.pdf

150 Source: *Federal Reserve Bank of St. Louis*, FRED Economic Data - graph: "Compensation of Employees: Wages & Salary Accruals (WASCUR)/Gross Domestic Product, 1 Decimal (GDP)", http://research.stlouisfed.org/fred2/graph/?g=2Xa

151 Source: *Federal Reserve Bank of St. Louis*, FRED Economic Data - graph: "Corporate Profits After Tax (CP)/Gross Domestic Product, 1 Decimal (GDP)" http://research.stlouisfed.org/fred2/graph/?g=fNA

152 David Cay Johnston, "Idle corporate cash piles up", *Reuters*, July16, 2012, http://blogs.reuters.com/david-cay-johnston/2012/07/16/idle-corporate-cash-piles-up/

153 *Organization for Economic Cooperation and Development* report: "OECD Health Data 2012 - How Does the United States Compare", http://www.oecd.org/health/health-systems/BriefingNoteUSA2012.pdf

154 Source: *Organization for Economic Cooperation and Development* — "OECD Health Data 2012 - Frequently Requested Data", http://www.oecd.org/els/health-systems/oecdhealthdata2012-frequentlyrequesteddata.htm

155 Armando Roggio, "Comparing UPS, FedEx, and USPS: Which is Best Now?" *Practical eCommerce*, November 8, 2011, http://www.practicalecommerce.com/articles/3156-Comparing-UPS-FedEx-and-USPS-Which-is-Best-Now-

156 H.R 6407 (109th Congress): "Postal Accountability and Enhancement Act", http://www.govtrack.us/congress/bills/109/hr6407

157 "Confidential Memorandum: Attack of American Free Enterprise System" prepared by Lewis F. Powell, Jr. for Eugene Syndor, Jr., Chairman, Education Committee, U.S. Chamber of Commerce, August 23, 1971

158 Kevin Bogardus, "Chamber of Commerce racks up $135 million lobbying tab for 2012" *The Hill*, January 22, 2013, http://thehill.com/business-a-lobbying/278533-chambers-of-commerces-lobbying-spending-topped-135-million-in-2012

159 From an editorial in the *National Review*, December 19, 2008, http://www.nationalreview.com/articles/226567/republican-stimulus-plan/mitt-romney

160 Brian Bender, "In 2010, Paul Ryan denied making appeals for stimulus funds", *The Boston Globe*, August 16, 2012, http://www.boston.com/politicalintelligence/2012/08/16/ryan/WEMawbCVyVTq2qi0pyBheK/story.html
Bureau of Labor Statistics, http://www.bls.gov/home.htm

161 Source: *Bureau of Labor Statistics*, http://www.bls.gov/home.htm

162 Source: *Bureau of Economic Analysis*, Table 1.1.5. Gross Domestic Product (A) (Q) http://www.bea.gov/iTable/iTable.cfm?ReqID=9&step=1

163 American Recovery and Investment Act of 2009, https://www.gpo.gov/fdsys/pkg/BILLS-111hr1enr/pdf/BILLS-111hr1enr.pdf

164 *Congressional Budget Office*, report: "Estimated Impact of the American Recovery and Reinvestment Act on Employment and Economic Output from October 2011 Through December 2011", February 2012, http://www.cbo.gov/sites/default/files/cbofiles/

attachments/02-22-ARRA.pdf

165 IGM Forum, University of Chicago Booth School of Business, survey on Economic Stimulus, http://www.igmchicago. org/igm-economic-experts-panel/poll-results?SurveyID=SV_ cw5O9LNJL1oz4Xi

166 Ibid.

167 James Newton, "Uncommon Friends : Life with Thomas Edison, Henry Ford, Harvey Firestone, Alexis Carrel & Charles Lindbergh" (1987) p. 31

168 Source: *U.S. Energy Information Administration*, Annual Energy Review for 2011, p. 3, Figure 1.0 "Energy Flow, 2011", http://www.eia.gov/totalenergy/data/annual/pdf/aer.pdf

169 Source: *U.S. Energy Information Administration*, International Energy Statistics,http://www.eia.gov/cfapps/ ipdbproject/IEDIndex3.cfm?tid=6&pid=29&aid=12

170 Source: *Global Wind Energy Council*, Global Wind Statistics 2011, http://gwec.net/wp-content/uploads/2012/06/GWEC_-_ Global_Wind_Statistics_2011.pdf

171 "American wind power reaches major power generation milestones in 2013," *American Wind Energy Association* (accessed May 5, 2016), http://www.awea.org/MediaCenter/pressrelease. aspx?ItemNumber=6184

172 *National Renewable Energy Lab*, http://www.nrel.gov/csp/ solarpaces/project_detail.cfm/projectID=40

173 Erik Kirschbaum, "Germany sets new solar power record, institute says", *Reuters*, May 26, 2012, http://www.reuters.com/ article/2012/05/26/us-climate-germany-solar- idUSBRE84P0FI20120526

174 Dan Lafontaine, "Army scientists develop deployable renewable-energy solutions", *RDECOM (U.S. Army Research, Development and Engineering Command)*, May 10, 2012, http:// www.army.mil/article/79471/Army_scientists_develop_deployable_ renewable_energy_solutions/

175 Amaani Lyle, "Service Officials Affirm Commitment to Renewable Energy", *Armed Forces Press Service*, June 12, 2012,

http://www.army.mil/article/81886/Service_Officials_Affirm_
Commitment_to_Renewable_Energy/

176 Rob McIlvaine, "Army, Air Force Will Power Fight with
Alternative Fuels" *Army News Service*, July 19, 2011, http://www.
army.mil/article/61879/Army__Air_Force_will_power_fight_with_
alternative_fuels/

177 *Defense Science Board* report: "More Capable Warfighting
Through Reduced Fuel Burden" May 2001, http://www.dtic.mil/cgi-
bin/GetTRDoc?Location=U2&doc=GetTRDoc.
pdf&AD=ADA392666

178 Denver Beaulieu-Hains, "Army to field energy-saving
systems to deploying BCT" *JMTC PAO, The Official Homepage of
the United States Army*, March 13, 2012, http://www.army.mil/
article/75607/

179 *National Renewable Energy Laboratory* report: "U.S.
Renewable Energy Technical Potentials: A GIS-Based Analysis" by
Anthony Lopez, Billy Roberts, Donna Heimiller, Nate Blair, and
Gian Porro, http://www.nrel.gov/docs/fy12osti/51946.pdf

180 *U.S. Energy Information Administration*, Annual Energy
Review 2011, Table 1.1 "Primary Energy Overview, Selected Years,
1949-2011" released September 27, 2012, http://www.eia.gov/
totalenergy/data/annual/pdf/aer.pdf

181 *International Energy Agency,* "World Energy Outlook
2012", http://www.iea.org/publications/freepublications/publication/
English.pdf

182 Cory Budischak, DeAnna Sewell, Heather Thomson, Leon
Mach, Dana E. Veron, Willett Kempton, "Cost-minimized
combinations of wind power, solar power and electrochemical
storage, powering the grid up to 99.9% percent of the time" *Journal
of Power Sources, Volume 225,* March 1, 2013, Pages 60-74, http://
www.sciencedirect.com/science/article/pii/S0378775312014759

183 Ibid.

184 Yvonne Y. Deng, Kornelis Blok, Kees van der Leun,
"Transition to a fully sustainable global energy system" *Energy
Strategy Reviews, Volume 1, Issue 2*, September 2012, Pages 109—

121, http://www.sciencedirect.com/science/article/pii/
S2211467X12000314

185 Mark Z. Jacobsonand Mark A. Delucchi, "A Plan to Power
100 Percent of the Planet with Renewables" *Scientific American
Magazine*, November 2009, http://www.scientificamerican.com/
article.cfm?id=a-path-to-sustainable-energy-by-2030

186 source: *International Organization of Motor Vehicle
Manufacturers*, http://oica.net/category/production-statistics/

187 Source: *National World War II Museum*, http://www.
nationalww2museum.org/learn/education/for-students/ww2-history/
ww2-by-the-numbers/wartime-production.html

188 "OPEC spare capacity in the first quarter of 2012 at lowest
level since 2008", *U.S. Energy Information Administration*, May 24,
2012, http://www.eia.gov/todayinenergy/detail.cfm?id=6410

189 Jeff Rubin, "How High Oil Prices Will Permanently Cap
Economic Growth" *Bloomberg View*, September 23, 2012, http://
www.bloomberg.com/news/2012-09-23/how-high-oil-prices-will-
permanently-cap-economic-growth.html

190 source: *U.S. Energy Information Agency*, http://www.eia.gov/
petroleum/data.cfm

191 Brad Tuttle, "2011 Is Priciest Year Ever for Gasoline: $3.53
Per Gallon, Over $4K Spent Per Household", *Time Magazine*, Dec.
20, 2011, http://business.time.com/2011/12/20/2011-is-priciest-year-
ever-for-gasoline-3-53-per-gallon-over-4k-spent-per-household

192 "Hidden Costs of Energy: Unpriced Consequences of Energy
Production and Use" by The Committee on Health, Environmental,
and Other External Costs and Benefits of Energy Production and
Consumption of the National Research Council, 2010, *The National
Academies Press*, http://www.nap.edu/openbook.php?record_
id=12794

193 Paul R. Epstein et al., "Full cost accounting for the life cycle
of coal", *Annals of the New York Academy of Sciences*, 1219 (2011)
p. 73—98, http://solar.gwu.edu/index_files/Resources_files/epstein_
full% percent20cost% percent20of% percent20coal.pdf

194 Source: *Michigan Public Service Commission,* "Report on

the Implementation of the P.A. 295 Renewable Energy Standard and the Cost-Effectiveness of the Energy Standards" February 15, 2012, http://www.michigan.gov/documents/mpsc/implementation_PA295_renewable_energy2-15-2012_376924_7.pdf

195 Jeff Tollefson, "Air sampling reveals high emissions from gas field", *Nature*, February 7, 2012, http://www.nature.com/news/air-sampling-reveals-high-emissions-from-gas-field-1.9982

196 Jeff Tollefson, "Methane leaks erode green credentials of natural gas - Losses of up to 9% percent show need for broader data on US gas industry's environmental impact", *Nature*, January 2, 2013, http://www.nature.com/news/methane-leaks-erode-green-credentials-of-natural-gas-1.12123

197 "Renewables 2012 Global Status Report", *Renewable Energy Policy Network for the 21st Century,* http://www.ren21.net/REN21Activities/GlobalStatusReport.aspx

198 Zachary Shahan, "Negative European Power Prices Seen Sunday Through Thursday Due To Strong Wind Power Supply", *CleanTechnica*, December 29, 2012, http://cleantechnica.com/2012/12/29/negative-european-power-prices-seen-sunday-through-thursday-due-to-strong-wind-power-supply/

199 Elizabeth Souder, "Wholesale power cost nothing last night", *Dallas Morning News*, October 14, 2011, http://energyandenvironmentblog.dallasnews.com/archives/2011/10/wholesale-power-cost-nothing-1.html

200 Martin Lamonica, "The Dog Days of Solar", *MIT Technology Review*, July 26, 2012, http://www.technologyreview.com/news/428583/the-dog-days-of-solar/

201 "Exxon Outspends Clean-Energy Industry on Washington Lobbying", *Bloomberg News*, July 30, 2009, http://www.bloomberg.com/apps/news?pid=newsarchive&sid=aPuYDoceYMe0

202 Alexandra Twin, "Dow Tumbles 7% percent", *CNN Money*, October 9, 2008, http://money.cnn.com/2008/10/09/markets/markets_newyork/index.htm

203 Alexandra Twin, "Dow, S&P break records", *CNN Money*, October 9, 2007, http://money.cnn.com/2007/10/09/markets/

markets_0500/index.htm

204 Henry Blodget, "Corporate Profits Just Hit An All-Time High, Wages Just Hit An All-Time Low," *Business Insider*, Jun. 22, 2012, http://www.businessinsider.com/corporate-profits-just-hit-an-all-time-high-wages-just-hit-an-all-time-low-2012-6

205 Source: *US Small Business Administration* - http://www.sba.gov/advo/press/06-17.html

206 Source: *Bureau of Economic Analysis* - http://www.bea.gov/national/nipaweb/SelectTable.asp?Popular=Y

207 Bruce Bartlett, "Reagan's Forgotten Tax Record", *Capital Gains and Games*, February 22, 2011, http://capitalgainsandgames.com/blog/bruce-bartlett/2154/reagans-forgotten-tax-record

208 Source: *Office of Management and Budget* Historical Tables, table 1.3

209 "Federal Receipt and Outlay Summary, 1940-2020", *Tax Policy Center*, http://www.taxpolicycenter.org/statistics/federal-receipt-and-outlay-summary

210 Milton Friedman Speaks: Lecture 13, 'Who Protects the Worker'

211 Rebecca Rifkin, "Americans Say Federal Gov't Wastes 51 Cents on the Dollar," *Gallup*, September 17, 2014, http://www.gallup.com/poll/176102/americans-say-federal-gov-wastes-cents-dollar.aspx

212 "Poll: Most Americans say tax dollars are wasted," CNN, April 15, 2010, http://www.cnn.com/2010/POLITICS/04/15/poll.wasted.taxes/

213 Senator Tom Coburn M.D., *Wastebook 2014*, http://showmethespending.com/wp-content/uploads/2014/10/wastebook2014.pdf

214 Budget of the United States – 2010, *Office of Management and Budget*, http://www.gpoaccess.gov/usbudget/fy10/pdf/fy10-newera.pdf

215 "Poll: Americans way off on public boradcasting funding," *Politico*, April 1, 2011,http://www.politico.com/blogs/onmedia/0411/Poll_Americans_way_off_on_public_broadcasting_

funding.html ; CNN/Opinon Research poll conducted March 11-13, 2011, published April 1, 2011, available at: http://i2.cdn.turner.com/cnn/2011/images/03/31/rel4m.pdf

216 Bruce Bartlett, "Are Taxes in the U.S. High or Low?" *New York Times – Economix Blog*, May 31, 2011, http://economix.blogs.nytimes.com/2011/05/31/are-taxes-in-the-u-s-high-or-low/

217 Source: *Tax Foundation*, "U.S. Federal Individual Income Tax Rates History, 1862-2013 (Nominal and Inflation-Adjusted Brackets)" October 17, 2013, http://taxfoundation.org/article/us-federal-individual-income-tax-rates-history-1913-2011-nominal-and-inflation-adjusted-brackets/

218 source: *Congressional Budget Office*, via *Tax Policy Center*: http://www.taxpolicycenter.org/taxfacts/displayafact.cfm?Docid=456

219 Office of Management and Budget, Historical Tables

220 Source: *Tax Policy Center*, "Historical Average Federal Tax Rates for All Households 1979-2011", http://www.taxpolicycenter.org/taxfacts/displayafact.cfm?Docid=456

221 Dennis Cauchon, "U.S. tax burden at lowest level since '58", *USA Today*, May 6, 2011, http://www.usatoday.com/money/perfi/taxes/2011-05-05-tax-cut-record-low_n.htm

222 "KPMG's Individual Income Tax and Social Security Rate Survey 2012," *KPMG International*, https://www.kpmg.com/CN/en/IssuesAndInsights/ArticlesPublications/Documents/Individual-Income-Tax-Social-Security-Rate-O-201210.pdf

223 Source: *OECD* combined revenue statistics: http://stats.oecd.org/Index.aspx?DataSetCode=REV

224 Source: *OECD*, via *Tax Policy Center*: http://www.taxpolicycenter.org/briefing-book/background/numbers/international.cfm

225 Source: *Government Accountability Office* report "U.S. MULTINATIONAL CORPORATIONS Effective Tax Rates Are Correlated with Where Income Is Reported", August 2008, http://www.gao.gov/new.items/d08950.pdf

226 David Cay Johnston, "9 Things The Rich Don't Want You

To Know About Taxes", *Willamette Week*, April 12, 2011, http://
www.wweek.com/portland/article-17350-9_things_the_rich_dont_
want_you_to_know_about_taxes.html

227 Source: *OECD* combined revenue statistics: http://stats.oecd.
org/Index.aspx?DataSetCode=REV

228 Jesse Drucker, "Google 2.4% Rate Shows How $60 Billion
Is Lost to Tax Loopholes" *Bloomberg Technology*, October 21,
2010, http://www.bloomberg.com/news/2010-10-21/google-2-4-
rate-shows-how-60-billion-u-s-revenue-lost-to-tax-loopholes.html

229 Christopher Helman, "What The Top U.S. Companies Pay In
Taxes", *Forbes*, April 1, 2010, http://www.forbes.com/2010/04/01/
ge-exxon-walmart-business-washington-corporate-taxes_print.html

230 Gallup poll conducted in April 2011: http://www.gallup.com/
poll/147152/americans-split-whether-taxes-high.aspx

231 "Briefing Book – Key Elements of the U.S. Tax System",
Tax Policy Center, (accessed May 30, 2016),http://www.
taxpolicycenter.org/briefing-book/key-elements/business/statutory.
cfm

232 Terry Krepel, "Hannity falsely claimed "50-percent of
American households no longer pay taxes", *Media Matters for
America*, April 9, 2010, http://mediamatters.org/
research/201004090085

233 Source: *Tax Policy Center* table: "Tax Units with Zero or
Negative Income Tax," http://www.taxpolicycenter.org/model-
estimates/tax-units-zero-or-negative-income-tax/tax-units-zero-or-
negative-income-tax

234 Source: *U.S. Census bureau* – http://quickfacts.census.gov/
qfd/states/00000.html

235 Source: *Institute on Taxation and Economic Policy* via
Citizens for Tax Justice – http://www.ctj.org/pdf/taxday2011.pdf

236 David Cay Johnston, "9 Things The Rich Don't Want You To
Know About Taxes", *Willamette Week*, April 12, 2011, http://www.
wweek.com/portland/article-17350-9_things_the_rich_dont_want_
you_to_know_about_taxes.html

237 Tiffany Hsu, "IRS: Nearly 1,500 millionaires paid no federal

income tax in 2009", *Los Angeles Times*, August 8, 2011, http://
latimesblogs.latimes.com/money_co/2011/08/nearly-1500-
millionaires-paid-no-taxes-in-2009-says-irs.html

238 *Citizens for Tax Justice*, chart: "Incomes and Federal, State &
Local Taxes in 2011", http://ctj.org/images/taxday2012table.jpg

239 *Congressional Budget Office*, Table: "Shares of Federal
Tax Liabilities for All Households, by Comprehensive Household
Income Quintile, 1979-2007," http://www.cbo.gov/sites/default/files/
cbofiles/attachments/Tax_liability_Shares.pdf

240 "Policy Basics: Where Do Federal Tax Revenues Come
From?" *Center on Budget and Policy Priorities*, March 4, 2016,
http://www.cbpp.org/research/policy-basics-where-do-federal-tax-
revenues-come-from

241 *Tax Policy Center*, Table: "Historical Top Tax Rate", http://
www.taxpolicycenter.org/taxfacts/displayafact.cfm?Docid=213

242 *Tax Policy Center*, table: Historical Effective Federal Tax
Rates for All Households
http://www.taxpolicycenter.org/taxfacts/displayafact.cfm?DocID
=456&Topic2id=20&Topic3id=22

243 *Tax Policy Center* report, "THE DISTRIBUTION OF
FEDERAL TAXES, 2009—12", Table 1: "Average Effective Tax
Rates Under Current Law, By Cash Income Percentile, 2009" http://
www.taxpolicycenter.org/UploadedPDF/411943_distribution_
federal.pdf

244 Avi Feller and Chad Stone "Top 1 Percent of Americans
Reaped Two-Thirds of Income Gains in Last Economic Expansion",
Center for Budget Policy and Priorities, September 9, 2009, http://
www.cbpp.org/cms/index.cfm?fa=view&id=2908

245 Joseph E. Stiglitz, "Of the 1%, by the 1%, for the 1%,"
VANITY FAIR, May 2011, http://www.vanityfair.com/society/
features/2011/05/top-one-percent-201105

246 Gus Lubin, "15 Mind-Blowing Facts About Wealth And
Inequality In America", *Business Insider*, April 9, 2010, http://www.
businessinsider.com/15-charts-about-wealth-and-inequality-in-
america-2010-4#half-of-america-has-25-of-the-wealth-2

247 Source: *Bureau of Labor Statistics*, http://www.bls.gov/lpc/data.htm

248 Source: *U.S. Census Bureau* http://www.census.gov/hhes/www/income/data/historical/index.html

249 Ilan Kolet and Bob Willis, "Minimum Wage in U.S. Fails to Beat Inflation: Chart of the Day", *Bloomberg.com*, December 28, 2011, http://www.bloomberg.com/news/2011-12-28/minimum-wage-in-u-s-fails-to-beat-inflation-chart-of-the-day.html

250 Source: *Central Intelligence Agency,* World Fact Book, https://www.cia.gov/library/publications/the-world-factbook/fields/2172.html

251 *Organization for Economic Cooperation and Development (OECD)*, table: "Income distribution — inequality, GINI coefficient (after taxes and transfers)", http://stats.oecd.org/Index.aspx?QueryId=26067&Lang=en

252 GDP figures: *Bureau of Economic Analysis*, http://www.bea.gov/national/

253 Robert Frank, "Gauging the Pain of the Middle Class", *New York Times*, April 2, 2011, http://www.nytimes.com/2011/04/03/business/03view.html

254 Source: *United States Department of Labor*, http://workforcesecurity.doleta.gov/unemploy/uitaxtopic.asp

255 Robert Frank, "The Fear and Loathing of the One Percent", *CNBC.com*, August 8, 2012, http://www.cnbc.com/id/48570985

256 Robert Frank, "The Job Worries of the One Percent", *Wall Street Journal*, March 14, 2012, http://blogs.wsj.com/wealth/2012/03/14/the-job-worries-of-the-one-percent/

257 Source: *Office of Management and Budget*, Budget of the U.S. Government, Fiscal Year 2013, Historical Tables, table 1.3 "SUMMARY OF RECEIPTS, OUTLAYS, AND SURPLUSES OR DEFICITS (—) IN CURRENT DOLLARS, CONSTANT (FY 2005) DOLLARS, AND AS PERCENTAGES OF GDP: 1940—2017" http://www.gpo.gov/fdsys/pkg/BUDGET-2013-TAB/pdf/BUDGET-2013-TAB.pdf

258 Source: St. Louis Fed graph: "Real Federal Consumption

Expenditures & Gross Investment, 1 Decimal (FGCEC1) 2009-01-01 to 2012-10-01", http://alfred.stlouisfed.org/graph/?id=FGCEC1,

259 Source: *Office of Management and Budget*, Budget of the U.S. Government, Fiscal Year 2013, Historical Tables, Table 1.2 "SUMMARY OF RECEIPTS, OUTLAYS, AND SURPLUSES OR DEFICITS (—) AS PERCENTAGES OF GDP: 1930—2017", http://www.gpo.gov/fdsys/pkg/BUDGET-2013-TAB/pdf/BUDGET-2013-TAB.pdf

260 Source: *Bureau of Labor Statistics*, via *St. Louis Fed*, Economic Data, http://research.stlouisfed.org/fred2/categories/32325

261 Dana Priest and William M. Arkin, "Top Secret America", *Washington Post*, July 19, 2010, http://projects.washingtonpost.com/top-secret-america/articles/a-hidden-world-growing-beyond-control/

262 "Election 2012: Voting Laws Roundup", *Brennan Center for Justice*, October 11, 2012, http://www.brennancenter.org/content/resource/2012_summary_of_voting_law_changes/

263 "State Policies in Brief: Targeted Regulation of Abortion Providers - as of March 4, 2016", *Guttmacher Institute,* https://www.guttmacher.org/sites/default/files/pdfs/spibs/spib_TRAP.pdf

264 Jones RK et al., "Abortion in the United States: incidence and access to services", *Perspectives on Sexual and Reproductive Health*, 40(1), (2008), 6—16.

265 "Adam Liptak, "The 14th Amendment, the Debt Ceiling and a Way Out", *The New York Times*, July 24, 2011, http://www.nytimes.com/2011/07/25/us/politics/25legal.html

266 Obama Administration white paper on Bulk Collection of Telephony Metadata Under Section 215 of the U.S.A. Patriot Act, August 9, 2013, https://www.aclu.org/foia-document/section-215-obama-administration-white-paper

267 *Office of the Clerk of the U.S. House of Representatives*, H R 3162 RECORDED VOTE, October 24, 2001, http://clerk.house.gov/evs/2001/roll398.xml

268 *Office of the Clerk of the U.S. House of Representatives*, H R 514 RECORDED VOTE, February 14, 2011, http://clerk.house.gov/evs/2011/roll036.xml

269 "McCain: Japanese Hanged For Waterboarding" *Associated Press*, June 18, 2009,

http://www.cbsnews.com/stories/2007/11/29/politics/
main3554687.shtml

270 Mark Mazzetti, "'03 U.S. Memo Approved Harsh Interrogations", *The New York Times*, April 2, 2008, http://www.
nytimes.com/2008/04/02/washington/02terror.html

271 Hearing before the Sub-Committee on the Constitution, Civil Rights, and Civil Liberties of the Committee on the Judiciary of the House of Representatives, June 18, 2008, http://judiciary.
house.gov/hearings/printers/110th/42972.PDF

272 "United Nations Convention against Torture and Other Cruel, Inhuman or Degrading Treatment or Punishment", http://
en.wikisource.org/wiki/Convention_against_Torture

273 *Americans for Tax Reform*, "Taxpayer Protection Pledge", http://www.atr.org/userfiles/Congressional_pledge(1).pdf

274 @IAVA, *Twitter*, September 19, 2012: https://twitter.com/
iava/status/248461535725355008

275 David Edwards, "Vets' group: 92 percent of 'D' or 'F' grades on supporting troops go to Republicans", *Rawstory.com*, October 22, 2010, http://www.rawstory.com/rs/2010/10/22/vets-group-142-republicans-d-f-veterans-affairs/

276 *IAVA (Iraq and Afghanistan Veterans of America)* 2010 Congressional Report Card, http://media.iava.org/iava_action/
IAVA_Action_2010_Congressional_Report_Card.pdf

277 Amy Belasco, "The Cost of Iraq, Afghanistan, and Other Global War on Terror Operations Since 9/11," *Congressional Research Service*, December 8, 2014, https://www.fas.org/sgp/crs/
natsec/RL33110.pdf

278 *Congressional Budget Office* cost estimate: "Preliminary Estimate of Changes to Direct Spending and Revenues Under S. 3457, the Veterans Jobs Corps Act of 2012, as Introduced on July 30, 2012", http://www.cbo.gov/sites/default/files/cbofiles/attachments/
S3457,paygo.pdf

279 Ramsey Cox, "G.O.P. blocks veterans jobs bill with budget

vote", *The Hill*, September 19, 2012, http://thehill.com/blogs/floor-actionsenate/250391-G.O.P.-kills-veterans-jobs-bill-with-budget-vote

280 "Budget Panel Eyes End to VA Care for 1.3 Million Vets", *Veterans of Modern Warfare*, http://www.vmwusa.org/index.php/healthcareservices/hcarticles/47-health/1079-va-care-end-eyed-for-13-million-vets

281 "Fact Sheet: Returning Heroes and Wounded Warrior Tax Credits", *The White House*, November 21, 2011, http://www.whitehouse.gov/the-press-office/2011/11/21/fact-sheet-returning-heroes-and-wounded-warrior-tax-credits

282 *U.S. Department of Veterans' Affairs*: Montgomery G.I. Bill, http://www.gibill.va.gov/benefits/montgomery_gibill/index.html

283 *U.S. Department of Veterans' Affairs*: The Post 9/11 G.I. Bill, http://www.gibill.va.gov/benefits/post_911_gibill/index.html

284 Bill Summary & Status 110th Congress (2007 - 2008) H.R.2642, http://thomas.loc.gov/cgi-bin/bdquery/z?d110:H.R.2642:

285 Dr. Margaret C. Harrell and Nancy Berglass, "Losing the Battle:
The Challenge of Military Suicide", *Center for a New American Century,* October 2011, http://www.cnas.org/losingthebattle

286 Robert Burns, "2012 military suicides hit record high of 349", *The Associated Press*, January 14, 2013, http://www.armytimes.com/news/2013/01/ap-2012-military-suicides-hit-record-high-349-011413/

287 Frank Newport, "Military Veterans of All Ages Tend to Be More Republican", *Gallup*, May 25, 2009, http://www.gallup.com/poll/118684/military-veterans-ages-tend-republican.aspx

288 Stephen Dinan, "Retired top military brass push for Romney", *The Washington Times*, November 4, 2012, http://www.washingtontimes.com/blog/inside-politics/2012/nov/4/retired-top-military-brass-push-romney/

289 Zachary Fryer-Biggs, "U.S. Firms Spending More On Lobbying", *Defense News*, July 7, 2012, http://www.defensenews.

comarticle/20120707DEFREG02/307070001/U-S-Firms-Spending-More-Lobbying

290 Reid Pillifant, "Architect of Obama's Health Care Plan Fears Political Decision by the Supreme Court, Says Romney's Lying", *capitalnewyork.com*, http://www.capitalnewyork.com/article/politics/2011/11/4156059/architect-obamas-health-care-plan-fears-political-decision-supreme-

291 "Our Position on Climate Change", *ExxonMobil*, http://corporate.exxonmobil.com/en/current-issues/climate-policy/climate-perspectives/our-position

292 James E. Hansen, "Climate change is here — and worse than we thought", *The Washington Post*, August 03, 2012, http://articles.washingtonpost.com/2012-08-03/opinions/35491435_1_climate-change-climate-model-normal-climate

293 Source: *George Mason Center for Climate Change Communication* and *Yale Project on Climate Change Communication* report, "Climate Change in the American Mind: Americans' Global Warming Beliefs and Attitudes in May 2011", p. 5, http://environment.yale.edu/climate/files/ClimateBeliefsMay2011.pdf

294 Source: *National Oceanic and Atmospheric Administration (NOAA)*, National Climatic Data Center: "State of the Climate Global Analysis for November 2012", http://www.ncdc.noaa.gov/sotc/global/2012/11

295 Steve Graham, "John Tyndall (1820 – 1893)", *NASA Earth Observatory*, October 8, 1999, http://earthobservatory.nasa.gov/Features/Tyndall/

296 Source: *National Oceanographic and Atmospheric Administration (NOAA)*, "Trends in Atmospheric Carbon Dioxide – Recent Monthly Average Mauna Loa CO2", http://www.esrl.noaa.gov/gmd/ccgg/trends/

297 "WORLD MOTOR CAR CENSUS; Total Estimate 12,588,949 Vehicles, of Which 10,505,660 Are in United States", *New York Times,* February 26, 1922, http://query.nytimes.com/gst/abstract.html?res=F60B14FC355810738DDDAF0A94DA405B828

EF1D3

298 source: *International Organization of Motor Vehicle Manufacturers*, http://oica.net/category/production-statistics/

299 John Sousanis, "World Vehicle Population Tops 1 Billion Units", *WardsAuto*, Aug. 15, 2011, http://wardsauto.com/ar/world_vehicle_population_110815

300 source: *U.S. Energy Information Administration (EIA)*, International Energy Statistics: Total Carbon Dioxide Emissions from the Consumption of Energy, http://www.eia.gov/cfapps/ipdbproject/iedindex3.cfm?tid=90&pid=44&aid=8

301 Intergovernmental Panel of Climate Change (IPCC), http://www.ipcc.ch/

302 Solomon, S., D. Qin, M. Manning, Z. Chen, M. Marquis, K.B. Averyt, M. Tignor and H.L. Miller (eds.), "Contribution of Working Group I to the Fourth Assessment Report of the Intergovernmental Panel on Climate Change, 2007", *IPCC*, http://www.ipcc.ch/publications_and_data/ar4/wg1/en/contents.html

303 website of *The [California] Governor's Office of Planning and Research*, "The Scientific Consensus", http://www.opr.ca.gov/s_scientificconsensus.php

304 Peter T. Doran and Maggie Kendall Zimmerman, "Examining the Scientific Consensus on Climate Change", *Department of Earth and Environmental Sciences, University of Illinois at Chicago, EOS volume 90 number 3*, January 20, 2009, http://tigger.uic.edu/~pdoran/012009_Doran_final.pdf

305 William R. L. Anderegga, James W. Prall, Jacob Harold, and Stephen H. Schneider, "Expert credibility in climate change", *Proceedings of the National Academy of Sciences*, June 4, 2010, http://www.pnas.org/content/early/2010/06/04/1003187107.full.pdf+html

306 James Lawrence Powell, "Why Climate Deniers Have No Scientific Credibility - In One Pie Chart", *Desmog*, November 15, 2012, http://www.desmogblog.com/2012/11/15/why-climate-deniers-have-no-credibility-science-one-pie-chart

307 Richard A. Muller, "The Conversion of a Climate-Change

Skeptic", *The New York Times*, July 28, 2012, http://www.nytimes.
com/2012/07/30/opinion/the-conversion-of-a-climate-change-
skeptic.html

308 "Business Resilience in an Uncertain, Resource-Constrained
World: CDP Global 500 Climate Change Report 2012, on behalf of
655 investors with assets of US$ 78 trillion", *The Carbon Disclosure
Project*, https://www.cdproject.net/en-US/Pages/global500.aspx

309 Andrew Montford, "The Royal Society and Climate Change
– GWPF Report 6", *The Global Warming Policy Foundation*, 2012,
http://www.thegwpf.org/images/stories/gwpf-reports/montford-
royal_society.pdf

310 reported remark to Treasury Secretary Paul O'Neill: Rebecca
Leung, "Bush Sought Way to Invade Iraq?" *60 Minutes – CBS News.
com*, January 9, 2004, http://www.cbsnews.com/news/bush-sought-
way-to-invade-iraq/

311 David Stockman, "Four Deformations of the Apocalypse",
New York Times, July 31, 2010, http://www.nytimes.
com/2010/08/01/opinion/01stockman.html

312 Source: Budget of the U.S. Government Fiscal Year 2017,
Historical Tables — Table 1.3 "Summary of Receipts, Outlays, and
Surpluses or Deficits in Current Dollars, Constant (FY 2009)
Dollars, and as Percentages of GDP — 1940-2021" *Office of
Management and Budget*, https://www.whitehouse.gov/sites/default/
files/omb/budget/fy2017/assets/hist.pdf

313 Source: Treasury Direct, "Historical Debt Outstanding -
Annual 1950 - 1999," *U.S. Department of the Treasury*, http://www.
treasurydirect.gov/govt/reports/pd/histdebt/histdebt_histo4.htm

314 Source: Budget of the U.S. Government Fiscal Year 2017,
Historical Tables — Table 7.1 "Federal Debt at the End of the Year
— 1940-2021," *Office of Management and Budget*, https://www.
whitehouse.gov/sites/default/files/omb/budget/fy2017/assets/hist.pdf

315 Source: *Office of Management and Budget*, 2011 Budget-
Summary Tables -Table S-3, http://www.whitehouse.gov/sites/
default/files/omb/budget/fy2012/assets/tables.pdf

316 *Office of Management and Budget*, Historical Tables, Table

1.2—Summary of Receipts, Outlays, and Surpluses or Deficits (-) as Percentages of GDP: 1930—2017, http://www.whitehouse.gov/omb/budget/Historicals/

317 "Employers Tax Guide", *Internal Revenue Service*, http://www.irs.gov/pub/irs-pdf/p15.pdf

318 Source: CPI Inflation Calculator, *Bureau of Labor Statistics* (accessed May 9, 2016), http://www.bls.gov/data/inflation_calculator.htm

319Source: 2011 OASDI (Old-Age, Survivors, and Disability Insurance) Trustees Report, *Social Security Administration*, http://www.ssa.gov/oact/tr/2011/II_D_project.html

320 National Commission on Social Security Reform, https://www.ssa.gov/history/greenspn.html

321 Source: The 2011 Annual Report of the Board of Trustees of the Federal Old-Age and Survivors Insurance and Federal Disability Insurance Trust Funds, http://www.ssa.gov/OACT/TR/2011/tr2011.pdf

322 Mary Williams Walsh, "Social Security to See Payout Exceed Pay-In This Year", *New York Times*, March 24, 2010, http://www.nytimes.com/2010/03/25/business/economy/25social.html

323 Source: 2011 OASDI Trustees Report, http://www.ssa.gov/oact/tr/2011/II_D_project.html

324 Jeff Zeleny, "Santorum Cites a Local Legend", *New York Times,* January 12, 2012, http://thecaucus.blogs.nytimes.com/2012/01/12/santorum-cites-a-local-legend/

325 *Office of Management and Budget*, Historical Tables,Table 1.2—Summary of Receipts, Outlays, and Surpluses or Deficits (-) as Percentages of GDP: 1930—2017 http://www.whitehouse.gov/omb/budget/Historicals/

326 *Office of Management and Budget*, http://earmarks.omb.gov/earmarks-public/

327 source: *Citizens Against Government Waste*, http://www.cagw.org/newsroom/releases/2010/earmark-spending-165.html

328 The Website of the Republican Majority in Congress, Conference Blog, March 11, 2010, http://www.G.O.P..gov/

blog/10/03/11/house-republicans-unilaterally-ban-all

329 Applewhite vs. The Commonwealth of Pennsylvania, July 12, 2012, http://pilcop.org/wp-content/uploads/2012/05/Exhibit-3-Applewhite-Stipulation-copy.pdf

330 *Brennan Center for Justice* at *NYU School of Law*, http://www.truthaboutfraud.org/case_studies_by_state/

331 Eric Lipton and Ian Urbina, "In 5-Year Effort, Scant Evidence of Voter Fraud", *The New York Times*, April 12, 2007, http://www.nytimes.com/2007/04/12/washington/12fraud.html

332 Rick Hasen, "Important District Court Opinion, Relying on Bush v. Gore, Issued in Ohio Hunter Litigation," *Election Law Blog*, http://electionlawblog.org/?p=29505

333 Lorraine C. Minnite Ph.D., "The Politics of Voter Fraud", *Project Vote*, http://www.projectvote.org/images/publications/Policy% percent20Reports% percent20and% percent20Guides/Politics_of_Voter_Fraud_Final.pdf

334 Justin Levitt, "The Truth About Voter Fraud," *Brennan Center for Justice at NYU School of Law*, November 9, 2007, https://www.brennancenter.org/publication/truth-about-voter-fraud

335 "Policy Brief on the Truth About 'Voter Fraud'", *Brennan Center for Justice*, September 12, 2006, http://www.brennancenter.org/content/resource/policy_brief_on_the_truth_about_voter_fraud/

336 Dan McGrath, "Felon Voter Fraud Convictions Stemming from Minnesota's 2008 General Election," *Minnesota Majority*, October 13, 2011, http://www.electionintegritywatch.com/documents/2011-Report-Voter-Fraud-Convictions.pdf

337 "2008 November General Election Turnout Rates," *The United States Elections Project, George Mason University*, last updated March 31, 2012, http://www.electproject.org/2008g

338 Kristen Mack, "In trying to win, has Dewhurst lost a friend?", *Houston Chronicle*, May 18, 2007, http://www.chron.com/news/article/In-trying-to-win-has-Dewhurst-lost-a-friend-1815569.php

339 Comprehensive Database of U.S. Voter Fraud compiled by News21, http://votingrights.news21.com/article/election-fraud/

340 Ibid.

341 "History of Voter ID," *National Conference of State Legislatures*, April 18, 2016, http://www.ncsl.org/research/elections-and-campaigns/voter-id.aspx

342 "Gun lobby targets Gore, Democrats", *CNN.COM*, May 23, 2000, http://articles.cnn.com/2000-05-23/us/nra.politics_1_nra-president-nra-officials-national-rifle-association

343 Patrick Jonsson, "President Obama Has Only Ever Signed Gun Laws That Expand Owners' Rights"
Christian Science Monitor, September 10, 2012, http://www.businessinsider.com/obama-vs-romney-gun-control-2012-9

344 *Brady Campaign to Prevent Gun Violence* press release: "Weaker Gun Laws, Lack Of Leadership Earn President Obama A Failing Grade", January 19, 2010, http://www.bradycampaign.org/media/press/view/1214/

345 Darren Samuelsohn, "Why Gun Lovers Still Fear President Obama" by July 19, 2012, *Politico*, http://www.politico.com/news/stories/0712/78696.html

346 Richard Florida, "The Geography of Gun Violence",
The Atlantic, July 20, 2012, http://www.theatlanticcities.com/neighborhoods/2012/07/geography-gun-violence/2655/

347 Richard Florida, "The Geography of Gun Deaths", *The Atlantic*, January 13, 2011, http://www.theatlantic.com/national/archive/2011/01/the-geography-of-gun-deaths/69354/

348 Gun Owners Poll, prepared for *Mayors Against Illegal Guns* by Frank Luntz, July 2012, http://www.mayorsagainstillegalguns.org/downloads/pdf/poll-07-24-2012.pdf

349 Quinnipiac University poll released, February 7, 2013, http://www.quinnipiac.edu/institutes-centers/polling-institute/national/release-detail/?ReleaseID=1847

350 Annual Lobbying by the National Rifle Association, *Center for Responsive Politics,* http://www.opensecrets.org/lobby/clientsum.php?id=D000000082

351 Peter Robison and John Crewdson, "NRA Raises $200 Million as Gun Lobby Toasters Burn Logo on Bread", *Bloomberg*

News, December 29, 2011, http://www.bloomberg.com/news/2011-12-29/nra-raises-200-million-as-gun-lobby-toasters-burn-logo-on-bread.html

352 Wayne LaPierre, "Stand and Fight", *The Daily Caller*, February 13, 2013, http://dailycaller.com/2013/02/13/stand-and-fight/

353 Angel Shamaya, "NRA Supported the National Firearms Act of 1934", *KeepAndBearArms.com*, March 29, 2002, http://www.keepandbeararms.com/information/XcIBViewItem.asp?id=3247

354 *U.S. Constitution, Article 1, Section 8,* https://www.law.cornell.edu/constitution/articlei#section8

355 Patrick Henry, Speech in the Virginia Ratifying Convention, June 5th, 1788, via *The Founders' Constitution*, Article 1, Section 8, Clause 16, Document 10, http://press-pubs.uchicago.edu/founders/documents/a1_8_16s10.html

356 John Hagan and Alberto Palloni: *Sociological Criminology and the Mythology of Hispanic Immigration and Crime*, Social Problems, Vol. 46, No. 4 (Nov., 1999), pp. 617-632, http://www.jstor.org/pss/3097078

357 Tim Wadsworth, "Is Immigration Responsible for the Crime Drop? An Assessment of the Influence of Immigration on Changes in Violent Crime Between 1990 and 2000", *Social Science Quarterly Volume 91, Issue 2, pages 531–553,* June 2010, http://onlinelibrary.wiley.com/doi/10.1111/j.1540-6237.2010.00706.x/abstract

358 Source:*Federal Bureau of Investigation*, http://www.fbi.gov/about-us/cjis/ucr/crime-in-the-u.s/2010/crime-in-the-u.s.-2010/index-page

359 Source: *The Bureau of Justice Statistics*, http://www.bjs.gov/index.cfm?ty=daaSearch/Crime/State/TrendsInOneVar.cfm

360 Walter A. Ewing, Ph.D., Daniel E. Martínez, Ph.D., and Rubén G. Rumbaut, Ph.D., "The Criminalization of Immigration in the United States", *American Immigration Council*, July 2015, http://immigrationpolicy.org/special-reports/criminalization-immigration-united-states

361 Source: Bureau of Justice Statistics, http://bjs.ojp.usdoj.gov/content/pub/press/pim09stpy09acpr.cfm

362 http://www.theagitator.com/2011/05/11/more-immigrants-less-crime/

363 Source: *UNODC (United Nations Office on Drugs and Crime)* 2011 Global Study on Homicide, available at http://www.unodc.org/unodc/en/data-and-analysis/statistics/crime/global-study-on-homicide-2011.html

364 Robert J. Samson, "Open Doors Don't Invite Criminals", *The New York Times*, March 11, 2006, http://www.nytimes.com/2006/03/11/opinion/11sampson.html

365 Ibid.

366 Source: *Death Penalty Information Center*, "Murder Rates Nationally and By State", http://www.deathpenaltyinfo.org/murder-rates-nationally-and-state

367 Source: *Death Penalty Information Center*, "Deterrence: States Without the Death Penalty Have Had Consistently Lower Murder Rates", http://www.deathpenaltyinfo.org/deterrence-states-without-death-penalty-have-had-consistently-lower-murder-rates

368 Source: FBI data via *Amnesty International*, "The Death Penalty and Deterrence", http://www.amnestyusa.org/our-work/issues/death-penalty/us-death-penalty-facts/the-death-penalty-and-deterrence

369 Michael L. Radelet & Traci L. Lacock, *Do Executions Lower Homicide Rates: The Views of Leading Criminologists*, The Journal of Criminal Law & Criminology, vol. 99, No. 2 (2009) (http://www.law.northwestern.edu/jclc/backissues/v99/n2/9902_489.Radelet.pdf)

370 Source: FBI Uniform Crime Report, via *Death Penalty Information Center*, http://www.deathpenaltyinfo.org/law-enforcement-views-deterrence

371 "Police Chiefs Reject Death Penalty as Useful Tool", *Death Penalty Information Center,* October 20, 2009, http://www.deathpenalty.org/article.php?id=406

372 Source: *FBI* "Crime in the United States – Expanded Homicide Data, table 12: Murder Circumstances 2005-2009",

http://www2.fbi.gov/ucr/cius2009/offenses/expanded_information/
homicide.html

373 Brian Knutson, "Sweet Revenge?", *Science*, Vol. 305, Issue 5688, pp. 1246-1247, August 27, 2004,
http://www.sciencemag.org/content/305/5688/1246.summary

374 Source: *Global Terrorism Database*, http://www.start.umd.edu/gtd/

375 "Deadly Attacks Since 9/11," *New America Foundation*, (accessed May 10, 2016), http://securitydata.newamerica.net/extremists/deadly-attacks.html

376 *National Counterterrorism Center Annual Report for 2011*, http://www.nctc.gov/docs/2011_NCTC_Annual_Report_Final.pdf

377 Source: *National Safety Council*, http://www.nsc.org/news_resources/injury_and_death_statistics/Pages/InjuryDeathStatistics.aspx

378 *Consumer Product Safety Commission*, 2011 report: "Instability of Televisions, Appliances and Furniture: Estimated Injuries and Reported Fatalities", available at http://www.cpsc.gov/library/foia/foia11/os/tipover2011.pdf (via Micah Zenko, http://blogs.cfr.org/zenko/2012/02/24/america-is-a-safe-place/)

379 John Mueller and Mark G. Stewart, "Terror, Security, and Money: Balancing the Risks, Benefits, and Costs of Homeland Security",March 20, 2011, http://polisci.osu.edu/faculty/jmueller/MID11TSM.PDF

380 Interview with Fareed Zakaria on CNN, February 19, 2012, http://edition.cnn.com/TRANSCRIPTS/1202/19/fzgps.01.html

381 Spencer Ackerman, "Calm Down. Iran's Missiles Can't (and Won't) Hit the East Coast", *Wired*, February 24, 2012, http://www.wired.com/dangerroom/2012/02/iran-icbm/

382 Robert Einhorn, "Debating the Iran Nuclear Deal," *The Brookings Institution*, August 2015, http://www.brookings.edu/research/reports2/2015/08/iran-nuclear-deal-battleground-issues-einhorn#bgissue1

383 source: Sixth annual report of the International Panel on Fissile Materials (2011), available at http://fissilematerials.org/

library/gfmr11.pdf

384 "Halevy: Iranian nuke not existential threat to Israel," *The Jerusalem Post*, August 4, 2012, http://www.jpost.com/Breaking-News/Halevy-Iranian-nuke-not-existential-threat-to-Israel

385 Ali Gharib, "Report: Israel Intel Chief Says Nuke-Armed Iran Not An Existential Threat," *ThinkProgress.com*, December 29, 2011, http://thinkprogress.org/security/2011/12/29/395711/mossad-israel-iran-existential-threat/

386 "Report: Barak Says Iran Is Not Existential Threat to Israel", *Reuters*, September 17, 2009, http://www.haaretz.com/news/report-barak-says-iran-is-not-existential-threat-to-israel-1.7710

387 Eli Clifton, "Chairman Of Joint Chiefs Of Staff Stands By Assessment That Iran Is A Rational Actor", *Think Progress*, March 1, 2012, http://thinkprogress.org/security/2012/03/01/435346/dempsey-iran-rational-actor/

388

389 Rahel Gebreyes, "General Stanley McChrystal Says Iran Is 'Obviously' A Rational Actor," *Huffington Post*, May 14, 2015, http://www.huffingtonpost.com/2015/05/14/stanley-mcchrystal-iran_n_7284630.html

390 Source: *C-Span* July 18, 2011, available at http://www.c-spanvideo.org/program/CoburnB

391 "Major Holders of U.S. Securities," *U.S. Department of the Treasury*, (accessed May 10, 2016) http://ticdata.treasury.gov/Publish/mfh.txt

392 Source: *U.S. Treasury*, http://www.treasurydirect.gov/govt/reports/pd/mspd/mspd.htm

393 Marc Labonte, Jared C. Nagel, "Foreign Holdings of Federal Debt," *Congressional Research Service*, March 28, 2016, http://www.fas.org/sgp/crs/misc/RS22331.pdf

394 Source: "China Foreign Exchange Reserves 1980-2016," *Trading Economics*, (accessed May 10, 2016) http://www.tradingeconomics.com/china/foreign-exchange-reserves

395 Seung Min Kim, "Romney's 'get rid of' Planned Parenthood remark becomes Dem fundraising tool", *Politico*, March 14, 2012,

http://www.politico.com/blogs/on-congress/2012/03/romneys-get-rid-of-planned-parenthood-remark-becomes-117503.html

396 Source: *U.S. Energy Information Administration* data: "U.S. Imports by Country of Origin," (accessed May 11, 2016), http://www.eia.gov/dnav/pet/pet_move_impcus_a2_nus_ep00_im0_mbbl_a.htm

397 "Crude Oil Export Licensing Policy," *Bureau of Industry and Security, U.S. Department of Commerce*, (accessed May 8, 2016), https://www.bis.doc.gov/index.php/crude-oil-export-licensing-policy

398 "Annual Energy Outlook 2015," *Energy Information Agency*, April, 2015, http://www.eia.gov/forecasts/AEO/pdf/0383(2015).pdf

399 "Crude Oil Prices - 70 Year Historical Chart," *Macrotrends*, http://www.macrotrends.net/1369/crude-oil-price-history-chart

400 Jack Gillum and Seth Borenstein, "FACT CHECK: More US drilling didn't drop gas price", *Associated Press*, March 21, 2012, http://news.yahoo.com/fact-check-more-us-drilling-didnt-drop-gas-065231245.html

401 Jack Gillum and Seth Borenstein, "FACT CHECK: More US drilling didn't drop gas price", *Associated Press*, March 21, 2012, http://news.yahoo.com/fact-check-more-us-drilling-didnt-drop-gas-065231245.html

402 "Energy Security in the United States", *Congressional Budget Office*, May 2012, http://www.cbo.gov/sites/default/files/cbofiles/attachments/05-09-EnergySecurity.pdf

403 "Statement on Signing International Security and Foreign Assistance Legislation, December 29, 1981," The Public Papers of President Ronald W. Reagan, *The Ronald Reagan Presidential Library*, https://reaganlibrary.archives.gov/archives/speeches/1981/122981d.htm

404 Source: *U.S. Department of State,* "Congressional Budget Justification — Foreign Assistance, FY 2015," http://www.state.gov/documents/organization/224071.pdf

405 Source: *U.S. Department of the Treasury*, "Historical Debt

Outstanding - Annual 2000 — 2015," retrieved March 31, 2016, https://www.treasurydirect.gov/govt/reports/pd/histdebt/histdebt_histo5.htm

406 "American Public Opinion on Foreign Aid", *WorldPublicOpinion.org*, November 30, 2010,
http://www.worldpublicopinion.org/pipa/pdf/nov10/ForeignAid_Nov10_quaire.pdf

407 Bianca DiJulio, Jamie Firth, and Mollyann Brodie, "Data Note: Americans' Views On The U.S. Role In Global Health," *Henry J. Kaiser family Foundation*, January 23, 2015, http://kff.org/global-health-policy/poll-finding/data-note-americans-views-on-the-u-s-role-in-global-health/

408 Charles Kenny, "On Foreign Aid, the Candidates' Rhetoric Doesn't Match Reality," *BLOOMBERG-BUSINESS WEEK*, October 7, 2012, http://www.businessweek.com/articles/2012-10-07/on-foreign-aid-the-candidates-rhetoric-doesn-t-match-reality

409 Julia Simon, "Egypt May Not Need Fighter Jets, But The U.S. Keeps Sending Them Anyway," *NPR NEWS*, http://www.npr.org/blogs/money/2013/08/08/209878158/egypt-may-not-need-fighter-jets-but-u-s-keeps-sending-them-anyway

410 Source: U.S. Air Force fact sheet: "F-16 Fighting Falcon," published September 23, 2015, http://www.af.mil/AboutUs/FactSheets/Display/tabid/224/Article/104505/f-16-fighting-falcon.aspx

411 Charles Kenny, "On Foreign Aid, the Candidates' Rhetoric Doesn't Match Reality," *BLOOMBERG-BUSINESS WEEK*, October 7, 2012, http://www.businessweek.com/articles/2012-10-07/on-foreign-aid-the-candidates-rhetoric-doesn-t-match-reality

412 *U.S. AID (U.S. Agency for International Development*, https://www.usaid.gov/what-we-do/global-health/hiv-and-aids

413 Bendavid E, Bhattacharya J. "The President's Emergency Plan for AIDS Relief in Africa: An Evaluation of Outcomes" Annals of Internal Medicine, 150:688-695, 2009, http://annals.org/article.aspx?articleid=744499

414 Source: PEPFAR funding fact-sheet, retrieved March 31, 2016, http://www.pepfar.gov/documents/organization/252516.pdf